Britten and the Guitar:

Critical Perspectives for Performers

Britten and the Guitar:

Critical Perspectives for Performers

Benjamin Dwyer

Carysfort Press

A Carysfort Press Book in association with Peter Lang

Britten and the Guitar: Critical Perspectives for Performers

by Benjamin Dwyer
First published in Ireland in 2016 as a paperback original by
Carysfort Press
58 Woodfield
Scholarstown Road
Dublin 16, Ireland

ISBN 978-1-78997-076-0

Typeset by Carysfort Press
Cover design by eprint limited

Contents

Acknowledgements

Aspects of *Chapter Three* were published in *The Musical Times* (Summer 2012) under the title '"Within it Lie Ancient Melodies"—Locating Dowland's Musical Rhetoric in Britten's *Songs from the Chinese*', and in a 2014 lecture of the same title at DePaul University, Chicago. Elements of *Chapter Five* have been incorporated into lectures given at the 2012 Annual Conference of the Society for Musicology in Ireland (Dundalk Institute of Technology), the Royal Irish Academy of Music, Dublin (2013) and at the University of Iowa (2014) under the titles 'Overt Simplicity, Covert Complexity: Britten's Recalibration of Variation Form' and 'Transcendence as a System: Britten's Reverse Variation Form'. All this material has undergone revision for reasons of broader contextualization and integration into this book.

Thanks are due to the staff of the Britten-Pears Library, in particular Dr. Nicholas Clarke who was always at hand to assist me in my research at the Red House. Thanks also to the staff at the British Library. I am grateful to Middlesex University for its fulsome support of my research and creative work.

Special thanks go to Faber & Faber and Boosey & Hawkes for permission to publish musical examples, and the Britten-Pears Library for permission to publish letters, MSS and photographs from the Britten-Pears archive.

I am indebted to Dr. Barra Ó Séaghdha whose critical survey of this book was enormously helpful.

I would like to offer special thanks to friends and colleagues who have supported me over the years: David Adams, Siobhán Armstrong, James Blennerhassett, Lorraine Byrne Bodley, John Buckley, Phil Buckley, Darby Carroll, Jonathan Creasy, Dan Farrelly, Peter Fribbins, Mark Fitzgerald, Bridget Flannery, Dylan Griffith, Barry Guy, Johannes Heisig, Niamh Holland, Maya Homburger, Marion Hyland, Pavlos Kanellakis, Brian Kavanagh, Deborah Kelleher, Garth Knox, Antonio de Linares, Rossi McAuley, Margaret Nolan, Wolfgang Marx, Billy O Hanluain, Gavin O'Sullivan, Chrissie Poulter, Marco Proietti, Nick Roth, Atoosa Sepehr, Peter Wells and Caroline Wynne have all offered me kindness and encouragement. Finally, I would like to thank my family who have always been very supportive of my creative and academic work.

For my brother Brian

List of Plates and Figures

Introduction

> *Nocturnal, after John Dowland* deserves a far higher place in the common view of Britten's achievement than it has yet gained'[1]

Despite the prodigious attention Benjamin Britten has received from musicologists over the past fifty years or so, very little research has focused on those works he composed for and with guitar. The fact that the guitar still resides very much on the periphery of the classical music world has probably nurtured this curious myopia. Additionally, Britten's accomplishment in situating English opera as a vital force in 20th-century music has rightly received the bulk of musicological attention. Britten's guitar works have thus been largely sidelined in light of more prominent achievements. However, marginal as they might be, I will argue that they are more significant than heretofore recognized because they emerge out of and feed into the most essential aspects of Britten's compositional character in ways that make us look at them anew. I have thus explored the guitar works within the context of these crucial features, which include Britten's aesthetic relationship with the music of the Elizabethan and Jacobean periods (and in particular his connection with John Dowland), his project to revitalize vocal forms in 20th-century English music, his melancholic obsessions with dream, sleep and death as conduits for cathartic release, and his methods of 'unconcealing' secret messages in his music that otherwise could not be explicitly articulated, most pertinently relating to his homosexuality.

This book focuses upon the unique ways in which Britten's guitar works highlight these central themes. Their tangential position within his overall output means that what they bring to this project has so far

[1] Peter Evans, *The Music of Benjamin Britten* (London: J.M. Dent, 1979), 333.

escaped serious consideration. However, what they expose are surprisingly fresh perspectives and insights into what I call Britten's unique musical idiolect. Just as the chromatic limitations of the harp encourage Britten to create a kind of elementary harmonic language for *Curlew River*, the guitar's idiosyncrasies, even its limitations, force Britten to work in a particularly concise and distilled manner. We thus experience Britten's guitar music as somewhat different; we hear it as a condensed exemplar, a hypostatized articulation of his musical thought, as music rendered through more focused and concentrated processes than much of his other work. Britten was a composer who constantly strove for a refinement of musical thought; so when he states that 'music for me is clarification; I try to clarify, to refine, to sensitise...My technique is to tear all the waste away; to achieve perfect clarity of expression, that is my aim', we can appreciate that the guitar is in many respects an ideal medium for him.[2] Since the restrictions of the instrument prohibit Britten from enriching his language exorbitantly, it provides him with a readymade conduit to achieve the 'perfect clarity' he seeks. In this regard, I shall argue that Britten's music for guitar often tells us more about his compositional *raisons d'être* than many of his larger works.

There are also numerous compositional innovations that are unique to Britten's guitar works, which make a study of them valuable for a better understanding of the composer. While Britten employs a reverse variation format in two other pieces, Op. 70's reverse structure is demonstrated here as being particularly distinctive in its sophisticated sub-structural configuration. The *Nocturnal*-passacaglia is also unique among Britten's many passacaglias in the way the 'rigid principle' of the ground collapses in an extended technical process of imminent self-destruction. In both *Nocturnal* and *Songs from the Chinese* we see exemplary confirmation of Britten's intuitive use of musical rhetoric, which he absorbed from Elizabethan and Jacobean models. The *Folksong Arrangements* for tenor and guitar also offer outstanding illustrations of Britten's sweeping renovation to folk-song setting that fashioned, in fact, a hybridized form. Through rhetorically charged accompaniments the folksong is fused with lieder models to create a sophisticated and distinctive form *sui generis* in song genres.

As a composer, guitarist, teacher and musicologist, I am convinced that a multi-perspectival approach to the study of a given musical subject draws out insights, often complex and even contradictory, that

---

[2] Murray Schafer, 'British Composers in Interview', in *Remembering Britten*, Alan Blyth (London: Hutchinson, 1981), 66.

deeply enrich appreciation. I therefore explore Britten's guitar works through numerous lenses. Music is not composed in a vacuum; a score is not merely an intricate code of musical symbols unreflective of its generator's existence. A piece of music is an overt demonstration of aesthetic attitudes, a unique and unrepeatable moment in the expressive consciousness of a creative artist, and a reflection of a composer's intellective and emotional development. No matter how abstract, music discloses information about a composer's social and political philosophies, historical and artistic influences, and psychological and spiritual predicaments.

In this book, therefore, analyses are not undertaken to produce objective empirical data about Britten's compositional methodologies but rather conducted within broader perspectives of significance often of a contextual, metaphoric and even philosophical nature. For example, two technical analyses (*Songs from the Chinese* and *Nocturnal*) are conducted through the lens of musical rhetoric, which strengthens our understanding of Britten's connection with the musical aesthetics of the English Renaissance and Baroque. An introductory exploration of Chinese poetics enhances an understanding of Britten's skill for creating multi-layered narratives in his sophisticated settings of text. A clarification of the social, political and musical environments in which Britten emerged in the inter-war years as a composer supports our understanding of his radical, almost anarchic approach to folksong setting. An appreciation of the Gnostic influences that darkened Dowland's music feeds into our comprehension of Britten's correlating obsessions with death; a philosophical enquiry into both composers reveals how their musical death wishes are paradoxically quests for transcendental catharsis. All these subjects and ideas interface with each other to create a *bricolage* of interpretation and perspective that I hope will achieve a richer understanding and appreciation of Britten's guitar works for guitarists, singers, teachers and those who simply enjoy listening to great music.

Chapter One: Setting Contexts

As the title implies, Chapter One is intended to provide a framework within which this book ought to be read and understood. Whereas it should be expected that Julian Bream and Peter Pears would be the focus of attention in any project relating to the guitar works of Benjamin Britten, to this triumvirate I wish to add a fourth protagonist—the English lutenist and composer John Dowland (1563-1626). Under consideration here, the five works composed by Britten for guitar are the 'Second Lute Song of the Earl of Essex' (from the opera *Gloriana*, 1953),[3] *Songs from the Chinese*, Op. 58 (1957), *Courtly Dances* 'Aldeburgh Version' from *Gloriana* (1957),[4] *Folksong Arrangements Volume VI* (1961) and *Nocturnal, after John Dowland*, Op. 70 (1964). While three of these works—Op. 70, the 'Second Lute Song' and the 'Aldeburgh Version'—are clearly associated with the musical world of Dowland, if not directly inspired by him, it is my contention that the remaining two works—*Songs from the Chinese* and *Folksong Arrangements*—are also indebted to Dowland through Britten's intuitive use of musical rhetoric as a means to musically amplify text.

Before Britten composed anything for the guitar, both Dowland and Henry Purcell (1659-1695) were already central figures for him. Reconnecting with the 'golden age' of Elizabethan and Jacobean music was vitally important for Britten not only as a means of forging a new English vocal tradition but also as an opportunity to renovate earlier

3 Sanctioned by Britten, the exact date of this arrangement by Bream is unclear. It was recorded by Bream and Pears in 1963 (RCA SB 0021 LSC 2718) and published in 2003 by Boosey & Hawkes (BH 11929).

4 This is an unpublished and virtually unknown work for guitar and small orchestra rediscovered by the present writer at the Britten-Pears Library archive.

compositional types such as passacaglia and variation form as vital components within his own musical language. An early example of an overt association with Dowland is seen in *Lachrymae, reflections on a theme of John Dowland* for viola and piano, composed in 1950. While Britten's interest in early music was wide-ranging and undogmatic, I wish to argue that Bream's unique skills as a lutenist and guitarist encouraged the composer to specifically invoke Dowland when he wrote for the guitar. Dowland is thus situated in this study as an abiding influence in all the works that Britten composed for the instrument.

Chapter One is intended to provide a general introductory perspective that illuminates the historical and circumstantial conditions that led to Britten's guitar compositions, the role Bream played in the composer's plans for early and new music, and how Britten's complex, obsessive personality brought him into a coterminous relationship with Dowland's melancholic fixations. It thus sets out by providing a short survey of the development of the guitar's repertoire and the instrument's historic relationship with England. Building on the achievements of the Spanish guitarist Andrés Segovia who effectively established the guitar worldwide as a respected concert instrument, Bream broke new ground through his development and expansion of the guitar's modernist repertoire. I argue that his advocacy for new English music in particular was such that he single-handedly created what may be described as an English school of guitar composition. Bream's efforts in building a body of new English guitar works were paralleled by a desire to rejuvenate the rich vein of Elizabethan lute-song and instrumental music. This had profound implications for Britten's relationship with the guitarist and his contribution to the instrument's repertoire.

In this regard, Bream, the lutenist, played a crucial role for Britten. I argue that Britten and Pears saw Bream as emblematic of Dowland and thus the perfect linchpin for their project to connect with Elizabethan and Jacobean music. I examine the ways in which the tenor and the lutenist worked tirelessly to introduce early music to 20th-century audiences. Their efforts also helped to build a historical foundation upon which Britten would create and develop his individual musical signature. The alliance had the dual benefit of reinvigorating the greatest achievements in early English music while simultaneously evolving a new phase of 20th-century works. The guitar became the net beneficiary of this unique collaboration, as Britten answered Bream's requests for new music. While the lute was used to excavate England's past in the music of Dowland and his fellow composers, the guitar was employed to help create the future of English music in the works of Britten and his contemporaries.

Aside from absorbing specific aspects of musical techniques and aesthetics, Britten's association with Dowland further extends to more philosophical and psychological factors. These are exemplified by their shared obsessions with darkness, dream, sleep, death and what might be described as the pursuit through music of the unattainable, and indeed the quest for ultimate silence by way of a desired abstention from musical discourse, or what Heidegger relates to us as *Lichtung*—a 'clearing' of existence. This close philosophical bond cannot be underestimated. There are few examples in the history of music where one composer has so profoundly integrated with the inner motivations of another: Bach's assimilation of Vivaldi or Stravinsky's recalibration of Pergolesi do not match Britten's musical and psychological communion with Dowland. Given this close affiliation, no study of Britten's personal obsessions and how they impact his music can be conclusive without a comparative assessment of Dowland's personal preoccupations and the phenomenon of Elizabethan melancholy.

Indeed, the two composers' shared obsession with melancholy and their striking ability to compose music particularly suggestive of darkness, give to their chosen themes of death, dream, sleep and nothingness a peculiar physical and mesmeric presence. These fixations are so intense and pervasive that they can be distinguished as essential components of their work—what I call their musical idiolects. This is why it is essential to explore the socio-cultural, intellectual, religious, political and psychological circumstances that fed such compulsions. For Britten, early psychological traumas and ongoing internal conflicts surrounding his homosexuality play a large part in his musical attempts to escape into dark regions. For Dowland, dangerous political times and a desire for metaphysical truth impact his compositional personality. For both, melancholia is a touchstone for creative practice.

The chapter concludes by observing this shared melancholia through a philosophical lens in an effort to understand how it influences the music of both composers and our reception of it. Frameworks are sought for understanding the apparent contradiction in that a musical death wish may also serve as a conduit for transcendental release. It is essential to make these connections because the obsessions Dowland and Britten had with melancholic themes can then be seen in less negative terms. This study will show that at the core of such pessimistic fixations lies a paradoxical imperative to engage music as a positive mode of transcendental catharsis.

The Guitar, Bream and the 'English School'

When the Spanish vihuelist and composer Alonso Mudarra published his *Tres libros de música en cifra para vihuela* in 1546, he included within it six works for a four-course 'guitarra'—four *Fantasías*, a *Pavana* and a *Romanesca*.[5] This is not only the earliest known published source for the guitar, it is also one of the few examples before modern times of music written for the instrument by a composer who was not himself a guitarist. As Mudarra *did* play the vihuela, an instrument superficially related to the guitar, this point might appear to be somewhat academic. However, since a central focus of this study is the contribution made to the repertoire by composers who were not guitarists, Mudarra's publication becomes all the more pertinent.

For some four hundred years thereafter, music for the instrument was composed almost exclusively by guitarists. Not surprisingly, this resulted in a body of work largely comprising solo virtuosic music. The concentration on virtuosic solo repertoire tended to draw a *cordon sanitaire* around the instrument, discouraging non-guitarist composers from writing for it. It consequently steered the guitar away from developing potentially interesting chamber music combinations and undermined its prospect as an effective accompaniment instrument. While the guitar *is* found in these ensemble combinations, its predominant function as a solo instrument paradoxically inhibited the advancement of a more sophisticated and intricate repertoire. It is no accident that the extraordinary rise of the guitar in the 20th century directly parallels the expansion of the instrument's repertoire through the music of non-guitarist composers.

Manuel de Falla's *Homenaje, pour le tombeau de Claude Debussy* was the first work for the guitar that signalled this new development. Following the death of Debussy in 1918, Henri Prunières, the editor of the prominent *Revue Musicale*, asked Falla to contribute to a memorial issue planned for 1920. Instead of writing an article as requested, Falla composed *Homenaje*, which also gave him an opportunity to respond to a request for a guitar work by the Catalan guitarist and composer Miguel Llobet. It may be argued that Falla's *Homenaje* represents the beginning of a renaissance in the history of guitar music. It is not only a significant work in itself—Britten described it as 'a twenty-minute piece condensed and distilled into four minutes'—but it also marks a moment in the history of the repertoire when the guitar emerged from the

---

5 The *Romanesca* is a set of variations on the well-known Spanish song *O guárdame las vacas.*

parochial world of the guitarist-composer.[6] This is important, as it initiated a movement away from music ensuing from the prodigious dexterity of the virtuoso and the idiosyncrasies of the fret board to music that arose out of independent musical thought, music of a broader and more expansive semantic lineage. Free from the cult of the virtuoso, which saw its apogee in 19th-century virtuosi such as Mauro Giuliani, Fernando Sor and Giulio Regondi, *Homenaje* is the first guitar work that belongs to the more comprehensive world of music at large.

Despite his successful collaboration with Falla, Llobet failed to contribute more to the guitar repertoire apart from his own compositions, which, though they display a refined musical personality and an insider's knowledge of the fret board, are little more than attractive miniatures. Thus, it was left to Andrés Segovia to activate the project of expanding and improving the instrument's repertoire. He did this for decades with great diligence building a catalogue of new guitar works by composers such as Joaquín Turina, Heitor Villa-Lobos, Manuel Ponce, Maria Castelnuovo-Tedesco and Joaquín Rodrigo. This list, however, is telling. Segovia, who always maintained something of a 19th-century persona, surrounded himself with composers who were largely conservative in relation to the aesthetic, harmonic, structural and philosophical revolutions that were taking place in music throughout the 20th century.

There is no doubting Segovia's exceptional contribution to the development of the repertoire through his commissioning of works by non-guitarist composers, many of which are of considerable quality. However, it must also be acknowledged that he not only missed opportunities to encourage some leading figures to write for the instrument, he actually rejected some significant music by a number of prominent composers, presumably on the basis that it was too 'modern'. His dismissal of *Quatre pièces brèves* by Frank Martin and *Tombeau de Robert de Visée* by André Jolivet, to name just two, gives us some indication of Segovia's regrettable shortsightedness and conservatism.

---

[6] Tony Palmer, *Julian Bream: A Life on the Road* (London: MacDonald, 1982), 51. Bream paraphrases Britten in this passage. The significance of *Homenaje, pour le tombeau de Claude Debussy* can also be considered in light of Falla's own appraisal of it. In 1920, he made an arrangement of the work for piano, and another version became the second movement of his *Homenajes* for orchestra (1938/9). Its title, 'À Claude Debussy (Elegía de la guitarra)' pays tribute not only to Debussy but also to the instrument for which the original was composed.

Segovia's reactionary disposition is put into relief when we consider that Schoenberg's *Pierrot lunaire* was written in 1912, Stravinsky's *Le Sacre du printemps* was premiered in 1913, that serialism had been broadly accepted as a key movement in composition since the early 1920s, and that the Darmstadt School was making its impact from the early 1950s. Thus, by the time Julian Bream embarked upon his performing career in mid-century, modernism in music was well and truly established. In stark contrast, it must be recognized that, as a direct result of Segovia's explicitly conservative tastes, by the 1950s the guitar repertoire was, with some notable exceptions, effectively a catalogue of rather traditional miniatures written by composers who had not actively engaged with the modernist enterprise and its radical transformations that had been implemented since the turn of the century.

While it cannot be said that Bream was a champion of the most revolutionary manifestations of modernist experimentalism, he was at least aware of the conservatism that dominated guitar music up to the mid-century. His efforts to expand the repertoire are marked by an acknowledgement of the aesthetic developments that had long been established in other musical arenas and a belief that not all guitar music had to have a Hispanic dialect. Bream was also a lutenist, and while the exploration of early music for the lute might not appear to be an influential factor in the development of new guitar music, in his case and context, the two elements are directly connected. As we shall see, this interrelationship was strengthened by Bream's close working partnership with Britten and Pears who provided the focus for Bream's exploration of English music, past and contemporary. At this juncture, I wish to explore Bream's conscious efforts to develop the guitar repertoire from the late 1940s onwards, which took on a distinctively English character. Bream's initiative not only represented a potentially rich vein of music to be explored, but also marked a new affiliation that English composers, as a collective entity, would have with the instrument.

Historically, the guitar had always had a chequered relationship with England largely due to the prominence of the lute in northern Europe and the southern-European associations of the guitar, which gave to the instrument an 'exotic' quality that was deemed foreign to English sensibility. This 'othering' of the instrument more or less guaranteed the guitar's virtual absence from England throughout the Renaissance, Baroque and Classical periods. However, there were some notable exceptions. Charles II was an enthusiast who played the instrument.

When he reclaimed the throne in 1660, the guitar accordingly enjoyed a prominent if short-lived role in the Royal Court during his rule. Not surprisingly, in the years following the king's reign, the guitar declined again in popularity. The instrument's presence in England thereafter principally depended upon visiting composer-guitarists such as the Italians Francesco Corbetta, Nicola Matteis, Giacomo Merchi and Giulio Regondi, and the Catalan, Fernando Sor, who kept this 'exotic' instrument in vogue as a tangential novelty within the broader classical music arena.[7] Although amateur enthusiasts and societies in England maintained an abiding interest in the guitar well into the 20th century, no significant English composer before 1950 took it seriously. Seen in this context, Bream's achievement in developing an entirely native English repertoire is of historic importance.

By no means did Bream eschew the traditional repertoire. On the contrary, once he had established himself as a major figure in the guitar world, he became a leading interpreter of most of the Segovian catalogue. Significantly, as a performer he was a progressive, and his willingness to explore beyond the Hispanic paradigm fastidiously guarded by Segovia had a profound and positive impact on the instrument. As one commentator put it,

> Bream's achievement in the early fifties was not simply that he introduced the guitar as a classical instrument to an ever-growing public, but that because of his own eclectic and wide-ranging taste in music, he transformed the repertoire of the guitar.[8]

That transformation was initiated as far back as the late 1940s, when Bream embarked upon an almost messianic project to nurture an entirely new type of repertoire for the instrument. This new music was not only broadly modernist in its aesthetic character and language, it was also decidedly English. The first composer to respond to Bream's request for new music was Reginald Smith Brindle, who wrote a short piece in 1947 entitled *Nocturne*. Stephen Dodgson, who was at that stage a fellow student of Bream's at the Royal College of Music, followed up with a short *Suite*. As inconspicuous as these two diminutive works are, they represent the foundation upon which Bream was eventually to build a significant body of English music for the instrument. Progress was slow, but Bream's resolve was firm:

---

7 For a detailed history of the guitar in England see James Tyler and Paul Sparks, *The Guitar and its Music* (Oxford: Oxford University Press, 2002).

8 Tony Palmer, *Julian Bream: A Life on the Road*, 35.

> It wasn't until the mid-fifties, when my recording career got under way, that I could actually afford new pieces...In 1957, Lennox Berkeley wrote a Sonatina for me, although that was commissioned by the BBC...and then Malcolm Arnold...wrote the well known Concerto...In fact, his Concerto was the first major British Concerto ever written for the guitar.[9]

Although Arnold's jazz-inflected tonal language can hardly be described as avant-garde, Bream was clearly interested in building a new repertoire that took some cognizance of musical developments in the 20th century and that did not predictably regurgitate clichéd Spanish idioms. Consequently, more adventurous music such as Smith Brindle's 1956 work, *El Polifemo d'Oro* came to Bream. Although based on the poem *Adivinanza de la Guitarra* by Federico García Lorca, *El Polifemo d'Oro* was music that decidedly did not speak Spanish. Another distinctly modernist work for the guitar came in the form of Richard Rodney Bennett's serial-based *Five Impromptus*, composed in 1968. With these two works, which Segovia would never have performed, the guitar finally caught up with modernist developments in music. In the four decades that followed, Bream continued to arduously build upon these pioneering achievements by encouraging more and more English composers of note to write pieces for him. In those years, figures such as James Bernard, Peter Racine Fricker, Tristram Cary, Tom Eastwood, William Walton, Humphrey Searle, Mátyás Seiber, Alan Rawsthorne, Giles Swayne, Peter Maxwell Davies, Michael Tippett, Lennox Berkeley and Michael Berkeley added important new music to this 'English' catalogue.

Of course, in developing the repertoire for the guitar, Bream did not restrict himself to the English scene. He also made many attempts to entice some of the century's foremost international composers to write new works for him. While he made some significant breakthroughs with leading figures such as Hans Werner Henze, Tōru Takemitsu and Leo Brouwer, he was not always successful in his efforts to expand the repertoire. A request to Stravinsky to write for him remained unanswered,[10] and while plans to commission a new work by Frank Martin were initiated, the composer unfortunately died before the project could be started. Further invitations submitted directly to Hindemith and Lutoslawski were courteously declined. Even Shostakovich was approached while on a visit to England. Bream cheerfully comments that, 'eventually [I] asked him to write a piece for

---

[9] Ibid., 80-81.

[10] *Julian Bream: My Life in Music*, DVD (Avie Productions, 2004).

the guitar. I knew it wouldn't come off. But there's nothing like a try, is there?'[11]

It would therefore be incorrect to suggest that Bream was concerned solely with creating an English school of guitar music, or that he was being consciously nationalistic to the point of excluding international figures. This is certainly not the case. However, while his efforts to encourage new music for the guitar led to a number of significant works by international composers, Bream's influence as a conduit for new music was felt most strongly among his fellow countrymen and it is here that his major contribution to new music for the guitar can be most appreciated. It is my contention that the collective body of work written for Bream by English composers is of such extensive range and distinction that it can quite legitimately be described as a 'school' of guitar composition. I further suggest that Britten's contribution to this school represents its highest peak.

Britten's rather extensive body of work for the guitar might lead one to assume that he was an untiring advocate for the instrument, but evidence suggests a more complex relationship. Bream's initial connection to Britten came through his musical partnership with Peter Pears as an accompanist on the lute, not as a guitarist. It is worth noting that the guitar, at least in the early years, was not at the forefront of the musical triumvirate that was Britten, Pears and Bream. Indeed, indications are that Britten was at the very least ambivalent about the guitar at this time. In a diary entry for 3 April 1934, the composer writes: 'We go to a Segovia recital at Patti palace at 9.0; but get bored and leave after one third of it...of course he is a superb player, but I don't like the Guitar as a solo inst[rument].'[12] These are hardly the comments of an enthusiastic guitar advocate or of the composer who would go on to produce one of the towering masterpieces in the repertoire. The truth is that Britten's exposure to the guitar came about more as a result of practical circumstances than through any abiding affection for the instrument. One of the central reasons for this exposure was the result of Britten's growing success as a composer, which placed increasing demands upon his time and prevented him from accepting concert engagements as an accompanist to Pears. Consequently, Pears was forced to search out alternative musicians to work with including the pianist Noel Mewton-Wood, the harpist Osian Ellis and Bream on the guitar and lute.

---

[11] Tony Palmer, *Julian Bream: A Life on the Road*, 92.

[12] John Evans, ed., *Journeying Boy: The Diaries of the Young Benjamin Britten 1928-1938* (London: Faber & Faber, 2009), 206.

In this respect, Britten's loss was Bream's gain, as Pears increasingly concertized with the guitarist and lutenist while the composer was busy writing music. Britten describes how the working relationship altered:

> ...[Pears'] flexible voice, with from the beginning an excellent technique, enabled us to explore music from widely different styles: from the early lutenists (which in those early days, before the advent of Julian Bream, I used to play for him on the piano).[13]

These were the circumstances under which Britten's first original composition for guitar, *Songs from the Chinese*, emerged. Once Bream was established as a core musician within Britten's circle, other works naturally followed including 'Aldeburgh Version', the 'Second Lute Song' and the *Folksong Arrangements*. Bream's comments on the matter are enlightening, not only in highlighting Britten's pragmatic attitude to the guitar but also in exposing his actual preference for the lute:

> I asked him originally in the mid-fifties, if he would write a solo piece for me...He said he would, although in fact I waited almost ten years for it. Around that time I was giving a lot of recitals with Peter Pears...For our concerts together Britten had written us a beautiful song cycle called *Songs from the Chinese*. But I suspect that for Britten the guitar was not much more than an 'interesting' instrument, almost too exotic in fact...As a plucked instrument, the harp was much more Britten's taste, more abstract, and his use of that instrument particularly in his chamber operas is as adroit as it is inspired. At first he thought he might write a lute piece for me. He adored the lute. I said, well, that would be marvelous, but there are not many lute players around, so if you're going to write a piece that has a chance of being heard and played regularly, then the guitar is the instrument. He too was a very practical man, and I think he got the point.[14]

If practicalities provided much of the incentive for Britten to write for the guitar, he nonetheless found a way to bring the instrument around to his way of thinking (or hearing). Bream reveals that in writing Op. 70,

> [Britten] obviously thought about the piece for a long time, and obviously still had the sound of the lute in his head, because towards the end of *Nocturnal*, he uses the guitar in such a way that you can almost believe you're listening to a lute. In other words, he made the guitar sound the way *he* wanted it to sound.[15]

---

[13] Paul Kildea, ed., *Britten on Music* (Oxford: Oxford University Press, 2003), 310.

[14] Tony Palmer, *Julian Bream: A Life on the Road*, 87.

[15] Ibid.

In this respect, Britten's relationship to the guitar was akin to that which I highlighted earlier about the broader reception of the instrument historically in England—as something of a foreign curiosity. Had Bream not been intimately involved with Pears and Britten, it appears unlikely that the latter would have composed anything for the guitar at all. Thankfully, Britten was a composer who developed close relationships with a small coterie of performing musicians for whom he wrote numerous compositions over an extended period of time. Given the international calibre of the performers mentioned in the following statement by Britten, we can reflect on the esteem in which Bream was held:

> I've learned a great deal from many artists I've written for and worked with, singers particularly (Joan Cross, Ferrier, Fischer-Dieskau, Vishnevskaya), some instrumentalists (Dennis Brain, Rostropovich, and many young English instrumentalists like Julian Bream and Ossian [sic] Ellis...[16]

Bream was thus fortunate to have had the benefit of Britten's friendship and professional approval, to have had the opportunity to become a close working partner to Pears and to be viewed as a significant participant in Britten's project to fuse his compositional signature to the musical aesthetics of the English Renaissance. This close relationship resulted in a remarkable body of music for the instrument culminating in a masterpiece for solo guitar. The significance of this work is articulated in a letter written by Bream to the composer in 1965 in which he states that he had performed *Nocturnal* no less than twenty-six times on his tour of the United States, and that it was received on every occasion with great enthusiasm. Bream further remarks in this letter that Op. 70 is, even at this early stage, considered to be a 'classic' in the repertoire and requests Britten to consider writing another work.[17] Having built a substantial body of guitar music written by some of the finest English composers of the 20th century, it is evident that Bream considered Britten's contribution as the jewel in the crown. It should come as no surprise therefore that the guitarist continued to push Britten for a new work in order to strengthen and develop this English school he had instigated and nurtured. Alas, it was a request that was to remain unanswered.

---

[16] Paul Kildea, ed., 248-9.

[17] Letter from Julian Bream to Benjamin Britten, 14 April 1965. Source: Britten-Pears Library archive.

Britten, Pears and Bream: Connecting to the Golden Age of English Song

One of Britten's compositional stances in relation to broader English trends may be best characterized in his opposition to the use of folksong as a basis for art composition.[18] As his diaries attest, this viewpoint seems to have established itself at an early stage in Britten's musical development. Some entries graphically highlight the young composer's concerted opposition to the determination of Vaughan Williams and others to forge a national tradition of art music developed from English folksong.[19] However, there were other factors at play here, not least those of a socio-political kind. It is worth noting that Britten would have been instinctively uncomfortable with some of the rhetoric used to promote folk-based art music that linked it to a belief in a particular sort of English identity. Notions of English racial superiority over other groups occasionally accompanied such rhetoric in the inter-war years. Even if unintentional, a tendency towards right-wing thinking would have made Britten, a homosexual and, at the time, a left-wing sympathizer, feel somewhat isolated and defensive.

From a purely musical perspective, Britten's position was based on his unwillingness to accept the limitation of modal material as a core foundation for composition. Despite the popularity and influence of modal-based music in England in the first half of the 20th century, from an early age Britten developed alternative aesthetic and cultural viewpoints that emanated from an unusual combination of national and international influences. He consciously drew inspiration from a number of contemporaneous cosmopolitan sources and cleverly circumvented the pastoral school, of which Vaughan Williams was a leading advocate. He achieved this by innovatively modifying his music through the forging of a deep connection with the great English composers of the late-Tudor and Stuart periods. Vocal music was at the core of this project and the undisputed gifts of Dowland and Purcell as song composers positioned them as superlative models. Though not

---

[18] While this statement asserts a general position, it simplifies Britten's relationship to folksong. As we shall see, Britten developed a strong attachment to the genre, which is evidenced by the significant number of arrangements that he made.

[19] On 28 December 1934, Britten wrote in his diary: 'Job of Vaughan Williams seemed interminable. There are some nice things in it if you aren't tired of folk song modalism – but most of it is heavy, dull, imitative & amateurish...It is concerts like this which make me absolutely despair of English Music and its critics.' John Evans, ed., *Journeying Boy: The Diaries of the Young Benjamin Britten 1928-1938* (London: Faber & Faber, 2009), 240.

noted for making overt commentaries about his own music, Britten was unambiguous about situating himself as key to reinstating English vocal music as a major component of 20th-century musical art: 'One of my chief aims is to try and restore to the musical setting of the English language a brilliance, freedom and vitality that have been curiously rare since the days of Purcell.'[20]

This statement reminds us that, in England, song as a genre declined after the death of Purcell. The tremendous success of Handel's dramatic works had a weakening impact on the more intimate form. All over Europe, the expansion of the public concert as an established trend, the creation of larger concert halls and the advancement in instrumental construction brought purely abstract music to new heights of importance. As a result, song was increasingly confined to private performance—a practice, which in Viennese society reached its pinnacle in the celebrated *Schubertiads*. There were in England, however, no composers of Schubert's stature, and it was not until the late 19th and early 20th centuries that song made something of a comeback with composers such as Frederick Delius, Arnold Bax and John Ireland, and with the folksong revival led by Cecil Sharp and Vaughan Williams among others. Britten, however, rejected both impressionistic, pastoral idylls and folk-based art songs, and consciously established a direct connection between his aesthetics and the exemplary music of the Elizabethan and Jacobean periods. While others were convinced that the rejuvenation of English music could only happen through the aestheticization of the ethnic repertoire, Britten saw the integration of Elizabethan forms into contemporaneous compositional practice as the most constructive rebuttal of the accusation that England was 'Das Land ohne Musik'.[21] While it would be wrong to suggest that he singlehandedly brought England's 17th-century rhetorical tradition to an overdue re-evaluation, it is true that because Britten wrote so brilliantly and extensively for the voice he can justifiably be seen as the first

---

[20] Benjamin Britten, 'Preface to Peter Grimes', in *Benjamin Britten's Poets: The Poetry He Set to Music*, ed., Boris Ford (Manchester: Carcarnet Press, 1994) xi.

[21] *Das Land ohne Musik* (*The Land Without Music*) is the title of a book published in 1904 by the German author and philosopher Oskar Adolf Hermann Schmitz (1873-1931). A barely concealed declaration of Germany's cultural superiority, it reinforced a perception of England that held sway in many parts of Europe during the latter half of the 19th century. Such as they were, English sensitivities were progressively relieved by the emergence of strong musical voices at the end of the 19th century and throughout the 20th.

composer since Purcell to advance English song as a significant facet of European music.

Much has been made of Purcell's incisive influence on Britten's vocal music. It was the belief that the former had 'never been matched in his ability to write the greatest of melodies that musically "speak" the English language' that had such a profound effect'.[22] This influence can also be seen in Britten's idiosyncratic realizations of numerous works by Purcell, from *Dido and Aeneas* and other stage works to individual songs. Current musicologists and performers who engage with historically informed practice sometimes dismiss Britten's Purcell reconstructions as anachronistic and inauthentic—their dramatic character and distinctive harmony illustrate Britten's imprint as much as they exhibit Purcell's. These works do, however, point to an extraordinary interpenetration of the two composers' compositional styles and underscore the deep association Britten felt with Purcell. If such symbiosis is a measure of a composer's influence upon Britten, then Dowland must also be seen in similar light, though with this signal distinction: Britten's relationship with Dowland is most effectively demonstrated in the works he wrote for and with guitar.

Even before Pears met Britten, the young tenor's connection to Elizabethan vocal music was firmly established, as he had been a member of the English Singers ensemble from the mid-1930s through which he had become familiar with the entire Elizabethan madrigal repertoire. Pears, therefore, was not only a hugely talented singer with whom Britten could have a successful and long-term musical partnership, he genuinely shared the composer's fascination with the music of England's past, and became a central advocate for his project to re-establish song as a major component of new English music following centuries of effective absence. Starting in 1954 and lasting twenty years, Bream's collaboration with Pears was also of great significance in this regard, as he played a pivotal role both as solo lutenist and as lute accompanist to Pears in bringing the music of Dowland and other Renaissance composers to new audiences following decades of neglect.

While Bream's interpretations on the lute would not necessarily adhere closely to historically informed practice, early-music advocates will admit that they nonetheless represent a significant initial

[22] Rodney Farnsworthy, "Hither, This Way': A Rhetorical-Musical Analysis of a Scene from Purcell's 'King Arthur',' *The Musical Quarterly* Vol 74, No. 1 (1990): 93.

development in the history of that renewal.[23] As we have already noted, Bream's influential work in Renaissance English music meant that his career was defined by a two-pronged strategy. His desire to develop a new English school of guitar composition was equalled by a determination to introduce to broader audiences the music of early English masters such as Dowland, Thomas Morley, Thomas Campion and Thomas Ford.

This strategy is evidenced in Bream's debut LP from 1955 entitled *An Anthology of English Song*, which was recorded on the lute accompanying Pears.[24] Bream's dual trajectory can be observed in subsequent years, as he shifted from lute to guitar and back again. Following a number of guitar albums, he returned to the lute in a 1957 recording entitled *Bream plays Dowland*.[25] The apparent reincarnation of the Elizabethan lutenist in the guise of a modern virtuoso appears to have had a considerable impact on Britten whose core aesthetic drive, as we have noted, was the recapturing of early English music within his own compositional aesthetics. A review of this album not only gives us some flavour of how novel this music was to listeners in the late 1950s but also intimates the paucity of such dedicated recordings at this initial stage of the early-music revival:

> This is one of the few recitals on an old instrument that can be heard from start to finish in one sitting, and with unalloyed enjoyment. [It] shows us that Dowland is no musty historical figure, but a composer of first-rate importance and one of the greatest musical figures in Elizabethan and Jacobean times.[26]

Bream plays Dowland was quickly followed in 1958 by another recording with Pears, entitled *A Recital of Lute Songs*.[27] Again, while the following review of the album sheds light on Bream's idiosyncratic interpretations, it also indicates how these early recordings allowed listeners, even professional ones, to re-evaluate the complexity of the lute accompaniments:

---

[23] See Appendix I for a selected discography of Julian Bream's recordings on the lute as solo instrument, as an accompanist to Pears and in larger ensembles featuring the music of Dowland and his English contemporaries.

[24] Decca LW 5243 (mono).

[25] Westminster XWN 18428 (mono)

[26] John Duarte (writing under the pseudonym 'Discus'), *Banjo, Mandolin and Guitar* (1960): 23; cited in Graham Wade, *The Art of Julian Bream*, (Blaydon on Tyne: Ashley Mark Publishing Company, 2008), 62.

[27] Decca LXT 5567.

> Peter Pears' voice is the perfect instrument for these songs in its flexibility; whilst Bream (a lutenist of world ranking even though he plays it like a guitar) could hardly be bettered as his accompanist. In many of the songs it is not really accompaniment in the usual sense; the lute has contrapuntally-moving parts to play which weave one fabric with the thread of the voice.[28]

In the following years, Bream continued to make numerous recordings on the lute as solo instrument, as an accompanist to Pears and in larger ensembles featuring the music of Dowland and his English contemporaries.[29] Alongside his live performances, the repertorial breadth of these recordings demonstrates that Bream's work in this area from the 1950s onwards can be evaluated as a major contribution to the revival of the early music scene in Europe. This is the very reason why he played such an important role for Britten.

In Bream, Britten and Pears not only recognized someone who was undoubtedly a virtuoso performer of great musical depth and personality, but also a musician who understood the nature and value of the Elizabethan and Jacobean traditions.[30] Bream thus created a valuable link in the project connecting Britten to his historical antecedents. The acute paucity of professional lute and guitar virtuosi in the early 1950s gave to Bream's artistry a deeply symbolic importance—a factor to which I think Pears and Britten were acutely sensitive. In a programme note for a concert in Aldeburgh on 22 June 1963 celebrating the 400th anniversary of Dowland's birth, Pears gives us an indication of the emblematic position Bream had begun to occupy in his mind and, doubtless, in Britten's also:

> Dowland certainly knew how to play his own lute music, but we had to wait three [sic] hundred years for his successor, and it is one of the achievements of his successor of today that he can reveal to us the rich and subtle counterpoint and sustain it, by means of a 'modern' colour-and-dynamic technique wholly right for this expressive music. Thus the 400-year-old composer—and his dear instrument—still lives.[31]

---

[28] John Duarte, *Banjo, Mandolin and Guitar* (1960): 23; cited in Graham Wade, *The Art of Julian Bream*, (Blaydon on Tyne: Ashley Mark Publishing Company, 2008), 62.

[29] See Graham Wade, *The Art of Julian Bream*, (Blaydon on Tyne: Ashley Mark Publishing Company, 2008); see also Appendix I.

[30] The accomplishments of both the countertenor Alfred Deller (1912-1979), and the lutenist and guitarist Desmond Dupré (1916-1976) in the project to rejuvenate English music at this time should be acknowledged.

[31] Peter Pears, 'John Dowland', in *The Sixteenth Aldeburgh Festival of Music and the Arts* (programme booklet), 27, in Graham Wade, *The Art of Julian Bream*, (Blaydon on Tyne: Ashley Mark Publishing Company, 2008), 74.

That Bream was able to make a substantial contribution to the first major celebration of Dowland in modern times is notable. As that 400th-anniversary festival also served as a public demonstration of Britten's aesthetic affiliations, Bream's presence takes on a more symbolic and significant meaning; hence the comments by Pears that Dowland 'still lives'. This projection from the past to the present is paralleled in the number of newly composed works that Pears and Bream jointly commissioned for voice and guitar throughout the 1950s and 1960s. These include *Shepherd's Warning* by James Bernard, which was premiered in the Wigmore Hall on 12 November 1952, *Four French Folksongs* by Mátyás Seiber, published by Schott in 1959, and *Anon. In Love* by William Walton, given its first performance in 1960 at the Aldeburgh Festival.[32] Here we see Bream's two-pronged approach to repertoire development feeding into his duo with Pears. The success in forging a new English song repertoire was perhaps exceptionally realized in a groundbreaking recording from 1963, *Music for Voice and Guitar*, which includes the Walton, Seiber and *O Mistress Mine* by Peter Racine Fricker. However, the album centrally features Britten's *Songs from the Chinese*, *Folksong Arrangements* and the 'Second Lute Song'.[33] Significantly, these compositions not only added to the repertoire for voice and guitar, but also bridged a historical gap of almost four hundred years to reinstate the English song tradition that was so exemplary of the Tudor and Stuart periods. In many ways, the 'Second Lute Song'—being an arrangement for tenor and guitar of an 'orchestrated' lute song, quite literally crossed both worlds. The composer for whom this connection meant most was, of course, Britten.

The concert in which the premiere of *Songs from the Chinese* took place in 1958 evidences Bream's symbolic importance. The programme itself can be interpreted as a mission statement conspicuously outlining the aesthetic connections Britten as a 20th-century composer wished to make with Dowland. Even the rhetorically driven arrangements of English folksongs (which we will discuss in Chapter Four) contribute to Britten's forging of a new 'guitar-song' genre that designated Dowland's lute-song genre as its aesthetic *fons et origo*.

---

32 In 1971 Walton re-scored *Anon. In Love* for tenor and small orchestra. Anxious to expand this repertoire, the duo also searched beyond the shores of England to seek new work from composers such as Hans Werner Henze who wrote (and dedicated to Britten) *Kammermusik 1958* for tenor, guitar and eight instrumentalists.

33 RCA SB 0021 LSC 2718.

Figure 1: Programme for Aldeburgh Festival recital at Glemham House, 17 June 1958

Peter Pears (tenor) and Julian Bream (lute)[34]

John Dowland — Fantasies, Galliards and Songs[35]

Flow my tears *and* Lachrymae Pavan
Fantasy for Lute solo
Fine Knacks for Ladies
Capt. Diggory Piper's Galliard *and*
If my complaints
The King of Denmark's Galliard
Die not before thy day
Now O now I needs must part *and* The Frog Galliard
What if I never speed?
The Earl of Essex Galliard

INTERVAL

[Britten][36] — Songs from the Chinese
[arr. Britten] — Folk Songs

The Shooting of his dear
Master Kilby
The Soldier and the Sailor [37]

Making these emblematic associations in the recital programme was important. When a reviewer for this concert stated that 'Julian Bream's lute and guitar playing has a quality of exquisite and timeless intimacy that conjures up equally well the melancholy of our own Dowland and of the classical Chinese poet', he was instinctively referencing the symbolic and aesthetic connections that the performers wished to convey between the lute and guitar on the one hand and Dowland and Britten on the other.[38]

As we have noted, those aesthetic connections are characterized by the obsession both composers had with themes of darkness, sleep, dreams and death. In the music of Dowland, the sheer number of songs that directly link to such themes demonstrates this fixation; indeed, the

---

34 Curiously, the programme here does not mention the guitar.

35 *The Aldeburgh Festival Programme Books 1954-1960*, held at the Britten-Pears Library, contain pencil annotations suggesting that some changes to the published programme were made.

36 Britten's name as composer and arranger (here placed in square brackets) does not appear on the programme.

37 Source: Britten-Pears Library archive.

38 Martin Cooper, *Daily Telegraph*, 18 June 1958. Source: Britten-Pears Library.

lutenist Anthony Rooley has highlighted up to fourteen.[39] These songs, alongside instrumental works that embody melancholia in their general mood, established a significant precedent for Britten, who, as we shall see, dwelt upon similar themes from a very early period in his creative output.

Melancholia and Musical Idiolect

> But night and dreams...I have had a strange fascination about that world since a very early age.[40]

> *Semper Dowland, semper dolens.*[41]

In situating Dowland as a seminal influence on Britten, it is useful to survey not only themes of common interest already outlined but also to investigate the particular socio-political, spiritual-religious and psychological factors that motivated the composers to develop such habitual obsessions. Despite the significant length of time that separates Britten from Dowland, and the obvious divergences in their modal and tonal languages, the degree to which melancholic motifs interpenetrate their work has given their musical aesthetics a very particular, identifiable and unique voice; a phenomenon that could be described as their shared musical idiolects.

In some respects, Britten's musical associations with dream, sleep and death are so much taken for granted that it comes as something of a surprise to observe in more detail the actual extent of these obsessions. The connection to melancholic subject matter is something of which Britten as a mature composer was clearly conscious. However, it is instructive to observe how these gloomy and nocturnal fixations instigated themselves at the preliminary stages in the young composer's development. A perusal of some early works will demonstrate the extent to which such dark and even adult motifs infiltrated the young composer's awareness.

---

39 'All ye whom love or fortune hath betrayed'; 'Would my conceit that first enforced my woe'; 'Flow my tears'; 'Sorrow stay! Lend true repentant tears'; 'Die not before thy day'; 'Mourn, mourn, day is with darkness fled'; 'If floods of tears could cleanse my follies past'; 'Toss not my soul'; 'Flow not so fast ye fountains'; 'Lend your ears to my sorrow, good people'; 'In darkness let me dwell'; 'Go nightly cares, the enemy to rest, From silent night, true register of moans'; and 'Come Heavy Sleep'. See Anthony Rooley, 'New Light on John Dowland's Songs of Darkness', *Early Music* Vol. 11, No. 12, (1983): 6.

40 Benjamin Britten and Donald Mitchell, *Owen Wingrave* (unpublished transcription of a BBC broadcast given in April 1971), 2.

41 'Always Dowland, always doleful'.

This is evidenced in a very early composition, *Quatre Chansons Françaises* of 1928, a setting of texts by Paul Verlaine and Victor Hugo. In the first song, *Nuits de Juin*, the dream-like atmosphere in the words, 'With eyes closed and ears half-open / Only a transparent half-sleep is possible', unmistakably invokes the nocturnal imagery of Dowland's 'Come Heavy Sleep' that Britten would later explore.[42] His setting of these words indicates clearly that the fifteen-year-old composer was already brooding on themes that were to remain central inspirations throughout his life. The third poem of the cycle, *L'enfance*, which juxtaposes the singing of a child with the 'death-rattle' of his mother, is particularly disturbing. It is remarkable that such dark subject matter should attract one so young, but all through his early life ruminations on the nocturnal continued to inhabit Britten's musical consciousness. This is seen in another early collection of songs entitled *Tit for Tat* for voice and piano on poems by Walter de la Mare.[43] One song from the set, 'Autumn', deals with the aftermath of a child's death, while another, 'Vigil', tells the story of the narrator attempting to read in the disappearing light of an approaching night. Themes of light and darkness, and the dissolution of consciousness are ones we will see Britten returning to habitually. Connected themes emerge in the title song, 'Tit for Tat', which provides the first indication of Britten's distaste for hunting and killing.

The hunting theme would return frequently, as it did in 1936 with the song cycle for high voice and orchestra, *Our Hunting Fathers*. Compiled by W.H. Auden, who was a significant influence on Britten at this early stage, the texts centre on the ethics of power and control relating to man and the animal world. They gave Britten an opportunity to explore images of pestilence, death and hunting through impressive orchestral writing, particularly in the 'Dance of Death' and the 'Epilogue and Funeral March'.[44] Britten also set a *danse macabre* by Auden in his 1939 composition for tenor solo, chorus and orchestra, *Ballad of Heroes*. The Second World War cannot have been far from Britten's thoughts in 1940 when he composed his largest orchestral work for the

---

42 Boris Ford, ed., *Benjamin Britten's Poets: The Poetry He Set to Music* (Manchester: Carcanet Press, 1994), 3 (translator not cited).

43 *Tit for Tat* was written between 1928 and 1931. Revised in 1968, Britten and John Shirley-Quirk first performed the collection on 23 June 1969 at the Aldeburgh Festival.

44 Just a few years earlier, Auden published a one-act play in verse and prose entitled *The Dance of Death*—a satire on the death of the capitalistic middle classes. Auden's belief in the transformational power of death was influential on the young Britten.

concert hall, *Sinfonia da Requiem*. Its three movements—'Lacrymosa', 'Dies Irae' and Requiem Aeternam'—take their headings from the Roman Catholic Mass for the Dead. An early connection with Elizabethan melancholy is made with the Dowland-associated first movement. In its total submersion in death, *Sinfonia da Requiem* can be seen as the culmination of Britten's pre-war melancholic obsessions.

Was there something about Britten's childhood that amplified the significance of darkness, dreams and melancholy in one so young? Perhaps the isolation of boarding school exacerbated the insecurities that most children experience at some stage in their development. Although not badly treated, his childhood diaries do indicate that while at Gresham's School in Holt, Britten experienced long periods of loneliness and sporadic bouts of depression. He was also prone to nightmares, as this excerpt from his diary shows: 'I really am getting alarmed at the lack of a letter from Mummy. Especially, as I dreamed about death 2ce [twice] last night, & both times tho' not she, it was connected with her.'[45] A little later, Britten recorded a dream that points to a deep trauma experienced as a result of being separated from his family:

> I really think that last night was the most miserable night of my existence. 1. I couldn't get to sleep (not. Usual). 2. I had literally about 6 terrible dreams, separated by ½ hour of sleeplessness. In 1. Mummy was killed by a chimney stack falling through the roof. 2. Pop was killed when driving a bus (!) over Kessinland dam. 3. Beth...was burned in the house catching fire.[46]

While it would be easy to exaggerate the stuffy and austere atmosphere of pre-war British boarding schools, these diary entries do indicate that the young Britten endured the trauma of long, secluded days and distressing, sleepless nights. That he could creatively work through this psychological anguish by composing—particularly the setting of texts that directly confront issues of death, loneliness, sleep, dreams, violence and repose—explains why, even as he got older, such a cathartic process became indispensible to his life. The procedure of encapsulating and exorcising traumatic experiences through music certainly delivered a psychosomatic and therapeutic release for Britten. Indeed, the practice became a requisite component of his work: by the time he was twenty-seven, interpenetrations of dream, sleep, death and

---

45 John Evans, ed., *Journeying Boy: The Diaries of the Young Benjamin Britten 1928-1938* (London: Faber & Faber, 2009), 30. The diary excerpt is dated 23 January 1929.

46 Ibid., 31. The diary excerpt is dated 11 February 1929.

all things nocturnal had established themselves in his psychological makeup to such an extent that they collectively acted as a hidden but dynamic teleological strategy in his music.

From this point on, melancholic fixations are more or less inseparable from Britten's music and run through his entire corpus. This is evidenced by the works that manifestly explore nocturnal themes such as *Serenade, Lachrymae, reflections on a song of John Dowland, Nocturne, A Mid-Summer Night's Dream, Nocturnal, after John Dowland* and *Death in Venice.* Set apart, this list is sufficient to establish Britten as 'an indefatigable walker in unlit places', to quote George Steiner. But Britten's melancholic reach into darkness also extends to other compositions. Even in those works whose central themes lie elsewhere, fixations of the darkest hue take hold in sub-texts and thematic interpenetrations. Here, Britten's melancholic addictions are touched upon, tantalizingly intimated or made inconspicuously implicit. For example, death and dreams pervade *Peter Grimes.* Death is told, 'be not proud', in *The Holy Sonnets of John Donne.* Disturbing night scenes haunt *The Rape of Lucretia. Winter Words* is a solemn rumination on physical and psychical deterioration. A madwoman finds the spirit of her dead child in *Curlew River.* Through metaphoric modes of undertone, death is enunciated in the 'poison tree' of *Songs and Proverbs of William Blake*; and the blood of dead children is just one dark image from a collection of melancholic ruminations—'Nightmare', 'Black Day' and 'Bed-time'—that permeate the cycle *Who Are These Children?*

This brief outline illustrates an unbroken continuum that gives Britten's melancholic work a perception and reach into the ineffable, dark regions of the psyche and the metaphysical that few composers, perhaps with the exceptions of Mahler, Berg and Crumb, rival with such consistent obsession. There are, of course, other fixations at play in Britten's music, not least those that emerge out of the disturbing conflicts he suffered as a homosexual in a heteronormative society. Britten's inability to outwardly express his most intimate concerns (even later in life when an increasingly liberal Britain allowed for such expression) was a powerful generator of musical schemata that embodied modes of conflict and irresolution. When these forces are most at play, antinomy becomes a cardinal feature. In Britten's music, such contradiction finds expression in the torsions between day and night, wakefulness and sleep, reality and dreams, and life and death.

As such conflicts also pervade Dowland's music, I wish to explore those aspects of his life and times that give his work a deep reach into melancholia. What were his beliefs and attitudes? What fed his psychological instabilities? What were the political and philosophical conditions that shaped his development as a composer? While this is not the place to embark on a biography of Dowland, there are four main issues that are, I think, central to answering these questions: Dowland's Catholicism, his failure to secure a position at the Court of Queen Elizabeth I; the collective spiritual and religious uncertainty of the period; and the composer's intellectual engagement with the philosophies of Neoplatonism that infiltrated deep into English artistic sensibility.

Dowland's decision to convert to Catholicism is a curious one, especially during this period of the Reformation wars when religious affiliation could have very grave personal and political consequences. The allure of the 'Mother Church' had to have been especially appealing considering the real and present danger in which his religious affiliation often placed him. Dowland would have been aware of this from an early age. While at Oxford, for example, he would have had to keep his Catholicism a secret, as the university required graduates to subscribe to numerous Articles of the Anglican Church. Even the revered status of England's foremost composer, the Catholic William Byrd, could not protect him whenever the Protestant Court decided to unleash its fury. In 1583, for example, Byrd's perceived affiliation with Thomas Paget, a key suspect in the Throckmorton Plot to kill the Queen, resulted in a temporary expulsion from Chapel Royal; and in the following year he was placed on the recusancy list for declining to participate in Anglican services. Adherence to Catholicism at this period was thus a choice that brought with it all sorts of potential hazards.

To make matters worse, Dowland seems to have been habitually prone to injudicious behaviour, which placed him in more than usual danger. His apparently naive involvement in 1595 with Catholic expatriates in Florence who were plotting to kill the Queen brought this home to him in no uncertain way. He had recently arrived in Italy with the ultimate aim to study in Rome with the renowned madrigalist Luca Marenzio. However, his association with traitors to the Crown, unintended or not, jeopardized his life. After writing a pleading letter to Sir Robert Cecil, he quickly returned to the court at Kassel to which he was contracted, and subsequently continued on to England. All this danger, potential or real, points to some deeply compelling motivation behind Dowland's decision to convert to Catholicism and to remain a Catholic throughout his life. As he had no misgivings about working at the Reformist courts of two German princes,[47] it is likely that his attachment to the 'old religion' had more to do with its mystical and ritualistic traditions than with any form of blind, militant allegiance.

Dowland's enticement back to England was also the result of a letter he received from Henry Noel, a prominent courtier and friend of Queen Elizabeth, suggesting that his return, in conjunction with Noel's active support, might result in a court position—something the lutenist had greatly desired for quite some time. When Noel died before he could arrange the appointment, it must have seemed to Dowland that fate was against him. To make matters worse, in 1594, when he applied for the prestigious post of court lutenist to the Queen, left vacant on the death of the previous occupant, John Johnson, his application was unsuccessful and the position continued to elude him. Much of Dowland's professional life and private anguish was thus affected by his failed attempts to advance in Elizabeth's Court. Numerous accounts attest to his tendency towards deep suspicion and the ensuing melancholy such reversals exacerbated. While his assertion that the Queen's rejection was a direct result of him being an 'obstinate papist' had some grounds,[48] his machinations with traitors to the Crown and his well-known proclivity for publicly criticizing fellow musicians cannot have helped his case.

Indeed, what we can gather from the evidence is that Dowland was something of a difficult personality who regularly had troubled relations with authority. While to an extent he may have been a victim of political and religious bias, it is also clear, for example, that he often unashamedly tested the conditions of his contracts of employment. On more than one occasion, he over-extended his leave of absence from Courts to such a degree that he jeopardized his often generous terms of employment. He was also a profligate spender and gambler, which resulted in recurring financial problems. Already prone to self-doubt and professional jealousy, Dowland's long-established belief that prestigious positions befitting his genius were intentionally refused him may have further contributed to his predisposition for melancholia. That such a predilection should manifest itself in his music is not surprising, as songs such as 'Unquiet Thoughts', 'In Darkness Let Me Dwell' and 'Come Heavy Sleep' demonstrate. Indeed, his internationally

---

[47] The Duke of Brunswick (at Wolfenbüttel) and the Landgrave of Hesse (at Kassel).

[48] Taken from a letter written by John Dowland to Sir Robert Cecil. Cited in Diana Poulton, *John Dowland* (Berkeley and Los Angeles: University of California Press, 1982), 38.

renowned *Lachrymae*, or 'Flow My Tears', came to epitomize the very essence of sorrow and sadness. Such was his fame for despondency that he wrote a consort piece with the title *Semper Dowland, semper dolens* (always Dowland, always doleful) and signed his name 'Jo: Dolandi de Lachrimae'.[49]

However, while generally accurate, the customary conflation of melancholia with Dowland must also be seen in broader contexts. Fascination with darkness and despondency, though much advanced in Dowland's character, was not a trait unique to him alone. Significantly, many artists, poets and composers of the period cultivated similar obsessions. Neither should we forget the fact that this was a period of recurrent plague and pestilence. It was a time when the average life expectancy was exceedingly low; to be sick at all was to genuinely court death. Profound psychological responses to rampant epidemics were recognized as major factors in shaping the mentality of the age, as John Donne clarifies: 'God hath accompanied, and complicated almost all our bodily diseases of these times, with an extraordinary sadness, a predominant melancholy, a faintnesse of heart, a chearlesnesse, [and] a joylesnesse of spirit.'[50]

Additionally, this was a period in English history of great intellectual and religious transformation. Science was also making an impact, and the reforming Protestant factions disseminating throughout Europe vied in ideological conflict not only with the Catholic church but also with numerous other religious movements and cults, many of which looked to the esoteric scriptures of the past for guidance. Burkhard Gladigow paints a complex picture of the times when he states:

> Renaissance Humanism and Romanticism took their alternatives to occidental Christian culture mainly from the sciences. A revived Platonism could subsequently be closely tied to Christianity—or it lived on as theory of magic and irrationalism right into the eighteenth century; Gnostic schemes and ideas of redemption could interfere with Asian religions that were imported through philologies; a monism could melt into a Christian pantheism or constitute a new religion.[51]

It may have been this extraordinary mix of ideas that created a sense

---

49 This appears in the *Album of Johannes Cellarius* (British Library MS Add. 27579, fol. 149v), c. 1600-1606.

50 Peter Holman, *Dowland Lachrimae (1604)*, (Cambridge: Cambridge University Press, 1999), 50.

51 Burkhard Gladigow, 'Europäische Religionsgeschichte', in *Locations of Knowledge in Medieval and Early Modern Europe: Esoteric Discourse and Western Identities*, ed. Kocku von Stukrad (Leiden: Brill, 2010), 21.

of deep insecurity within English *mentalité*. The volatility in intellectual, spiritual and political quarters was epitomized by Donne's laconic sentence: 'Tis all in pieces all cohaerance gone.'[52] This burgeoning sense of insecurity also found deep resonance in the arts through the expression of *contemptus mundi*, which was founded on the belief that the artifice of the material world, reinforced by the weight of science and technology, was little more than a delusionary attempt to hide from God by repressing a craving for goodness and holiness.

However, the widespread obsession with darkness and morbidity, particularly in relation to the arts, lies pertinently with Italian Neoplatonists such as Marsilio Ficino, Pico della Mirandola, Cornelius Agrippa and Pontus de Tyard, who influenced English intellectual society considerably. The subject of Neoplatonism is far too vast to fully elucidate here, but could in a sentence be described as a philosophical system, based on Platonism and assimilating aspects of alchemical studies, mysticism, cabalism and Christianity, which postulates a unified source from which all existence originates and with which an individual soul may be spiritually united. One of the most persuasive of these Neoplatonists was Ficino whose influence proliferated throughout Europe. As Robin Headlam Wells points out: 'by the end of the sixteenth century there were few major European poets who did not show some awareness of fundamental Neoplatonic ideas in however diluted a form.[53]

The impact Neoplatonism had on music was significant. Through the study of Hermetic texts, Ficino designated Orpheus as the inspirational source for any composer wishing to develop his art through Gnostic study.[54] The philosophy dictated that, in imitation of Orpheus, composers and performers should be able to create a divine aesthetic excitation. Bearing in mind the prevalent notion of *contemptus mundi*, we can see how Ficino's theory of divine aesthetic stimulation, through the cathartic power of melancholy, gained a foothold on certain personalities, Dowland included, who were clearly

52 Robin Headlam Wells, *Elizabethan Mythologies: studies in poetry, drama and music* (Cambridge: Cambridge University Press, 1994), 189.

53 Ibid., 192-3.

54 Robin Headlam Wells points out that the Hermetic tracts were actually composed by a number of unknown Egyptian writers in the second or third century CE. A fact of which Ficino was unaware, but one which somewhat undermined the credibility of Neoplatonic thought in Elizabethan times. See Robin Headlam Wells, *Elizabethan Mythologies: studies in poetry, drama and music* (Cambridge: Cambridge University Press, 1994), 191.

drawn to the more ritualistic and esoteric aspects of intellective thought. Dowland believed in the *mysterium tremendum* of music, its inherent capacity to act as a liberating force, its ability to release the mind and soul from the perceived treacheries of the material world and its potential to astonish: 'In a word [music] is so powerful a thing, that it ravisheth the Soule, and carries it beyond it selfe, helpes, elevates, extends it.'[55]

Expanding this point further, Anthony Rooley has argued that Dowland was particularly drawn towards a specific aspect of Neoplatonic Hermeticism, which counterpoised the tradition's essentially optimistic vision.[56] Pessimist Gnosis was a concept (introduced to Renaissance thought principally by Ficino) that viewed 'the material world as evil'; thus an ascetic life was encouraged that would enable the Hermetic philosopher to 'transcend contaminated matter and to rise into the spiritual world of the divine mind.'[57] Dowland was drawn to the notion that eminence in performance and composition would most likely be achieved through a cathartic conflation with desolation. As Rooley explains:

> Only by embracing the darkness wholly, by spurning all hope, can the troubled soul begin to wake from the deep sleep of ignorance...Eventually, the light of the divine so fills the soul's awareness that the dark, loathsome world of sense is seen for the treacherous unreality it is.[58]

Thus, the apparent contradiction here is that through the exploration of pure desolation and melancholic states, via the purgative experience of music, one can light the core of darkness and

> revive the languishing Soule, affecting not only the eares, but the very arteries, the vitall & animall spirits, it erects the mind, & makes it nimble. And this it will effect in the most dull, severe, and sorrowfull Soules, expell griefe with mirth, and if there be any clouds or dust, or dregs of care yet lurking in our thoughts, most powerfully it wipes them away.[59]

---

55 Robert Burton, *The Anatomy of Melancholy* (Oxford: Lichfield, Short and Cripps, 1621/Da Capo Press, 1971), 372.

56 Anthony Rooley, 'New Light on John Dowland's Songs of Darkness', in *Early Music* Vol. 11, No. 12 (1983): 17.

57 C.A. Patrides and R.B. Waddington, eds., *The Age of Milton: Backgrounds to Seventeenth-Century Literature* (Manchester: Manchester University Press, 1980), 152.

58 Anthony Rooley, 17-19.

59 Robert Burton, *The Anatomy of Melancholy* (Oxford: Lichfield, Short and Cripps, 1621/Da Capo Press, 1971), *372*.

The degree to which Neoplatonism influenced Dowland is hard to quantify. I suggest, however, that given his propensity to be moved by ideological arguments, his innate attraction to ritual and symbol, his conscious embodiment of a melancholy persona and the reference to Orpheus on the score of *The First Booke of Songes or Ayres*,[60] one can quite legitimately conclude that Ficino's philosophy, and in particular the Pessimist Gnosis branch of Hermeticism that he introduced, had a profound impact on Dowland's musical thinking and processes. Thus, clear explanations can be found for why Dowland's musical meditations upon sleep and death are so profoundly affecting. For him, the most direct route to divine aesthetic stimulation in composition and performance was by way of a deep, cathartic consideration of melancholy. These seminal aspects of Dowland's intellectual, philosophical and spiritual preoccupations, which feed directly into his musical idiolect, explain why his music, to this day, paradoxically makes such dark themes so powerfully attractive.

Between Presence and Absence

What are we to deduce from these melancholic obsessions of Britten and Dowland? Do these fixations amount to anything more than a perverse proclivity for despondency? In answering these questions, it should be kept in mind that while often obsessively focused upon darkness and death, the music of Britten and Dowland rarely submits to such negativity without recourse to some sort of transcendental aspiration. Additionally, the religious, environmental and metaphysical contexts within which Dowland's music was composed allows us to see his putative negativity in different light.

Britten's music, I believe, functions under similar strategies. Indeed, this connection lies at the heart of his instinctive desire to symbiotically connect to Dowland through a shared desire to transcend inner conflict through music. Both composers suffered from interior conflicts. While some were undoubtedly self-inflicted, others were caused by their complicated relationships to the socio-political environments with which they were forced to engage. This is the *fons et origo* of their perennial need for escape to silence, the source of their almost pathological attraction to nothingness through the abnegation of

---

60 An 'Epigram of Tho[mas] Campion on the innovation of the Author' quotes the following: 'The renown which posterity gave to Orpheus the music of Dowland better gives to herself. By arresting the fleeting notes in the printed signs she makes plain to our very eyes the delights she afforded to our ears.' See Diane Poulton, *John Dowland* (London: Faber and Faber, 1972), 220.

discourse. Dowland's 'In darkness Let Me Dwell' and 'Come Heavy Sleep' imply such negation in their very themes. Even in Britten's vocal works, a pressing drive towards silence is embedded in the writing, as Claire Seymour illuminates:

> 'Silence'—verbal, musical, spatial—is indeed at the heart of Britten's expressive method. His operas proliferate with mute or semi-articulate characters who are unable to give voice to their anxieties or relieve their psychological stress. In these cases the music must bear the dramatic burden.[61]

At the centre of Britten's obsessions, therefore, lies a search for a kind of pure existence that is free of confusion, conflict and a painful inability to express his most intimate needs. The natural inclination in Britten's musical personality for transparency and innocence, for release through silence and metaphorical death, displays close analogy to Heidegger's theory of pure being. This being, or *Dasein* (being there, or 'being-in-the-world'), is said to find fulfilment 'in an impassioned freedom toward death'.[62] George Steiner's negotiation of Heidegger's occasionally intractable meditations upon being also brings them into close affiliation with particular concerns that affected Britten and Dowland: an 'enslavement' to their own internal conflicts and a sense of being 'othered' ('theyness') by their socio-political or religious environments:

> The inalienability of death—the plain but overwhelming fact that each must die for himself, that death is the one existential potentiality which no enslavement, no power of 'theyness' can take away from individual man—is the fundamental truth of the meaning of being.[63]

We thus see that the music of Britten and Dowland can be appreciated as a journey towards, a striving for a transparency of existence unavailable to their situated, embodied lives—hence the perennial death wish. But it would be wrong to consider this notion as merely symbolic, some ethereal impression having no practical import. Heidegger presents *Dasein* as a real-world phenomenon:

> In his now well-known example of hammering in a workshop, [Heidegger] suggests that what we encounter when we are absorbed in such activity is not a 'hammer-thing' with properties to which we then

---

[61] Claire Seymour, *The Operas of Benjamin Britten: Expression and Evasion* (Woodbridge: The Boydell Press, 2004), 10.

[62] George Steiner: *Martin Heidegger* (Chicago: University of Chicago Press, 1978), 106.

[63] Ibid., 104.

> assign a use value. On the contrary, what shows up for us initially is the hammering, which is 'in order to' nail boards together, which is 'for' building a bookcase, which is ultimately 'for the sake of' being, say, a person with a neat study...Heidegger expresses this by saying that Dasein is an 'ability-to-be', which comes to realization only through the ways it is channeled into concrete 'possibilities'...This projection of possibilities opened by understanding is realized and made concrete in 'interpretation'...our way of 'explicitly appropriating' the world 'in preparing, putting to rights, repairing, improving...[64]

Transferring Heidegger's hammering motif, the notion of a practical *Dasein* to Britten, we can situate his music as an attempt to appropriate the world, his world, in order to put it right, to improve it, to transform it. Heidegger's distinctive language refers to active relations that have transformational agency: 'in order to', 'for the sake of', the 'ability-to-be', and to be 'channeled into'. These renovating processes imply a movement approaching some new condition and conjure up a peregrination towards a 'repairing', an 'improving'. Seen through a Heideggerian lens, Britten's music becomes an active agent of repair, a tool for healing, a process that offers him the 'ability-to-be' other than what he is, free of anguish; a state that for him is exemplified by 'an impassioned freedom toward death', to repeat a citation. It is Britten's peculiar psychological makeup that correlates death and nothingness (the unfinished Dowland cadence) with an improved futurity. Steiner clarifies this apparent contradiction:

> This 'nothingness', however, is not *nihil* ('nothing'), or *Vernichtung* ('annihilation'). It is *Nichtung*, an untranslatable neologism in which 'negation' is made an active, creative force. This negation takes from *Dasein* its self-evidence, its habitual inertia. It restores to *Dasein* its primal astonishment in the face of being.[65]

In this regard, Britten's music takes its cue from Dowland whose beliefs, as we have seen, were underwritten by his adoption of Pessimist Gnosis, which argued that the soul's liberation from oblivion could only be achieved through a cathartic engagement with desolation. Here we can begin to apprehend the similarities between Dowland and Britten, especially their shared belief in death as a type of ecstatic release. No enquiry, therefore, into Britten's melancholia and his desire for renovated being can be disconnected from the phenomenon of Elizabethan melancholic sensibility and its Gnostic-inspired affiliation

---

[64] Charles B. Guignon, ed., *The Cambridge Companion to Heidegger* (New York: Cambridge University Press, 2006), 9-10.

[65] George Steiner: *Martin Heidegger*, 115.

to death as a form of 'astonished' and transcendental release. Steiner's further clarification of *Dasein* brings these topics into closer focus:

> ...when [Heidegger] sees truth as an illumination, an epiphany and a self-disclosure in the 'clearing' of existence, he is varying on long-established theological and gnostic themes. His repeated conviction that the enterprise of philosophy is that of a pilgrimage toward, that the journey already enfolds within itself what we can grasp of its fulfillment, represents a precise simile to the religious figure of man's journey and to the religious-meditational striving after transcendence.[66]

This, I believe, provides the basis for the musical idiolect shared by Britten and Dowland; and much of the analysis in this book explores these connections structurally, rhetorically and symbolically. Both composers, through a shared melancholia, sought to employ music as an agent of transformation and as a means to alter awareness, experience and being. They saw silence and death as a place of renovation. Dowland achieved this through a deep engagement with Gnostic practices, Britten through a judicious application of structural schemata that literally 'channelled into concrete "possibilities" new potentialities of experience.' By virtue of a shared musical idiolect that seeks out silence, their work occupies interstitial spaces between presence and absence.

---

66 George Steiner, Martin Heidegger (Chicago: University of Chicago Press, 1978), 62.

Chapter Two: Courtly Connections—*Gloriana* and the Guitar

Benjamin Britten's opera *Gloriana* produced two unlikely works with guitar: the 'Second Lute Song of the Earl of Essex', in an arrangement for tenor and guitar, and an adaptation of *Courtly Dances* subtitled 'Aldeburgh Version', a virtually unknown work for guitar and small orchestra, which the present author rediscovered in the Britten-Pears Library in 2011 while researching for this book. That there are any works by Britten that exist separately in arrangements is highly unusual given the composer's predisposition for idiosyncratic writing that emerges directly from the distinctive characteristics of a given instrument or voice. As a result, works that could be called Britten's itinerant music are relatively few in number.

This chapter explores the motivations behind various arrangements of the 'Second Lute Song' and provides a background to the publication of the tenor and guitar version, which is connected with a visit Julian Bream made in 2003 to the Red House (Britten's home and the location of the Britten-Pears Library). As the song is now more likely to be played and heard outside the occasion of an opera production, a contextualization of the work that explores its themes and technical characteristics may be useful. The song is thus scrutinized through an examination of its Elizabethan source material, both textual and musical. A juxtapositional reading with the 'First Lute Song', which directly precedes the 'Second Lute Song' in the opera, reveals the central contradictory theme of private desire versus public responsibility—a theme that takes on broader resonances, as it underscores similar predicaments in Britten's personal life. Finally, the critical function of the 'Second Lute Song' within the opera is explored as a valuable framework for its interpretation as a stand-alone work.

A study of two MSS of the 'Aldeburgh Version' offers insights into Britten's approach to its rather pragmatic arrangement. Details relating to the work's scant performance history provoke questions concerning its future presentation and reception. Britten's treatment of generic forms in *Courtly Dances* raises points regarding compositional originality and techniques of pastiche. A discussion places the views of Britten and his amanuensis, Imogen Holst, against a broader assessment of 20th-century compositional practice. Questions of innovation or derivation in relation to the treatment of generic set pieces depend upon the degree to which such established structures are assimilated into the musical idiolect of a given composer—this is a benchmark used to assess Britten's *Courtly Dances*.

The 'Second Lute Song'—Sources and Contexts

The exceptional beauty and emotional depth of the 'Second Lute Song of the Earl of Essex' has secured its separate existence as a stand-alone work in a number of transcriptions, including one with guitar. However, as we have noted, this is far from common practice where Britten's music is concerned.

> I certainly write music for human beings—directly and deliberately. I consider their voices, the range, the power, the subtlety, and the colour potentialities of them...I consider the instruments they play—their most expressive and suitable individual sonorities...almost every piece I have ever written has been composed with a certain occasion in mind, and usually for definite performers.[67]

Britten's compositional approach gives his works a precision of character, a refined and sculpted craftsmanship honed to the particularities of a given instrument or vocal medium that resists transcription. When Britten writes for viola, we not only get a viola work but a piece of music that idiosyncratically embodies a distinct 'viola-ness'.[68] Composed directly out of the individual sonority of the instrument, this music would be radically altered by transcription, as seminal components embedded within it from the moment of its inception would be lost. Thus, it is difficult to imagine a flute arrangement of *Metamorphoses after Ovid*, for example; or to envisage *Serenade* in a version for tenor, trombone and strings. This point only serves to highlight the small number of exceptions to a general rule about Britten's music. The 'Second Lute Song' is among the few works

---

[67] Benjamin Britten, *On Receiving the Aspen Award* (London: Faber and Faber, 1964), 10-11.

[68] Britten's remarkable ability to write exceptional music directly emerging from the particular idiosyncrasies of the guitar is captured in two fascinating notes he sent to Bream. See Appendix II.

of his that appear in numerous guises and which are regularly performed outside their original setting. Indeed, *Gloriana* is the source of most of Britten's itinerant music, which includes *Symphonic Suite*, the 'Choral Dances', the 'Morris Dance' for two descant recorders and numerous versions of *Courtly Dances*.

The reason why *Courtly Dances* from *Gloriana* have reappeared in so many versions is due to the generic nature of the set pieces that comprise them; galliards and Morris dances function equally well inside or outside the circumstance of the opera's narrative. At the time of the opera's premiere, Britten's particular treatment of these Elizabethan forms drew some criticism from a number of commentators who characterized them as mere exercises in pastiche—a subject that will be discussed in due course. However, the 'Second Lute Song' has avoided such criticism, as Britten very successfully blended components of the original music upon which some of it is based with his own stylistic language and technique. As we shall see, the use of original textual and musical source material gives the work an authentic quality; indeed, the presence of both Dowland and Purcell hovers over the song. However, in its finely wrought melismatic vocal writing and its luscious if vaguely disquieting harmony, the music is pure Britten.

Any work of Britten's that claims to be a lute song was hardly going to miss the attention of Julian Bream. That this music is a 'contrived' lute song—in the opera, the lute is invoked by the orchestra's harp—further supports its potential realization as a 'real' lute song outside and beyond its original setting and context. However, the range and complexity of the accompaniment part denied the lute its place here and the guitar was the natural option for Bream and Pears to consider. As it turns out, the trajectory from operatic aria to intimate song for tenor and guitar is more complex than might be assumed.

The first extraction of the 'Second Lute Song' from the opera seems, in fact, to have been at the instigation of Imogen Holst. Indeed, she was decisive in the arrangement, promotion and dissemination of much of Britten's itinerant music.[69] However, it is still not known whether she

---

69 Imogen Holst (1907-1984) was more than just Britten's amanuensis. A close friend to him and Pears, she was also a composer and conductor in her own right, and an artistic director of the Aldeburgh Festival from 1956 to 1977. She had a particular interest in early music and her arrangement of William Byrd's *Sellinger's Round* for string orchestra formed the basis for *Variations on an Elizabethan Theme*, which was jointly composed by Britten, Berkeley, Tippet, Walton and Oldham. This work ties in with 'Courtly Dances' and *Gloriana*, as it was also premiered in 1953 to celebrate the coronation of Elizabeth II.

was the first to transcribe the 'Second Lute Song' or whether she was inspired to do so because Britten and Pears were already performing it in their concerts. The first appearance of the song as a stand-alone piece took place on 28 June 1953, when it was included in an operatic concert at the Aldeburgh Festival.[70] It may also have been performed a little later on 12 July at a similar concert given at the Queen's Hall, Barnstaple, as part of the Taw and Torridge Festival, with Britten accompanying the tenor Rowland Jones. An impromptu performance of it certainly took place at the King's Lynn Festival on 26 July 1953 with Britten and Pears. Though not listed in the programme, it was reported in the *Lynn News and Advertiser* as having been asked for: 'the request was not refused. And the song, magnificently sung by Mr. Pears, provided an impressive finale to a brilliant concert'.[71] Holst's arrangement derives directly from the vocal score except for the introduction and piano coda, which makes use of the corresponding music in the opera. However, it is not known if Britten used this arrangement for the performances mentioned above or whether he simply sight-read from the orchestral score. What is certain is that Britten and Pears recognized the song's exceptional qualities and sanctioned through their own concerts its performance as an individual set piece.

Once the piano arrangement existed, Bream must have seen an obvious opportunity, especially since it was at this time that he and Pears were actively seeking out new material. As we have noted in Chapter One, during the early 1950s when *Gloriana* was being composed, Pears was often left without Britten as his accompanist. Indeed, there is some evidence of tension between them relating to the problem of securing time for rehearsals and concerts. The tenor appears to have been unhappy about Britten's acceptance of the *Gloriana* commission, as a significant number of previously planned concerts had to be shelved or rearranged. The fact is that Pears had a performing career to manage and when composing commitments prevented Britten from fulfilling his obligations as accompanist, the singer was naturally forced to turn to others to maintain stability in his work schedule. In a letter written in November 1952, Britten complains about being unable to work with Pears: 'I must say we both miss our concerts together this year—but we shall go back to them next Autumn with renewed energy &

---

70 Paul Banks, 'Gloriana: A List of Sources' in *Britten's Gloriana: Essays and Sources'*, ed. Paul Banks (Woodbridge: Boydell/Britten-Pears Library, 1993), 124-125.

71 *Lynn News and Advertiser*, 28 July 1953; see ibid.

enthusiasm.'[72] The duo partnerships Pears created with Bream, Ellis and Mewton-Wood gave him the opportunity to explore repertoire different to that which he performed with Britten. Of course, Bream gave Pears access to the entire Elizabethan lute-song repertoire and new works for voice and guitar. In this context, the 'Second Lute Song' in a version for tenor and guitar serves as a hybrid of both genres.

The unease Pears felt about the disruption that the writing of *Gloriana* would cause to his concert career extended to doubts about his actual suitability for the role of the Earl of Essex. Notwithstanding, he clearly loved the 'Second Lute Song'; Holst recalled that 'Peter [was] very much moved by the Second Lute Song, and obviously [was] longing to begin work on his part'.[73] Thus, the opportunity to perform it with Bream must have seemed very attractive to Pears since singing it against the quieter accompaniment of the guitar would afford him the opportunity to explore more searchingly its intimate and contemplative themes. It would also allow for multiple performances—an unlikely occurrence with the opera.

One source indicates that Bream's arrangement of the 'Second Lute Song' dates from about 1962 or 1963,[74] while archival material in the Britten-Pears Library suggests that it is closer to 1957. It is more likely to be the latter, as it would seem improbable that Bream would have waited ten years after the initial piano arrangement was made before venturing one himself. There is little information regarding performances of the 'Second Lute Song' with Pears and Bream, so it is impossible to be conclusive about where and when it was premiered. However, if the Britten-Pears Library documents are accurate regarding the song's arrangement date as 1957, this would mean that the duo performed it before the premiere of *Songs from the Chinese* in June 1958. Bream's rather chaotic hand-written arrangement, which notates the guitar part only, provides little indication that he intended to make a full, legible version available to others and suggests that he may have wanted to maintain exclusive rights to the song's performance in this version; no attempt was made to publish the arrangement during his performance career.

---

72 Philip Reed, Mervyn Cooke & Donald Mitchell, eds., *Letters From A Life: The Selected Letters of Benjamin Britten Volume IV 1952-1957* (Woodbridge: Boydell Press, 2008), 97.

73 Ibid.

74 Paul Banks, 142-143. This assessment is possibly connecting the period of arrangement of the 'Second Lute Song' with that of its recording in 1963.

Plate 1: 'The Second Lute Song of the Earl of Essex', MS (excerpt) of Julian Bream's arrangement for guitar (and voice)[75]

[75] Source: Britten-Pears Library archive.

Indeed, were it not for certain circumstances surrounding a visit Bream made to the Red House as late as 2003, the 'Second Lute Song' in its version for tenor and guitar might never have been published. Bream visited the Red House to film part of a documentary about his life and work.[76] Nicholas Clarke, a librarian at the Britten-Pears Library, facilitated the guitarist's visit and provided him with the original scores and archival material that were to be used in the making of the film. Clarke's account of Bream's return to Britten's home provides insight into the guitarist's relationship with the composer and Pears at a time when they were all working together productively. Curiously, until this point Bream had not seen the MS for Op. 70: 'he'd never actually seen the composition sketch for *Nocturnal*. It was quite an amazing surprise and it brought back all sorts of memories for him.'[77] Following a long period of absence, Bream's visit to the Red House rekindled many memories, especially when he was shown some film footage he had never before seen:

> I had found some footage of Julian from a 1964 film where he'd been performing lute songs from the Renaissance with Peter Pears. We also found another clip of Pears from a 1970s film called *Music for a Royal Occasion*. Britten is conducting the English Chamber Orchestra in the suite from his coronation opera *Gloriana*. One of the key moments is the Earl of Essex's 'Second Lute Song'. I showed Julian both film clips—of him in 1964 performing with Peter Pears, which quite amused him, and also the lute song, where he sees Pears singing. I knew that he himself had actually done an arrangement of the lute song, and in fact I brought the manuscript out for him to look at. It was at that moment he became quite interested in publishing it. I think coming back to the Red House certainly reawakened his interest; it might have been something that was on his mind for some time, but I think if he hadn't come here it is possible it might not have happened.[78]

If Bream's plan to publish the 'Second Lute Song' was revived by his visit to the Red House and seeing the film footage of himself and Pears, it was also something that the Britten-Pears Library knew would be of practical importance, as over the years it had received numerous requests by guitarists and singers worldwide for a copy of the arrangement. Clarke's commentaries about Bream's visit also highlight some of the more relaxed times the guitarist shared with Britten and his friends:

---

[76] *Julian Bream: My Life in Music* (Avie DVD Productions, 2004).

[77] Interview with Dr. Nicholas Clarke conducted by the author at the Red House, 5 February 2011.

[78] Ibid.

> The previous time Julian had been at Aldeburgh, Peter Pears was still alive, which means it was some time before 1986—I don't think he had been here since then. So when he came back in 2003 it was obviously a poignant time for him. Very often in interview he tended to get emotional about the whole thing. You know, he was here during a very significant time. The photographer Clive Strut, who took a number of important photos of Britten and Pears, told me that he can remember coming here during the 1960s and Ben, Julian and Mstislav Rostropovich were all improvising blues and jazz. His one regret was that he didn't have his camera there that night.[79]

This story of Bream improvising blues and jazz with Britten and Rostropovich provides a more vivid picture of the close relationship the guitarist had with the composer than any official account of their personal and professional association might suggest. With this friendship came trust and with trust came the consent to transcribe and perform one of the composer's greatest works. Even if it was forty years from the composition of the 'Second Lute Song' before a published arrangement was made available to guitarists, we should be thankful to Bream, as it must stand as one of the most extraordinary songs in the voice and guitar repertoire. As a stand-alone work extracted from *Gloriana*, however, it is essential to situate the song and its themes in context. To this end, the following section provides a broad outline of the opera and the pivotal role the song plays within it.

The 'Second Lute Song'—Insights and Conclusions

> The 'Second Lute Song' is one of the most evocative set-pieces in all Britten's output, full of harmonic felicity and period details...This unruly curvaceousness is the planned anarchy of Baroque ornamentation, or rather Britten's version of it.[80]

The 'Second Lute Song of the Earl of Essex' is certainly the most important aria in *Gloriana*. Unique source materials give it an authenticity that allows it to operate integrally within the opera's period and milieu. For example, the text for the song is taken from a poem written by the original Earl of Essex—Robert Devereux (1565-1601). Devereux was a nobleman and a soldier, but like many aristocrats of the period, he was also an accomplished poet. By using a text written by a person characterized in the opera, Britten astutely taps into sources that give the dramatic work not only a literary veracity but also a

[79] Ibid.

[80] Graham Johnson, *Britten, Voice & Piano: Lectures on the Vocal Music of Benjamin Britten* (London: The Guildhall School of Music & Drama and Ashgate Publishing Limited, 2003), 109-117.

historical one. Significantly, a connection with John Dowland comes into focus, as many of Devereux's texts were set by Dowland, including a section of the lengthy poem 'The Passion of a Discontented Mind'. This is thought to have been written when Devereux was in prison awaiting execution. Dowland's setting appears in *A Pilgrimes Solace* published in 1612.[81] Dowland also rewrote his song 'Can she excuse my wrongs with virtue's cloak?' in an instrumental arrangement entitled 'The Earl of Essex, His Galliard'. In light of this entire study, the connection to Dowland supports the central argument of his recurrent presence in the work of Britten.

The 'Second Lute Song' creates a further sense of authenticity through its use of a musical source composed by the English madrigalist Thomas Wilbye (1574-1638). Isolating the first word from the opening line of Devereux's poem 'Happy were he could finish forth his fate', Britten employs a fragment of the composition entitled 'Happy, Oh Happy He' from Wilbye's *Second Book of Madrigals* (1608) whose four-part setting to these words (see X in Example 1) is replicated in all the strings of Britten's version (see Y in Example 2).

Example 1: John Wilbye, 'Happy, Oh Happy He'

81 Steven W. May, 'The poems of Edward de Vere, 17th Earl of Oxford and Robert Devereux, 2nd Earl of Essex', in *Studies in Philology* 77 (1980): 86.

Example 2: Britten, 'The Second Lute Song of the Earl of Essex', bars 1-4

Lasting only four bars, the quoted fragment forms the harmonic structure underpinning a melismatic vocal line for the tenor on the words, 'Happy, happy were he...' The result is a beautifully ornamented development upon Wilbye's opening phrase. As in Britten's use of Devereux's text, the ploy of initiating the 'Second Lute Song' with a musical quote from an authentic madrigal (composed just a few years after Elizabeth's death) gives to the work a distinct air of legitimacy, even as Britten goes on to develop the music in his own distinctive harmonic idiolect.

Aside from its inherent qualities as a poignant vehicle for characterizing the Earl's personality, the 'Second Lute Song' plays a significant structural role within the opera. Indeed, Britten employs the song on two occasions: in its first appearance in Act I scene ii and at the end of the opera when it returns in a fragmented version in the form of an Epilogue. This structural significance gives to the song the additional responsibility of conveying the central thematic and dramatic elements of the opera. In *Gloriana*, the ageing Queen Elizabeth loves the younger Earl of Essex, but she is forced to have him executed for treason. Thus, the opera's dramatic tension resides in the dichotomy between her private passion for the young suitor and her loyalty to the Realm and the duties that the monarchy demands of her:[82] 'I count in the glory of my crown that I have reigned with your love, and there is no jewel that I prefer before that jewel. Neither do I desire to live longer than that I may see your prosperity; and that's my desire.' The key to understanding Elizabeth's dilemma is outlined by Britten in an ingenious and stark juxtaposition of the 'Second Lute Song' with the preceding 'First Lute Song'. In Act I scene ii, the Earl of Essex is ushered in to see the Queen. Exhausted from her stately responsibilities, and apprehensive about an imminent Spanish invasion, she demands that he should sing a song to raise her spirits:

QUEEN: Cares of State eat up my days.
There lies my lute:
Take it and play.
ESSEX: (SONG: First Lute Song of the Earl or Essex)

'First Lute Song of the Earl of Essex'
Quick music is best
When the heart is oppressed,
Quick music can heal
With dancing, by night and by day.
Hallaloo, hallalay, Hallaloo, hallalay,
Halla la la la la la la la la loo laya.

Quick music is best
For the pipe, or the strings;
Quick music can heal
With dancing, the pleasure of kings:
Hallaloo, (etc.)

Donald Mitchell explains why Britten has juxtaposed these two lute songs:

> It was Britten's original intention that 'Happy were he' [the 'Second Lute Song'] should stand alone; [but he] realised at an early stage that another song was needed, to postpone the revelation of 'Happy were he', to introduce in fact a process of gradual self-revelation on Essex's part: that introspective 'other self' had as it were to be drawn out of him, not immediately vouchsafed. That, surely is the thinking behind the quick, shallow and unconvincing gay little song that is the First Lute Song, 'Quick music is best'.[83]

As they are so clearly connected in the opera, a contextualization of the

[82] See Appendix III for a short synopsis of *Gloriana*.
[83] Donald Mitchell, 'The Paradox of *Gloriana*: Simple and Difficult', in *Britten's Gloriana: Essays and Sources*, Paul Banks, ed. (Woodbridge: Boydell/Britten-Pears Library, 1993), 68.

'First Lute Song' will assist in a better understanding of the second. The tonality of the former, this 'shallow and unconvincing' dance-tune in triple time, is an optimistic E major, but a discordant E♭ in the bass undermines its lighthearted mood. The manipulation of tonalities a semitone apart is a common feature of Britten's music and he employs it here effectively to underscore a number of ideas and contradictions. Discordant harmony reflects the Queen's negative mood and the disparity of temperament between the older monarch and the younger courtier. Such incongruence will be a vital factor in the unfolding calamity they will both endure. Additionally, as Essex is in love with the Queen, performing the superficial 'First Lute Song' implies that he cannot, under coercion as it were, reveal his true feelings. As Mitchell has suggested, the discordant E♭ underpins the contradiction lying behind the surface gaiety of the song (see X at double basses in Example 3).

Example 3: Britten, 'First Lute Song', bars 25-31

Essex attempts to maintain the superficial happiness and even

> tries to give himself and the song a lift by jacking the song up a semitone, from E to F, only to find himself dogged by that unnervingly stubborn dissonant pedal, which merely follows suit, moving up from E♭ to E♮, in the context (now) of Essex's F [see Y at cellos in Example 3].[84]

[84] Ibid., 68-9.

The fundamental triviality of the 'First Lute Song' fails to lighten the Queen's sombre mood. She therefore makes a second command:

QUEEN: Too light, too gay:
A song for careless hearts.
Turn to the lute again,
Evoke some far-off place or time,
A dream, a mood, an air
To spirit us both away.

It is only at the opening of the 'Second Lute Song' that the grating pedal disappears and Essex is able to expose his deeper feelings without any distressing contradictions. Here we observe a more sensitive, thoughtful, even meditative personality (see Example 2 above).

ESSEX: **'Second Lute Song of the Earl of Essex'**
Happy were he could finish forth his fate
In some unhaunted desert, where, obscure
From all society, from love and hate
Of worldly folk, then might he sleep secure;
Then wake again and give God ever praise;
Content with hips and haws and brambleberry;
In contemplation spending all his days,
And change of holy thoughts to make him merry;
Where, when he dies, his tomb might be a bush
Where harmless robin dwells with gentle thrush.

The juxtaposition of these two rather disparate songs reflects a number of central themes in the opera. That Essex sang both in close proximity suggests that he is also of a dual character. This aspect of the Earl's personality is something that Britten discovered at the very early stages of preparation for the opera and felt would be representative of broader themes within the work. Britten had a copy of *Elizabeth and Essex: A Tragic History* written by Lytton Strachey—the book upon which the libretto for *Gloriana* was subsequently based.[85] In the margin of page 4, Britten marked a section describing the binary aspects of the Earl's character:

> The youth loved hunting and all the sports of manhood; but he loved reading too. He could write correctly in Latin and beautifully in English; he might have been a scholar, had he not been so spirited a nobleman. As he grew up this double nature seemed to be reflected in his physical complexion. The blood flew through his veins in vigorous vitality; he ran and tilted with the sprightliest; and then suddenly health would ebb

85 Lytton Strachey, *Elizabeth and Essex: A Tragic History* (London: Chatto, 1928).

away from him, and the pale boy would lie for hours in his chamber, obscurely melancholy, with a Virgil in his hand.[86]

Thus, the Earl's personality underscores the themes of conflict and contradiction that are central to the drama. As mentioned, the seminal role of the 'Second Lute Song' in *Gloriana* is highlighted by its re-emergence in the Epilogue. It does not appear as an exact replica of the original but is distorted and interspersed with other material, and only some of its text is articulated. This is the moment when Elizabeth has signed the death warrant for Essex; she is alone and falls into a trance where time and locus are suspended. The music eventually settles into a calm orchestral soundscape supporting the Queen's spoken words. Occasionally, she joins the orchestra's tune, singing intermittently to herself. An entourage of crowned kings and queens files past her in the background. Sir Robert Cecil appears, asking her to name her successor. She faces the audience with some words from her famous 'Golden Speech'.[87] To the side, an apparition of the Queen appears singing 'Mortua, sed non sepulta—'Dead, but not buried'.

The 'Second Lute Song' is used structurally here to counterpoise Elizabeth's flashbacks to her loving memories of Essex. Those words from the song that reappear include 'In some haunted desert', which are sung just as the ghostly entourage of monarchs passes by; and the line 'There might he sleep secure' underscores her imminent death. The song's return thus highlights with poignant emphasis the ironic discrepancy between Elizabeth's hope and desire for sexual contentment with Essex and the tragic reality that confronts her. The fragmentation of the work, its structural transformation from a lute-song into an indefinable open form, also suggests a disintegration of her physical and emotional stability. Although the disjointed song that, as listeners, we piece together is the one we recognize as that sung by Essex in Act I scene ii, it functions in the Epilogue as a précis of Elizabeth's entire existence. As Peter Evans suggests, it is 'the whole of

---

[86] Phillip Reed, 'The Creative Evolution of *Gloriana*', in *Britten's Gloriana: Essays and Sources*, Paul Banks, ed. (Woodbridge: Boydell/Britten-Pears Library, 1993), 21.

[87] Queen Elizabeth's 'Golden Speech' was delivered to Members of Parliament on 30 November 1601. Instead of discussing economic affairs, she surprisingly disclosed that it would be her final Parliament and the ensuing speech was an emotional declaration of the love and respect she had for the country, her position and the Members of Parliament.

her life that is passing in review before the dying Queen.'[88]

Elizabeth's statement, 'I grieve, yet dare not show my discontent', underpins the personal dichotomy that has been identified as the central theme of the opera. However, as this theme also pervaded Britten's personal life, particularly as a homosexual in a hetero-normative society, the opera's play on public and private worlds takes on even greater significance. Following quickly on the heels of a commission to compose *Billy Budd* for the Festival of Britain in 1951, the Royal Opera House's prestigious commission to compose *Gloriana* to mark the coronation of the Queen represented irrefutable testimony of Britten's ascent to the heights of the British artistic establishment. It marks the point from which he was generally acknowledged as the foremost English composer of his generation. Additionally, the extensive transformation from being a left-wing, Auden protégé of the 1930s to being a 'court composer' of the new Elizabethan age represents a radical modification of his relation with the state. In the decade following his return from America in 1942, we see a concerted effort by Britten to significantly recalibrate his position within British society. That process meant that many old friends and colleagues were discarded while influential establishment figures including Royalty were encouraged into his circle.[89]

In this context, the opera's public-private themes also reflect the mounting internal struggles Britten experienced as a homosexual who consciously embraced a conservative establishment and sought Royal approval. Indeed, this contradiction gives Britten's best music its

88 Peter Evans, 'The Number Principle and Dramatic Momentum in *Gloriana*', in *Britten's Gloriana: Essays and Sources*, Paul Banks, ed. (Woodbridge: Boydell/Britten-Pears Library, 1993), 90.

89 By the early 1950s, Britten was able to count among his close friends members of the extended Royal Family such as Lord Harewood and his wife (Harewood was the Queen's first cousin and his mother was the Princess Royal), and the Prince and Princess of Hesse and the Rhine (Peg and Lu). In a letter written to Erwin Stein in 1954, Britten paints a vivid picture of his newly-established circle of friends and acquaintances, and his current attitude to royalty—one that would have contrasted greatly with views he held in the 1930s: 'It has all been so interesting, and full of new experiences and atmospheres—a world in every sense alien to us but bound to us by the warmth and bigness of Peg and Lu. We have met so many people, familiar to you personally or by reputation. It is a curious, circumscribed, little world, this international Royal clan—there were, for instance, seven princes to the family Xmas dinner! Some are fascinating, Barbara of Prussia, and Francis of Barvaria...'. Letter to Erwin Stein, 1 January 1954, in Philip Reed, Mervyn Cooke & Donald Mitchell, eds., *Letters From A Life: The Selected Letters of Benjamin Britten Volume IV 1952-1957* (Woodbridge: Boydell Press, 2008), 199-202.

psychological intensity, as the desire to explicitly articulate core aspects of his personality is overpowered by a self-censoring tendency.[90] Such disturbing music emerges out of the psychological torsions created by Britten's irrational desire to embrace the very power structures that criminalized him.

Courtly Dances: 'Aldeburgh Version'—Rediscovery and Assessment

While in more recent years *Gloriana* has been slowly entering the repertory of opera houses and companies worldwide, it is arguably the least successful of Britten's dramatic works. Extracted from the opera, numerous versions of *Courtly Dances* have historically fared much better. According to archives, no less than nine different arrangements have been made of the work; each one differs in terms of orchestration, and the number and organization of its movements:[91]

Figure 2: Arrangements of 'Courtly Dances' from *Gloriana*

Gloriana: Symphonic Suite, op. 53a
'March' from *Courtly Dances* (arranged for orchestra)
'Morris Dance' (arranged for two descant recorders)
Courtly Dances (arranged for small orchestra)
Courtly Dances (arranged for lute and ensemble)
Five Courtly Dances from *Gloriana* (arranged for school orchestra)
Courtly Dances (arranged for chamber ensemble)
Gloriana: Symphonic Suite (version with chorus)
Courtly Dances—'Aldeburgh Version' (arranged for guitar and small orchestra)

The present author rediscovered *Courtly Dances*—'Aldeburgh Version' in February 2011 in the archives of the Britten-Pears Library while researching this project. Two MSS were uncovered: the first is a very rough and incomplete draft of an orchestral arrangement of *Courtly Dances* in Britten's hand (Plate 2); the second MS is a fair copy and completed version of the first in Imogen Holst's hand (Plate 3). The words 'Aldeburgh Version' are written in pencil on the front page of Holst's fair copy underneath the printed title *Courtly Dances*. This refers to the 1957 Aldeburgh Festival at which it was premiered. The words 'Aldeburgh Version' also appear on the bottom of the official programme for the 'Orchestral Concert' of the Festival and are

90 The ways in which this inner conflict impacted Britten's musical idiolect will be discussed in more detail in the section entitled 'The Perfect Lie' in Chapter Five.

91 Paul Banks, 95-181.

additionally printed in the programme note to the work.

> In the second act of *Gloriana* there is a scene in the great room of the Palace of Whitehall; an orchestra plays in the gallery, while Queen Elizabeth I and her courtiers and their ladies are dancing. The original stage orchestra consisted of only six players: later, a *Suite* for full orchestra was published. The Aldeburgh version to be played this evening has been specially orchestrated for this concert, to include all the players who have been gathered together for the rest of the programme.[92]

Plate 2: MS in Britten's hand of 'Galliard' (excerpt) from *CourtlyDances*—'Aldeburgh Version'[93]

[92] Source: Britten-Pears Library archive.
[93] Source: Britten-Pears Library archive.

Plate 3: MS of fair copy in Holst's hand of 'Galliard' (excerpt) from *Courtly Dances*—'Aldeburgh Version'[94]

'Aldeburgh Version' is thus the official subtitle assigned to the work by Britten and Holst to distinguish this arrangement of *Courtly Dances* from all others. It would appear that the work was rather quickly written to provide additional music for the concert, which featured Julian Bream on lute and guitar. The event took place on 23 June 1957 at the Jubilee Hall in Aldeburgh, featuring the Aldeburgh Orchestra

94 Source: Britten-Pears Library archive.

conducted by Charles Mackerras. While questions remain regarding the premiere date for the 'Second Lute Song', the programme below demonstrates that the 'Aldeburgh Version' is possibly the first work with guitar composed by Britten to be performed by Bream.[95]

The programme for this concert is another example of the two-pronged approach to repertoire exploration discussed in Chapter One, which Bream and Britten were keen to exploit. The concert is divided between Elizabethan and Jacobean works performed with lute, and recent or newly composed music featuring the guitar. As the 'Aldeburgh Version' is ostensibly a period consort work in which one would expect to hear the lute, but in this case is recast by Britten as a kind of guitar concerto, it serves as a hybrid of both. The 'Second Lute Song', as we have seen, serves a similar function.

Figure 3: Programme for the 'Orchestral Concert' of the 1957 Aldeburgh Festival[96]

Henry Purcell:	SUITE: Distressed Innocent
John Dowland:	Lachrimae (for lute and strings)
Franz Joseph Haydn:	Secular Cantata: Arianna a Nasso
Edward Elgar:	Serenade in E Minor
INTERVAL	
Hans Werner Henze:	Apollo and Hyacinth (for mezzo, harpsichord and 8 solo instruments)
Heitor Villa-Lobos:	Concerto for guitar and orchestra
[Britten]	The Courtly Dances from Gloriana (for chamber orchestra) March; Coranto; Pavane; Morris Dance; Galliard; La Volta.

In the 'Aldeburgh Version', the guitar plays a prominent solo role in all but one of the movements. Thus, while the work does not quite fit the general contours of a concerto, it bears comparison to a Baroque

95 Records at the Britten-Pears Library suggest that 'I will give my love an apple', 'The Soldier and the Sailor' and 'The Shooting of his Dear' were first performed at the Wigmore Hall on 6 May 1956. However, this is contradicted by the *Aldeburgh Festival Programme Books 1954-1960*, which states that 'The Shooting of his dear', 'Master Kilby' and 'The Soldier and the Sailor' were premiered on 17 June 1958 at Great Glemham House. It is thus impossible to be sure about which were the first works with guitar to be written by Britten. It would appear likely, however, that it is either *Courtly Dances*—'Aldeburg Version', the 'Second Lute Song' or one or more of the folksongs from *Folksong Arrangements Volume VI*.

96 Source: Britten-Pears Library archive.

concertante in the form of a suite. Scored for flute, oboe, bassoon, horn, trombone, guitar, harpsichord, percussion and strings, the 'Aldeburgh Version' incorporates the following dances from *Gloriana* in the given order: March, Coranto, Pavane, Morris Dance, Galliard, Lavolta, March. It is common practice in most versions of *Courtly Dances* to repeat the opening March at the end. Though it appears not to have been repeated in its premiere performance.

Scrutiny of Britten's MS and Holst's fair copy highlights Britten's working methods, which seem to be of a rather pragmatic nature. For example, we can see that Britten maintained the integrity of the strings as they appear in *Symphonic Suite*, Op. 53a and used them as a harmonic foundation upon which to create the new arrangement. The first page of Britten's MS, which is representative of the entire score, shows that, in the five staves at the bottom of the score where the string music should be, no notes are written for the most part. Instead, Britten scribbled the letters 'OS'. At the bottom of the page a note explains that OS signifies 'As in Orchestral Suite', meaning *Symphonic Suite*, Op. 53a. Occasionally, he does add separate lines for the double bass or cello. Thus, while preserving the majority of the string music from *Symphonic Suite*, Britten has added some nuanced touches (see Plates 2 and 3 above).

A critic for *The Scotsman* on 29 June 1957 gave a positive review of the 'Aldeburgh Version', stating that these dances

> were played in the opera by six players; in the orchestral suite the treatment was on the heavy side but this new arrangement, made for the combination of players available for this particular concert, comes off perfectly.[97]

Despite this endorsement, Bream never performed the 'Aldeburgh Version' again. It seems paradoxical that the version of *Courtly Dances* for lute and ensemble, which he arranged for the Julian Bream Consort, was regularly performed and even recorded while the 'Aldeburgh Version' for guitar and orchestra remained neglected. The work, however, did receive one other performance about eleven years after the premiere. This took place in a concert at the Queen Elizabeth Hall, London, on 10 January 1968 featuring the English Chamber Orchestra and the guitarist Desmond Dupré, conducted by Imogen Holst.

---

[97] Source: Britten-Pears Library archive.

Plate 4: Programme for second performance of Courtly Dances 'Aldeburgh Version' at the Queen Elizabeth Hall, London[98]

Benjamin Britten

THE COURTLY DANCES FROM GLORIANA
for chamber orchestra

First London performance in this Aldeburgh version

In the second act of 'Gloriana' there is a scene in the great room of the Palace of Whitehall; an orchestra plays in the gallery, while Queen Elizabeth I and her courtiers and their ladies are dancing. (When he was writing the opera in the winter of 1952-3, Britten suddenly said: 'I can't write tunes for all these dances unless I know about the steps and the figures'. I had recently begun working for him as amanuensis, and I knew that I'd got to do something about it quickly, so I rang up a friend and took several cross-country trains from Aldeburgh to Oxford and had a two-hour lesson and came back and taught him the dances.)
The original stage orchestra consisted of only six players: later, a 'Suite' for full orchestra was published. Britten wrote this third, unpublished, version for the last item of the final concert at the 1957 Aldeburgh Festival, to include all the instruments that were needed during the rest of the programme.
The 'March' is formal, for the ceremonial entry of the Queen. The 'Coranto' lives up to its reputation of being 'full of Sprightfulness and Vigour', while the 'Pavane' is a 'kind of staid musick, ordained for grave dancing'. The 'Morris' was danced at Court in the sixteenth century by a small boy with a blackened face, wearing tiny silver bells on his leggings: Britten's tune is founded on the rhythm of a traditional English morris dance called 'The Fool's Jig'. The earliest Galliards were lively, but after 1600 the dance became 'Grave and Sober'. The 'Lavolta' was danced 'high in the Italian mode'.
The Courtly Dances end with a repetition of the ceremonial 'March'.

Acknowledgments

Miss Imogen Holst and the ECO and MS would like to thank Benjamin Britten for allowing his unpublished 'Fanfare' to be played, Messrs Boosey & Hawkes, for permission to use the manuscript parts of the Aldeburgh version of the Courtly Dances from Gloriana, Faber and Faber Ltd, for permission to reproduce the facsimile of the 1923 Waltz from Imogen Holst's 'Britten' in their Great Composers series, Faber Music Ltd, for permission to use the manuscript parts of Capriccio (1932) before they are available on hire, and for permission to reproduce a fragment from the original rough sketch of the work.

Photo of Gustav Holst by John Gay
Photo of Imogen Holst by Godfrey Macdomnic

98 Source: Britten-Pears Library archive.

This concert is highly significant, as it means that Britten sanctioned a performance of the 'Aldeburgh Version' beyond the 'certain occasion in mind' for which it was originally composed. Given that the venue was London's prestigious Queen Elizabeth Hall and that the work was performed by the English Chamber Orchestra, it can be confidently assumed that Britten was convinced that this work stood on its own merits and was not merely the result of a pragmatic and short-term response to a local requirement in a given time and place.[99]

Courtly Dances—Innovation or Derivation?

The various set pieces that comprise *Courtly Dances* appear in Act II scene iii of *Gloriana* and provide the musical backdrop to a masque given by the Queen in Whitehall Palace. These dances were written to enhance our understanding of the lavish court life of Elizabeth I and as such they are not directly implicated in the drama of the opera. It could be argued that the amplification of the pageantry is to an extent a functional device that reinforces the ritual of the Queen's crucial role in English politics, but *Courtly Dances* do not psychologically or dramatically intensify any particular theme or sentiment in the story. Beyond the obvious role of the opera's dramatic narrative, Britten was also keen that *Gloriana* should have a festive character and a pageant-like atmosphere that would not only historically underpin the opera but would also provide a celebratory atmosphere for the coronation of Queen Elizabeth II, for which the opera was commissioned. Thus, Elizabethan musical forms such as the pavane, the galliard, the lavolta and the coranto are employed by Britten to act as the basis of a pageant that in fact celebrates both Elizabeths. However, challenges arise as to how such stylized forms may be integrated into the idiosyncratic language of a 20th-century composer.

Britten's dances do not quote original sources, but his generally unadulterated use of stylized forms raises questions of derivation.

[99] This point is worth making in the context of Britten's refusal in some cases to allow second performances of certain arrangements of *Courtly Dances*. For example, in 1963 John Dingle made a version of *Courtly Dances* for a small ensemble of flute, spinet, violin, viola, cello and tabor. Britten gave his consent for this arrangement on the provision that additional performances outside the one for which it was specifically made would not take place. This embargo was possibly imposed because of the unusual nature of the instrumentation; or it may have been insisted upon because Britten did not think the arrangement was of very good quality. For whatever reason, Britten's willingness to impose an embargo on some arrangements of *Courtly Dances* has obvious implications for those arrangements that he did allow to be performed again, including the 'Aldeburgh Version'.

Although Britten was keen to point out that he 'thought a great deal about [the Elizabethan period] to try to get the atmosphere', and that he had not 'half-timbered' his music',[100] it is perhaps not surprising that dance music of such unreflective character contained in a 20th-century opera might attract some disapproving commentary. As one critic pointed out: 'the bulk of the music is hardly more than pastiche, sometimes very clever pastiche, sometimes not so clever'.[101] Britten seems to have been aware of the potential dangers of falling into mere imitation with *Courtly Dances*. He told Lord Harewood in a letter that *Courtly Dances* had to be serious, not 'just folk dances and village green stuff';[102] and Imogen Holst remembers clearly Britten's request 'to swear to tell him directly...[if they] began to turn into pastiche'.[103]

This fear of merely creating derivative music might account for the apparent compositional difficulties Britten encountered, as work on *Courtly Dances* did not come easy. According to Holst, he was bogged down by concerns of tempo, performance style, the rhythmic characteristics of the dances and what type of orchestration would best replicate the Elizabethan sound world. At one stage, Holst went to Oxford to research the dance forms with some colleagues who were experts on the subject and even took lessons on dancing so that she could demonstrate to Britten their rhythmic characteristics.[104] Holst clearly felt that Britten 'got the right Elizabethan flavour with contemporary materials',[105] though, as we have seen, others disagreed. Perhaps this very desire to be 'authentic' led to the music being somewhat too stylized. As a result, we can see that much of the criticism directed at *Courtly Dances* stems from the conviction that these pieces exhibit more of the observable attributes of period dance forms than they do Britten's re-imagining of such forms within the framework of his own musical language.

The use of a sequence of self-contained set pieces such as *Courtly Dances* is unique in Britten's operatic output, as he normally employs

---

100 Antonia Malloy, 'Britten's Major Set-Back? Aspects of the First Critical Response to Gloriana', in *Britten's Gloriana: Essays and Sources*, Paul Banks, ed. (Woodbridge: Boydell/Britten-Pears Library, 1993), 60.

101 Ernest Newmann; cited in ibid.

102 Philip Reed, Mervyn Cooke & Donald Mitchell, eds., *Letters From A Life: The Selected Letters of Benjamin Britten Volume IV 1952-1957* (Woodbridge: Boydell Press, 2008), 63.

103 Ibid., 95.

104 Phillip Reed, 'The Creative Evolution of *Gloriana'*, in *Britten's Gloriana: Essays and Sources*, Paul Banks, ed. (Woodbridge: Boydell/Britten-Pears Library, 1993), 35.

105 Philip Reed, Mervyn Cooke & Donald Mitchell, eds., *Letters From A Life*, 95.

an unbroken-narrative technique. To an extent, however, the employment of set pieces created a fundamental problem relating to the organization of dramatic tension. In an opera that wanted to be both ceremonial (a national event celebrating the coronation) and a stand-alone dramatic work, conflicting prerequisites would inevitably be counter-productive. This inherent problem was reflected by the varying press commentaries *Gloriana* received. Some critics made allowances:

> It is a festival piece, such as eighteenth-century composers wrote for royal weddings—part pageant, part ballet, part cantata—an occasional work which should not be judged by the standards applicable to opera in general, where the music and the drama are their own masters.[106]

However, other critics were less sympathetic. Desmond Shaw-Taylor made the most serious accusation that

> in general, drama has been subordinated to spectacle and splendour...Masques, dancing, ceremony—all these were required, not only in homage to the present Queen, but in order to present a vivid picture of the Elizabethan Age. The familiar attributes of the principal figures are recognisably outlined; but the work remains essentially decorative, a lavish picture book.[107]

Such debate helps set the parameters for assessing the place and function of *Courtly Dances* within the opera. However, there are additional evaluations that need to be made in viewing the suite as a stand-alone work. Considered in terms of European developments in music during the 1950s, Britten's entire corpus (not to mention the 'period' *Courtly Dances*) would have been considered by many high modernists such as Boulez and Stockhausen as merely the vestige of an outdated tonality. On the other hand, in comparison to more traditional 20th-century composers such as Aaron Copeland, Joaquín Rodrigo or Heitor Villa-Lobos, *Courtly Dances* would be considered as merely the natural expression of late nationalism in music. Indeed, *Courtly Dances* accomplish something quite similar to Rodrigo's entire output—the preservation of national forms and traditional material within the context of the modern orchestra in compositions that judiciously recalibrate the music with occasional dissonances and rhythmic adjustments. In this regard, Rodrigo's courtly *Fantasía para un*

---

[106] Antonia Malloy, 'Britten's Major Set-Back? Aspects of the First Critical Response to Gloriana', in *Britten's Gloriana: Essays and Sources*, Paul Banks, ed. (Woodbridge: Boydell/Britten-Pears Library, 1993), 156.

[107] *New Statesman*: 13 June 1953; cited in ibid., 156-7.

gentilhombre, written a year after *Courtly Dances*, stands as a Spanish equivalent of Britten's masque suite. What this indicates is that the 20th century, even the mid-20th century, before postmodernism's fragmentation made its impact, was witness to a surprising variety of musical styles that were often diametrically opposed aesthetically and ideologically.

Therefore, the challenge of assessing *Courtly Dances* in terms of derivation is not so much a question of their relationship to tonality but rather one of the level of control and integration of source materials. In this regard, a comparison with *Wozzeck* (1922) may be instructive, as Berg also incorporated into his opera a number of established models such as passacaglia, prelude, fugue and even sonata form in a fully integrated manner while preserving his own harmonic distinctiveness. Berg, of course, was not attempting to reflect a given period from the past but he does provide a stratagem for renovating 'old' forms through their integration into an individual 20th-century voice. Stravinsky provides another interesting case with *Pulcinella* (1920, based on the music of Pergolesi, 1710-1736). While preserving much of the character of the original source material, Stravinsky recalibrates the music within newly devised structural and rhythmic contours and a wholly original harmonic framework that ingeniously reflects and preserves the individual signatures of both composers.

Viewed in light of these examples emanating from the serial and neoclassical idioms, *Courtly Dances* may indeed be seen as more pastiche than original, as they ultimately do not reflect the nuanced complexity of tonal and structural renovation for which much of Britten's music is notable. Additionally, there are numerous examples of Britten's ability to successfully integrate older forms into his musical idiolect. Indeed, the works for guitar discussed in this study provide some of the best examples of this process, including the 'Second Lute Song' and *Nocturnal*, which directly engage with Dowland and the Renaissance lute-song model, and the song cycles, which incorporate Dowland's techniques of musical rhetoric in more sublimated ways. In this regard, Britten differs considerably from Rodrigo, as the latter's music never distances itself appreciably from the traditional folk materials upon which it is based. Thus, in comparison to Britten's other works that engage with Renaissance sources, *Courtly Dances* begin to look somewhat contrived. Furthermore, since the 1950s the tremendous advances made in historically informed performance practice will likely not advance the case for *Courtly Dances*. Perhaps the work should ultimately be seen in terms of the history of early-music research and performance, and its broader reception. Within this historiographical context, Britten's renovations of Elizabethan music can be seen as serving a unique purpose in that they directed focus on a period of music that before 1950 was largely ignored and unappreciated. While in the context of contemporary performance practice, *Courtly Dances* might seem out-of-date and beside the point, Britten's efforts, alongside those of Holst, Pears and Bream, certainly provided a significant contribution to the initial stages of the project to perform and disseminate early music.

Chapter Three: *Songs from the Chinese*

To gain a comprehensive understanding of *Songs from the Chinese*, Op. 58 requires multi-perspectival readings, which this chapter undertakes in its four sections.[108] The first two provide contextual information; the second two present analytical studies of the score. As important as musical analysis is, it offers only one kind of knowledge; there are many other related narratives surrounding a musical subject that also need elucidation. Thus, the first section, entitled 'Understanding Chinese Poetry', enquires into Chinese poetics, explores the socio-cultural and political contexts within which classical Chinese poetry was written, offers some biographical information on the poets in question and briefly addresses the problematics of translation and the impact they may have on interpretation. Though Britten obviously had an intellectual and aesthetic understanding of Chinese poetry, it must be acknowledged that the study of the genre has advanced immensely in the half-century or so since Op. 58 was composed in 1957. Current research on Chinese poetry and translation allows us to contextualize the groundbreaking work of Arthur Waley and others like him—both their achievements and shortcomings.[109] My reading of Britten's engagement with Chinese poetry is necessarily connected with the level of understanding of the genre Western sinologists like Waley had in the 1950s. However, insights gleaned from current research in the discipline will also further enrich the interpretative scope of the music.

The second section of this chapter, '*Songs from the Chinese*: Questions and Speculations', looks at a number of issues pertaining to the premiere of Op. 58. It also examines the marginalia and

[108] Benjamin Britten, *Songs from the Chinese*, Boosey & Hawkes, 1959.

[109] Arthur Waley (1889-1966) was the eminent orientalist and sinologist upon whose numerous published books and articles on Chinese poetry Britten principally relied for source material and historical information.

annotations that Britten penciled into his copy of the Waley book *Chinese Poems*, which is the text source for the song cycle. These jottings give us a unique insight into Britten's creative decision-making practices that not only broaden our understanding of the choices he made, particularly in relation to structural design, but also pose tantalizing questions about choices he forewent.

The final two sections analyse *Songs from the Chinese* by addressing the score directly. 'Locating Dowland's Musical Rhetoric in *Songs from the Chinese*' reveals evidence of Britten's simulation of processes of musical rhetoric found in Dowland's lute songs, thereby providing verification of the shared musical idiolect discussed in Chapter One. While that chapter highlights how and why both composers were drawn to melancholy as a defining element of their musical language, this section focuses upon specific examples of musical rhetoric used by Dowland and replicated by Britten that give this melancholic idiolect its affective power. There is no evidence to suggest that Britten was academically aware that he was employing tools of musical rhetoric; and I do not suggest that he was attempting to consciously plagiarize Dowland. What I argue is that the considerable degree to which numerous technical features in *Songs from the Chinese* correlate to those found in some of Dowland's songs indicates how much Britten subconsciously assimilated the Elizabethan's musical language into his own.

The final section, 'A Closer Look at *Songs from the Chinese*', addresses structural, harmonic, melodic and rhythmic devices, as well as Britten's idiosyncratic writing for the guitar, all of which combine to reveal how his skilful manipulation of technical resources is put to the service of text illumination. The analysis will thus support another central theme in this study that Britten's approach to composition is so deeply connected to words and their meanings that his music could be said to be 'text-intrinsic', even in compositions where no text is set. The case for this last point will be made in Chapter Five, which focuses on the purely instrumental *Nocturnal*. However, in this section addressing *Songs from the Chinese*, the argument is supported by an inquiry not only into vocal writing and technical apparatuses, but also into Britten's striking illumination of the text through inspired accompaniment writing for guitar, which dynamically amplifies its meaning, and offers metaphoric sub-texts and counter-narratives.

Understanding Chinese Poetry

Britten's *Songs from the Chinese* is a setting of six Chinese poems translated by Arthur Waley. Two of these are by unknown poets and come from the ancient *Book of Songs*. Dating from later periods, the four remaining poems were written by three renowned poets—Wu-ti (156-87 BCE), Po Chü-i (772-846 CE) and Yu Lu (1125-1210 CE).[110] Before we discuss pertinent aspects of these poems and their authors, I would like to start by exploring some general characteristics of Chinese poetics.

Chinese poetry operates on different formal and figurative levels to Western poetry. Our classical inheritance sees poetry as an act of 'making', whereas the Chinese tradition regards *poïesis* as a process of apperception and enactment. Apperception is a method of understanding by which newly observed characteristics of an object are associated with a past experience. In Chinese poetry, this refers to the way 'one meaning carries resonances from one or more other meanings.'[111] Chinese poetry, therefore, does not engage with the imitation of certain aspects of reality, it is not concerned with *mimesis* per se, but rather with accounts of experiences that express the poet's connection to his or her reality; thus, it is of a subjective nature. Chinese poems typically engage in quiet and intimate modes of expression, and explore liminal states and the capturing of 'essences'. The result is a poetics that emphasizes mood, tone and atmosphere over more tangible narrative or symbolic elements. However, a real appreciation of Chinese poetry comes not only in comprehending the immediate circumstance described but also in deducing other possible interpretations emerging from broader contexts:

> skill in reading poetry (or listening to speech or song) meant skill in inferring, from the particular expression, a fullness of what the expressive act revealed, not only the poet's implicit intentions but more generally the world to which the poem responded.[112]

To gain a better understanding of this latent agency within Chinese poetics, we need to investigate the social and cultural practices that poetry served. As we have noted, two poems set in *Songs from the Chinese*—'The Big Chariot' and 'Dance-Song'—come from *The Book of*

---

[110] See Appendix IV for biographical notes on these poets.

[111] Robert Ashmore, 'Chinese Poetics', in *The Princeton Encyclopedia of Poetry & Poetics: Fourth Edition* (Princeton: Princeton University Press, 2012), 239.

[112] Ibid.

Songs, which was China's first great anthology of poetry. Known as the *Shī Jīng*, or 'song-word scripture', *The Book of Songs* was compiled some time after 600 BCE and comprises 305 very old 'poems' or 'songs'.[113] Some of these poems possibly date from as early as 1000 BCE, which likely accounts for the poets' anonymity. It is not known if Confucius selected the poems himself, as many contend; but he did give the *Shī Jīng* a central position in Confucian education and philosophy.[114] The songs from the anthology are varied in character but most pertain to some aspect of community life and may be divided into four general categories covering folksongs, festive songs sung at court celebrations, odes used for solemn ceremonies and eulogies performed at religious sacrifices. These song-poems reflect the broad aspects of daily life in Chinese society before the 6th century BCE: courtship, marriage, seasonal festivities, hunting, feasting, war and sacrifice. Many make use of repetitive sounds, onomatopoeic and alliterative techniques, and stock phrases, which often give the poems a formal, generic and ritualistic quality. They avoid personal sentiment in favour of communal pragmatism, in which respect they often served a diplomatic function. Confucius believed that proper study of the *Shī Jīng* requires

> being competent to act autonomously as the representative of one's ruler in diplomatic exchanges (*Analects 13.5*); indeed, formal performances from the *Shi* were often required at state banquets, demanding not only a command of the repertoire but an acute sensitivity for how contextual meanings might shift with circumstances of performances.[115]

This functional aspect of the poetry accounts for the rather unemotional quality it appears to display. However, the structural character of these poems also affects this perceived aloofness. When compared on a structural level to most Western poetry, these 'songs' are exceptionally terse and concise, especially if they are read in the original, where pronouns often disappear and grammatical connections are kept to a minimum. This is clearly demonstrated by 'Dance Song',

---

[113] *Shi* also refers to an ancient musical repertoire overseen by musicians of the Zhou court (1046-256 BCE). 'This repertoire...became central to the curriculum of traditionalist ritual and musical education. It became fixed over time, and as the old musical settings fell from memory on the Zhou's waning centuries, the remaining written text, and anthology of 305 poems, was known as the *Shijing* (...also known as the *Book of Songs*)'; cited in Robert Ashmore, 'Chinese Poetics', 239.

[114] Ibid., 238-239.

[115] Ibid., 239.

one of the two poems Britten chose from the *Shī Jīng*. An exact transliteration from the Chinese takes the following form:

Figure 4: 'Dance Song' from *The Book of Songs* [116]

Feet of lin[117]	many	duke's sons
Grieving: sad	lin	alas grieving lin
Brow of lin		kinsmen
		Alas grieving lin
Horns of lin		clansmen
		Alas grieving lin

As we can observe, the poetry is considerably pared down. Consequently, suggestion is favoured over exposition and explication. Furthermore, it is largely free of syntactical control. Like much of Chinese poetry, it seldom specifies prepositions or conjunctions and is essentially a series of images that exist outside notions of specific time. The Indo-European perception of past, present and future, which is expressed in the languages' verb tenses, can thus be seen as paradoxically limiting. In stark contrast, Chinese verbs tend to 'return to the Phenomenon itself, that undifferentiated mode of being, *which is timeless, the concept of time being a human invention arbitrarily imposed upon Phenomenon*'.[118]

An awareness of these issues assists in our understanding of Chinese poetics, the central tenet of which is the distinct lack of syntactical agency; perhaps the characteristic with which Indo-European sensibilities struggle most. For example, while the terseness of 'Dance Song' may be perceived as emotionally and dramatically redundant, these characteristics must not be confused with a paucity of meaning or evocative connotation. On the contrary, the actual lack of specificity in a classical Chinese poem is a direct invitation for readers to deduce additional and divergent interpretations. In fact, the poem's economy and reticence allows for an imagistic device known as *xing* to be activated—an allegorical connotation whereby poems metaphorically connect the natural world to the human condition.[119] The reader is thus

[116] Kyung Soo Moon, 'Balinese Influences in *Songs from the Chinese*' (PhD diss., University of Texas, 1993).

[117] A lin sometimes is referred to as a giraffe but in this context it really means the mythical lin, translated by Waley as a unicorn.

[118] Wai-Lim Yip, *Chinese Poetry* (Durham: Duke University Press, 1997), 3. The italics are the author's.

[119] Alex Preminger and T.V.F. Brogan, eds., *The New Princeton Encyclopedia of Poetry and Poetics* (New Jersey: Princeton University Press, 1993), 191.

encouraged to find the meaning of the poem not in the particular descriptions contained therein, but elsewhere. This is why, in Confucius's time, diplomats used *xing* as a means of making ambiguous allusions to sensitive political situations. It further explains why the poems from the *Shī Jīng* have traditionally been understood to have political and ethical meanings that clearly extend beyond their apparently naive descriptions of love or nature. Needless to say, this aspect of Chinese poetics has far reaching implications for our ability to satisfactorily interpret these texts as read poetry or in musical settings.

As certain images in Chinese poetry established metaphorical authority over time, Western readers need to be acquainted with the symbolic meaning this imagery was intended to invoke. For example, the blowing wind was regularly interpreted as sounds of sorrow; rain showers symbolized opulence and plenitude; and wet leaves referred to tearful cheeks. Even something as ordinary as grass served as a powerful symbol for separation, as every year grass disappears and returns like a traveller. Clouds and dust were employed as illustrations of sudden, unpredictable movement and instability. These metaphors serve to accentuate a number of constant themes that appear in Chinese poetry. The passing of time, for example, is a central motif. There are hundreds of poems that deal with themes of sorrow for the passing of spring, and grief over the coming of autumn, which were potent metaphors for the anxiety of impending age. This dread of passing time is frequently expressed in the poet's relationship to his social and political history; the rise and fall of dynasties, and heroic acts and battles are invoked to this end. Sometimes the poetry highlights the narcissism of human ambition by contrasting the glories of the past with the ruins of the poet's present. Naturally, love is a major theme in Chinese poetry and many poems deal quite transparently with the excitement of a first love, the ache for a lover, the agony of uncertainty, the ecstasy of desire and the distress of departure and separation.

Significantly, Chinese poetry often reflects a stoical resignation at the way things are, but this does not preclude the possibility of transcendental change. Freedom is sought, however, not in the speculation upon external elements (a particularly Western attribute) but rather by searching inwardly through reflection. However, this tendency towards the subjective does not assume a total dereliction of hope, as Western thought systems such as Existentialism and the attendant literature of negation it cultivates might understand it. While there may be philosophical acceptance, there is little desperation. This is a poetic attitude that is far from feeling (as, for example, Camus'

Myth of Sisyphus posits)[120] that life is a futile search for meaning, unity and certainty in the face of an unintelligible world devoid of God and eternal truths. In contrast, the Chinese ethos, reflected in its poetics, supports the notion that through honest self-reflection and analysis the darkest moments in life can at least be tolerated. The following poem by Po Chü-i entitled 'Resignation' (clearly modelled on 'The Big Chariot' from the *Book of Songs*) represents a good example of this resigned poetic attitude:

> Resignation
> Keep off your thoughts from things that are past and done;
> For thinking of the past wakes regret and pain.
> Keep off your thoughts from thinking what will happen;
> To think of the future fills one with dismay.
> Better by day to sit like a sack in your chair;
> Better by night to lie like a stone in your bed.
> When food comes, then open your mouth;
> When sleep comes, then close your eyes.[121]

It is anticipated that an enhanced appreciation of Chinese poetics, an understanding of the problematics surrounding the translation of Chinese poetry into English and an awareness that, through the process of *xing*, Chinese poems metaphorically connect the natural world to the human condition will provide useful contextual knowledge to support a broader understanding of the texts set by Britten in his Op. 58. I now wish to focus on an investigation of Britten's decision-making processes in relation to the cycle—one that, as the title of the section suggests, raises as many questions as it answers.

---

120 Albert Camus, *The Myth of Sisyphus*, trans. Justin O'Brien trans. (London: Penguin, 2005).
121 Arthur Waley, *Poems from the Chinese* (London: Ernest Benn, 1925), 25.

Songs from the Chinese—Questions and Speculations

> ...I plan my work away from the piano and away, moreover, from paper...[122]

In this section, with the help of correspondence and commentaries, I hope to offer some useful background information surrounding the premiere of *Songs from the Chinese*. I further wish to explore a number of relevant factors linked to the song cycle that pre-date its composition. For instance, samples of marginalia written by Britten into his copy of Waley's book may help us appreciate some of the choices he made in relation to poem selection. While investigations of this nature remain speculative, they do assist in a heightened appreciation of Britten's creative decision-making processes and further offer evidence of his approach to creating structural schemata.

As no evidence appears on the MS, establishing an exact commencement date for the composition of Op. 58 is difficult. However, from a letter written by Bream, we can surmise that Britten had been considering a number of songs by late May of 1957 at the very least.[123] Just over a year after Bream wrote this letter, he and Pears premiered the new song cycle at the 1958 Aldeburgh Festival. The concert took place in Great Glemham House on 17 June[124] and within a month the BBC had broadcast the performance.[125] The score is dedicated to Princess Margaret and Prince Ludwig of Hesse and the Rhine—their pet names, Peg and Lu, are inscribed in the published score. Their friendship with Britten had flourished since their recently shared trip to the Far East and his dedication of Op. 58 to them may be

---

122 P. Kildea, ed., *Britten on Music* (Oxford: Oxford University Press, 2003), 139. This is a transcript of a recording of Benjamin Britten interviewed by T. Birch on 25 February 1956.

123 Letter from Julian Bream to Benjamin Britten, 2 June 1957. Source: Britten-Pears Library archive.

124 Great Glemham House is situated a few miles outside Aldeburgh. The poet George Crabbe (1754-1832) lived there. His collection of poetry, *The Borough* (published in 1810), provided the source for Britten's opera *Peter Grimes*. The Earl of Cranbrook and his wife, Fidelity Cranbrook (Dowager Countess of Cranbrook) owned the house from the early 1930s onwards. She was a long-time friend of Britten and Pears, and was Chairperson of the Aldeburgh Festival for thirty-five years.

125 The BBC first broadcast *Songs from the Chinese* on 15 July 1958 through the BBC Midland Home Service. See Paul Banks et al., eds., *Benjamin Britten: A Catalogue of the Published Works* (Aldeburgh: The Britten–Pears Library for The Britten Estate Limited, 1999).

seen as an affectionate declaration of that closeness.[126]

Somewhat contrastingly, correspondences between Britten and Arthur Waley provide interesting insights into their rather formal if cordial relationship:

> I have recently given myself the pleasure of setting some of your fine Chinese translations to music. I have used only some of the shorter ones (1. The Big Chariot. 2. The Old Lute. 3. The Autumn Wind. 4. The Herd Boy. 5. Depression—'Turn to jade...'. 6. Dance Song), and set them with accompaniment for guitar. Peter Pears and Julian Bream propose to give the first performance at the forthcoming Aldeburgh Festival on Tuesday afternoon, June 17th.
>
> My publishers are, of course, in touch with George Allen & Unwin for formal permission, but I wanted to let you know personally, and hope you have no objection to my having used your poems.
>
> If, of course, you are free and inclined to come to the first performance we should be delighted, otherwise I hope it will not be too long before you hear a performance of these little songs.
>
> With best wishes.
> Yours sincerely,
> Benjamin Britten.[127]

Waley responded immediately, writing that, 'Nothing could delight me more, & I have told Unwin so. I shant [sic] be at the Festival, but hope to hear them later on.'[128] Having heard the songs on the BBC Radio broadcast, Waley wrote to Britten again making an interesting statement regarding his own translation of the poems, which he

---

126 In 1955, Britten and Pears undertook a five-month tour of the Far East accompanied by Princess Margaret and Prince Ludwig. They did not visit China, though Hong Kong was included in their itinerary. The friendship with 'Peg and Lu' was further acknowledged by Britten when he dedicated his only song-cycle in German, *Sechs Hölderlin-Fragmente* (1958), to the Prince with the inscription: 'Meinem Freund, dem Prinzen Ludwig von Hessen und bei Rhein, zum fünfzigsten Geburtstag'. Their friendship also developed into a professional collaboration, as in 1958 Princess Margaret established the Hesse Student Scheme (enabling young musicians to attend the Aldeburgh Festival). She was also President of the Festival from 1986 to 1997. Britten's decision to set the poems of Friedrich Hölderlin (1770-1843) was clearly a gesture towards Prince Ludwig's nationality but may also have been influenced by Hans Werner Henze's *Kammermusik 1958,* which includes in its score *Drei Fragmente Nach Hölderlin* (for tenor and guitar). It was the Prince and Princess who first introduced Britten to Henze.

127 Letter from Benjamin Britten to Arthur Waley, 3 April 1958. Source: Britten-Pears Library archive.

128 Postcard from Arthur Waley to Benjamin Britten, 5 April 1958. Source: Britten-Pears Library archive.

apparently now considered to be rather too prosaic. This comment suggests the possibility that Waley's approach to the translation of Chinese poetry may have altered somewhat since the publication of *Chinese Poems* in 1946. Though we cannot know for certain, it is at least possible that his opinions altered in light of newly acquired knowledge regarding translation and Chinese poetics:

> Dear Britten
> I enjoyed the Chinese songs very much, on the Third Programme. It was altogether a most lovely concert, and I want to thank you and Imogen for it. I liked the music of the songs, but I thought the words sounded abysmally prosy.[129]

Judiciously, Britten did not enter into extended debate regarding the alleged prosaic character of the translations choosing instead to concentrate on informing Waley of the many performances the songs were receiving and of the reception they engendered:

> Dear Arthur Waley,
> I was so pleased with your nice letter, and to learn that you like the music of the Chinese Songs. Peter Pears and Julian Bream are doing them many times, and they tell me the performances and the reception of the songs gets better and better. I am sorry you found the words 'prosy'; I think they are wonderful.[130]

That Britten had a broad interest in Eastern culture and Chinese poetry in particular is clear from the number of books on the subjects in his library at the Red House. These include *Dance and Drama in Bali*, *The Translations of Ezra Pound* and five books by Waley: *The Nō Plays of Japan*, *The Life and Times of Po Chü-I*, Wu Ch'eng-En's *Monkey*, *Ballads and Stories from Tun-huang* and *Chinese Poems*, from which Britten chose his six texts for Op. 58.[131]

On some pages of *Chinese Poems*, Britten wrote annotations that

---

[129] Letter from Arthur Waley to Benjamin Britten, 22 July 1958. Source: Britten-Pears Library archive.

[130] Letter from Benjamin Britten to Arthur Waley, 5 August 1958. Source: Britten-Pears Library archive.

[131] Beryl de Zoete and Walter Spies, *Dance and Drama in Bali* (London: Faber and Faber, 1938); Ezra Pound, *The Translations of Ezra Pound* (London: Faber and Faber, 1953); Arthur Waley, *The Nō Plays of Japan* (London: Allen & Unwin, 1921); Arthur Waley, *Chinese Poems* (London: Allen & Unwin, 1946); Arthur Waley, *The Life and Times of Po Chu-I* 772-846 A.D (London: Allen and Unwin, 1949); Wu Ch'eng-En, *Monkey*, trans. Arthur Waley (Harmonsworth: Penguin Books, 1961); and Arthur Waley, *Ballads and Stories from Tun-huang* (London: Allen and Unwin, 1960).

provide fascinating insights into his structural plans for the cycle. For instance, pencil markings on one of the index pages clearly indicate Britten's circling of two poems from the section entitled *The Book of Songs* with the numbers 1 and 6. From this we can confidently speculate that Britten had the clear and early intention of setting six songs and of opening and closing the cycle using the ancient poems from the *Shī Jīng*.

Plate 5: Arthur Waley, *Chinese Poems*, index pages[132]

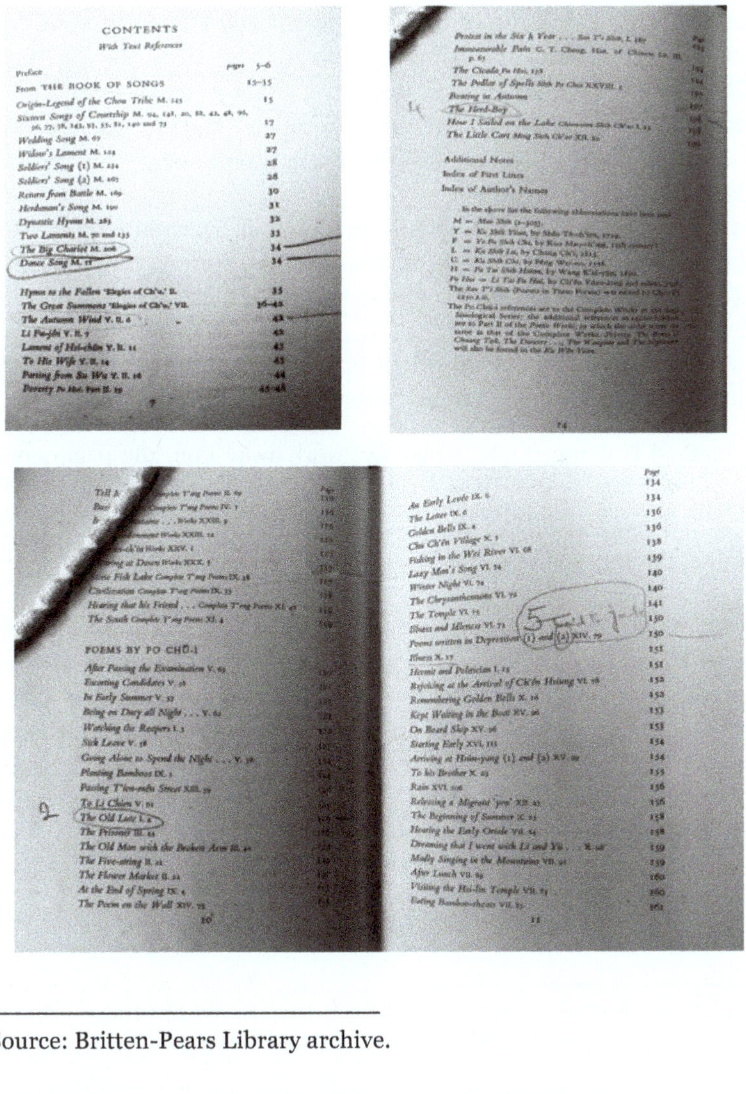

132 Source: Britten-Pears Library archive.

As we have noted, these anonymous poems from *The Book of Songs* are much more declamatory in character than the more recently composed poems chosen for the cycle. To reiterate what I have outlined previously, many of these older, epigrammatic poems employ repetitive sounds, onomatopoeic and alliterative techniques, and stock phrases, which bestow upon them a prescribed and ritualistic quality that appears to circumvent personal feeling and overt sentiment. It is clear that Britten intuitively felt that such pragmatic texts, strategically placed at the beginning and end of the cycle, would act as a kind of protective shield for the more emotionally wrought poems placed within. As we have noted, the remaining four poems that Britten positioned inside this protective frame were 'The Old Lute' written by Po Chü-i, the 'The Autumn Wind' by Wu-ti, 'The Herd Boy' by Lu Yu and 'Depression', also written by Po Chü-i. Plate 5 above clearly shows the numbers 2, 3, 4 and 5 pencilled beside the chosen poems, which illustrate that Britten's plans for the cycle's sequence were carefully considered.

However, the marginalia encourage further speculation. Britten's decision to select 'Depression' as the culmination of the four inner settings indicates that he recognized early on that this poem would have significant potential as a carrier of dramatic tension. Its strategic placement offers a schema that directs the four inner songs towards a dramatic and emotionally charged *dénouement* with 'Depression'.

> My method is quite simple. I plan my work away from the piano and away, moreover, from paper. I do ninety-nine per cent of my work thinking about it...Then when the music is fixed in my head I go to the paper and work out more precisely the details. I don't use the piano except at the very end when the work is more or less complete'[133]

As we have seen, marginalia can be very useful in developing a picture of Britten's decision-making processes. They can also present a number of dilemmas, as do those written into other pages of Waley's book, which raise a number of tantalizing questions about Britten's ultimate objectives regarding structure and poem selection—questions that cannot this time be so easily answered. For example, on the very last blank page of the book Britten wrote the following list:

---

[133] P. Kildea, ed., *Britten on Music*, 139. This is a transcript of a recording of Benjamin Britten interviewed by T. Birch on 25 February 1956.

Plate 6: List written in Britten's hand on final page of Arthur Waley, *Chinese Poems*[134]

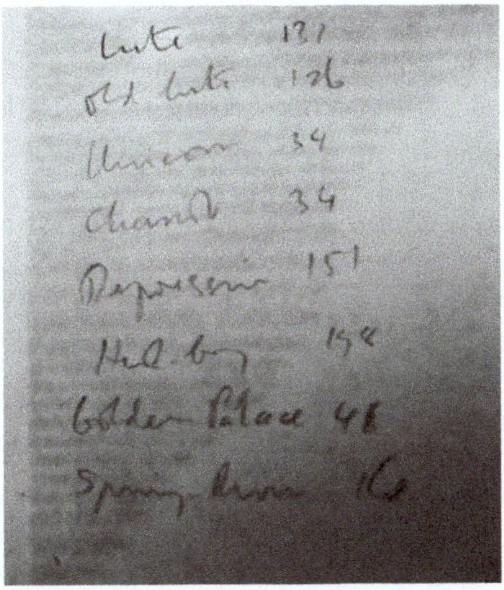

Lute
Old Lute
Unicorn
Chariot
Depression
Herd-Boy
Golden Palace
Spring River

With the addition of three extra poems and a different order for the original six, this list clearly suggests that Britten was at some point considering a longer cycle for Op. 58. Are there three songs for voice and guitar somewhere in the archives of the Britten-Pears Library that Britten, for one reason or another, decided not to include in his final selection? Though unlikely, this actually occurred with the song cycle *Winter Words*, Op. 52. Written in 1953, *Winter Words* is a setting of eight Thomas Hardy poems that was premiered by Britten and Pears at the Leeds Festival that year. Subsequent to the premiere, two further settings were discovered. Originally intended to be part of *Winter Words*, both were finally discarded when the ultimate form of the cycle was decided upon.

---

[134] Source: Britten-Pears Library archive.

Even if three other guitar songs do not exist, it is highly instructive in our study of *Songs from the Chinese* to know what other poems Britten was seriously considering for the cycle (for this reason I include the three poems in Appendix V). One poem by Po Chü-i, 'The Five-String', is a useful tool by which to understand the other 'lute' poem Britten in fact employed. 'The Old Lute' is terse and short; it suggests rather than delineates its themes, which are more fully developed in 'The Five-String'. The other poem by Po Chü-i considered by Britten is 'The Spring River'; a meditation on age and the desire to reject the superficialities of life; its themes would have been aptly suited to the cycle's obsessions with death and the passing of youth. The third poem on the annotated list is 'The Golden Palace', a rather odd, formal poem about ritual and honour, which is somewhat similar to the ceremonial aspect of the final chosen poem in the set, 'Dance Song'.

I do not believe that too great an emphasis should be placed on these three poems (unless, of course, manuscripts of their settings are discovered). However, they do offer insights into why Britten ultimately chose the poems he did. While the rejected texts would have replicated the central concerns of the cycle—themes of death, the passing of time, the struggle to accommodate new trends, the sadness of lost youth and the futility of official patronage and bureaucracy—they were unlikely to have enhanced those themes more effectively than the chosen texts were expected to do. Both 'The Five-String' and 'The Spring River' may ultimately have been rejected because of their length. As he hints in the letter to Waley cited above—'I have used only some of the shorter ones'—in all probability, Britten felt that the guitar as an accompaniment instrument did not have sufficient resonance or harmonic breadth to sustain songs of extensive structural length; poems of this range would have either created a formal imbalance within the cycle or would have required an extended and more complex harmonic structure.

In this regard, Britten can be admired for not only knowing what the guitar could achieve, but also for intuiting what it perhaps could not. In my analysis of 'Dance Song' below, I suggest that it is not only a veiled tribute to the dedicatees of the cycle, but also a covert homage to their royal pedigree. If my speculation is accurate, 'The Golden Palace' may have been considered for possible inclusion in this light. However, I think the poem was ultimately rejected for purely aesthetic reasons, as it is simply inconceivable that Britten could bring himself to set the line, 'Pounded beef and boiled pork and mutton'.

Locating Dowland's Musical Rhetoric in *Songs from the Chinese*

As we have seen in Chapter One, the connections that Britten made with Dowland were unambiguous. The songs 'If My Complaints Could Passions Move' and 'Flow My Tears' are used in *Lachrymae, reflections on a song of John Dowland*; 'Come Heavy Sleep' is the theme upon which *Nocturnal, after John Dowland* is based; and the dangerous politics of Dowland's Elizabethan world is the setting for the opera *Gloriana*. Tellingly, Britten returned to Dowland in the last year of his life when, close to death, he composed a version of his *Lachrymae* for viola and strings. This tells us that Dowland was a perennial presence for Britten. He not only provided him with extraordinary examples of English settings in a genre, the lute song, which offered a powerful outlet for deeply expressive musical gestures, but he also embodied a figure with whom Britten could feel an emotional and psychological connection.

Although Chinese texts might seem worlds away from early English music, the second poem of Op. 58, 'The Old Lute', in a setting by Britten naturally invokes Dowland.

> Of chord and cassiawood is the lute compounded;
> Within it lie ancient melodies.[135]

The lute was rarely absent from Britten's consciousness and this line in particular must have resonated with him, calling to mind the emotional poignancy of Dowland's 'ancient melodies'. Indeed, it was through the expert practice of musical rhetoric that Dowland was able to make his lute songs so expressive and affecting. Nothing had quite prepared England for music so unprecedented in its depth of emotional power. Dowland's uncanny ability to amplify the meaning of texts by composing correlating and affective musical *figurae* was an emerging phenomenon that met with great enthusiasm. Freed from the interpretative and technical strictures that governed the well-established motet and madrigal, the lute song, with its frequently explosive rhetorical expressiveness, initiated a completely new musical encounter, which gave a unique and personal experience to the performers and, cathartically, to the listeners. The degree to which this exciting new genre enhanced Dowland's prestige is shown by the remarkable success *The First Booke of Songes or Ayres* had when it was

---

135 Arthur Waley, *Chinese Poems* (London: Allen & Unwin, 1946). All the chosen poems set in *Songs from the Chinese* are taken from these translations.

published in 1597, and by the subsequent reprints that were made in 1600, 1603, 1606, 1608 and 1613.

The historic connection between text and music is grounded in the fact that music was part of the *Seven Liberal Arts*—theories of education based on Classical ideals that were codified in Europe around the 5th century and which, by the early Renaissance, had become increasingly established in the canon of higher learning. The *Seven Liberal Arts* consisted of *The Trivium* and *The Quadrivium*: the former were the three lower arts—Grammar, Rhetoric and Logic, which constituted the basic educational foundation for the higher arts—Arithmetic (number in itself), Geometry (number in space), Music (number in time) and Astronomy (number in space and time). Until relatively late in its history, music was predominantly vocal. Because of this long and close association with text, music was heavily influenced by the practice of rhetoric, and consequently, theories of musical rhetoric became a significant and influential branch of the discipline. By the time Dowland published *The First Booke of Songes or Ayres*, England was very much a culturally aware environment in terms of those philosophies that underpinned musical rhetoric.

Traditionally, the art of rhetoric was divided into five areas: *inventio*, *dispositio*, *elocutio*, *memoria* and *pronunciatio*. *Inventio* was the discovery of the material to be used. *Dispositio* was concerned with the arrangement of that material. *Elocutio* (or *decorativo*) was the embellishment, amplification and decoration of the text with exemplary words and sentences. The resulting discourse was then memorized (*memoria*) and delivered orally (*pronunciatio*). As we have seen, the Classical age's reverence for Orpheus as the ultimate poet and musician led to the belief that music was a powerful tool of communication and could arouse any emotion in its listeners. For musicians of the Renaissance and Baroque, the use of musical rhetoric allowed them to identify the emotional content represented by a given text and to communicate that to an audience. For example, the composer and poet Thomas Campion (1567-1620) makes this clear when he says:

> Happy is hee whose words can move,
> Yet sweet Notes help perswasion.
> Mixe your words with Musicke then,
> That they the more may enter.[136]

---

[136] Thomas Campion, 'The Description of a Maske...At the Marriage of the Right Honourable the Earl of Somerset, London, 1614', in Robert Toft, *Tune Thy Musicke To Thy Hart: The Art of Eloquent Singing in England 1597-1622* (Toronto: University of Toronto, 1993), 4.

It was widely believed that only by strict adherence to the laws of rhetoric could an aesthetic excitation and direct communication be achieved. Music could not automatically 'speak for itself', but rather, it needed to be imbued, as the lutenist Thomas Mace (1613-1706) suggested, with a variety of elements that would extricate and articulate the expressive meaning inherent in its construction.

> There is in Musick...such a wonderful-various-way of Expression, even as in Language, Unbounded, and Unlimited; and we may as properly, and as Aptly take a Subject Matter to Discourse upon...and show as much Wit, and Variety, as can the Best Orator, in the way of Oratory: And I would, that this were better known, and more put into Practice...'[137]

Dowland responded to the rhetoric of the language in his chosen texts by composing musical settings that were themselves imbued with potent musical rhetoric. Indeed, he was renowned for his skill in this regard; the poet and writer, Henry Peacham the Younger (1576-1643), referred to 'Master Doctor Douland' as 'inferior to none in the world...for depth of skill and richness of concept'.[138] Dowland amplified the meaning of texts with a diversity of musical *figurae*, transforming both into what would in his time have been called 'eloquent song'. Even when texts were not extraordinary in themselves, composers such as Dowland used musical embellishments in order to transform them into profoundly affecting songs. Indeed, simple texts that followed an established pattern often allowed for greater rhetorical expansion by a composer.

Where are these techniques of musical rhetoric located in Britten's *Songs from the Chinese*? Not surprisingly, the first place to look is in the song that tells of the lute's 'ancient melodies'—'The Old Lute':

> **'The Old Lute'**
> Of chord and cassiawood is the lute compounded;
> Within it lie ancient melodies.
> Ancient melodies – weak and savourless,
> Not appealing to present men's taste.
> Light and colour are faded from the jade stops;
> Dust has covered the rose-red strings.
> Decay and ruin came to it long ago,

137 Judy Tarling, *The Weapons of Rhetoric: A Guide for Musicians and Audiences* (Hertfordshire: Corda Music, 2004), 105.

138 Henry Peacham the Younger, *The Compleat Gentleman* (London: 1622, facsimile Amsterdam: 1968), in Robert Toft, *Tune Thy Musicke To Thy Hart: The Art of Eloquent Singing in England 1597-1622* (Toronto: University of Toronto, 1993), 12.

But the sound that is left is still cold and clear.
I do not refuse to play it, if you want me to;
But even if I play people will not listen.

How did it come to be neglected so?
Because of the Ch'i-ang flute and the zithern of Ch'in

All the vocal and harmonic components of 'The Old Lute' are constructed from five melodic fragments derived from the Lydian mode starting on the note E.

Example 4: Britten, 'The Old Lute', *Songs from the Chinese*, (polyphonic stratification)

This construct of stratified polyphony created from the combined voices of the guitar and tenor part is clearly a reference to similar structures that characterize the lute-song genre and may well have been employed to subliminally invoke Dowland—an apt intervention in a song that is, at least on one level, about the decline of the lute as a fashionable instrument. In light of this, it is worth remembering that many of the accompaniments that support Dowland's lute songs do more than simply add harmonic foundation to the vocal part. Analogous to the construct of stratified polyphony above, Dowland's accompaniments frequently weave numerous contrapuntal lines that pre-empt, interlace and reiterate those of the voice. This feature of polyphonic stratification was clearly understood by Britten, as comments made by Pears at the Aldeburgh Festival in 1963 attest.[139]

Thus, the polyphonic nature of 'The Old Lute' demonstrates Britten's unambiguous reference to the musical construction of the lute song genus most typified by Dowland. This point underscores the fact that

139 See comments by Pears on page 20.

the lute songs of those composers immediately succeeding Dowland display a reduced concern for complex polyphony. The highly restricted range of each modal fragment (the notes in brackets in Example 4 are only arrived at after some time), allied to the marking 'slow and remote' creates a static harmonic environment that gives the song a deeply immanent character—a technical device that musically reinforces the diminished status and bleak prospect for the instrument in the Chinese poem.

There are two specific details here that show the characteristics of musical rhetoric in action: the use of the Lydian mode and the reiteration of falling intervals. As we have noted in Chapter One, composers of the Renaissance and Baroque periods utilized certain modes in order to create specific affective states pertinent to the mood and character of a given work. Received opinion assigned affects to each mode, dictating that, for example, the use of the Phrygian mode would incite frenzy and inspire emotionally charged states. By the seventeenth century, this mode was thought to aggressively arouse the spirit and imbue the listener with courage and masculinity. The Lydian mode, on the other hand, was understood to have the opposite effect: encouraging gravity and solemnity, it was thought to infect the mind with a kind of uncontrollable ecstasy.[140] In this respect, Britten's intuitive use of the Lydian mode for 'The Old Lute' suggests a practice of musical rhetoric most appropriate to the solemn nature of words that speak of loss and decay.

140 Judy Tarling, *The Weapons of Rhetoric: A Guide for Musicians and Audiences* (Hertfordshire: Corda Music, 2004), 76.

Example 5: Britten, 'The Old Lute', *Songs from the Chinese*

Recalling Morley's insistence that 'where your ditty speaketh of 'descending', 'lowness', 'depth', 'hell', and others such, you must make your music descend', we can see how Britten intuitively follows such instruction. Example 5 demonstrates how a drop in pitch completes numerous phrases in 'The Old Lute'. The reiteration of descending intervals is a technique of musical rhetoric that subtly intimates the old lute's fall from grace and gives to the song an appropriate sense of decay.

Example 6: Britten, 'The Old Lute', *Songs from the Chinese*, bars 30-34

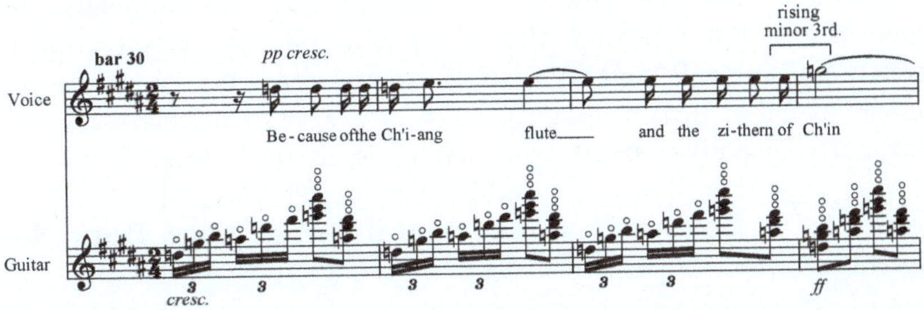

For this reason, the final phrase of the song, which breaks with that mood, comes as a total surprise. The abrupt transition to a new tempo ('Quick', crochet = 104) and fast harmonics conjures up the world of the novel instruments spoken of in the poem, the dazzling confusion they induce in the old poet and the unexpected change in society for which shifting fashion is a powerful indicator. The poet's world, which has been turned upside-down, is rhetorically captured by Britten when the previously falling 3^{rds} of the vocal line are literally turned upside-down by the arrival of these newfangled instruments, which now make the end of the phrase rise a minor 3rd. 'The Old Lute' is a short song of only thirty-seven bars, but through its effective use of stratified polyphony it demonstrates how Britten instinctively absorbed into his own musical idiolect the lute-song derivations and techniques of musical rhetoric typical of Dowland's music.

Another direct influence from Dowland can be observed in the cycle's opening song, 'The Big Chariot'. In the third stanza, Britten resorts to the repetition of certain word phrases. This technique of reiteration is a foundational component of musical rhetoric theory known as *subjunctio* (*epizeuxis*).

> Don't help on the big chariot;
> You will only make yourself dusty.
> Don't think about the sorrows of the world;
> You will only make yourself wretched.

As the Elizabethan writer and critic George Puttenham (1529-1590) asserts: 'the figure that worketh by iteration or repetition of one word or clause doth much alter and affect the eare and also the mynde of the hearer, and therefore is counted a very brave figure both with the Poets and the rhetoriciens.'[141] Dowland's effective employment of iteration to amplify sexual longing is one that, I suggest, Britten understood intuitively. It is a technique that can often create great intensity; thus when words are repeated 'the affect is amplified, useful both for "vehement" appeals and in a softer appeal for pity. The voice may appear to fail at peak volume through excess of strong emotion, as in Dowland's sexually charged "to see, to heare, to touch, to die"'.[142]

Example 7: Dowland, 'Come Again! Sweet Love Doth Now Invite'

Similarly, the repeat Britten employs at bars 28-29 ('The big chariot, the big chariot') emphasizes the size and weight of the chariot and consequently the hardship it imposes. When he uses duplication in the phrase 'You'll be stifled with dust, be stifled with dust' (bars 31-32) it gives the impression that the singer is running out of breath; the voice is so stifled by the obligation to articulate all the repeated words within a short time frame that the vocal line is forced to descend and diminish under the strain.

Additionally, the specific use of repetition of the opening lines, 'Don't think about the sorrows of the world', as they appear for the third time (that is, in the third verse), is directly influenced by Dowland's use of the technique known in rhetoric as *reduplicatio* (*anadiplosis*). This is the repetition of the last word of one phrase at the beginning of the next. A perfect example can be found in Dowland's 'In Darkness Let Me Dwell', where the lines,

> The roofe Dispaire to barre all cheerfull light from mee
> The wals of marble blacke that moistned still shall weepe

---

[141] George Puttenham, *The Arte of English Poesie*, ed. Baxter Hathaway (London: 1589/Kent: 1970), in Robert Toft, *Tune Thy Musicke To Thy Hart: The Art of Eloquent Singing in England 1597-1622* (Toronto: University of Toronto, 1993), 21.

[142] Judy Tarling, *The Weapons of Rhetoric*, 224.

are transformed through the process of *reduplicatio* into

> The roofe Dispaire to barre all, all cheerfull light from mee
> The wals of marble blacke that moistned, that moistned still shall weepe, still shall weepe

Similarly, from bar 35 Britten amplifies the essential theme of 'The Big Chariot' through an effective use of *reduplicatio*; though he applies the technique to a single line, the effect is identical:

> Don't think about the sorrows of the world
> think about the sorrows of the world
> the sorrows of the world

Britten makes a number of repetitions of the line diminishing its length each time, which simultaneously increases the fervor of the admonition. Furthermore, this practice very astutely creates in the ear a fourth concise sub-text that cautions 'Don't think sorrows'. These lines are set in melismatic figurations so effectively and naturally that they provide undeniable evidence of Britten's distinctive ability to transform ancient techniques of musical rhetoric into ingenious settings that are equally convincing and seductive when heard through his own musical language.

Dowland's influence is demonstrated once more when Britten employs a variant of *reduplicatio* in 'The Autumn Wind' from bar 51:

> Youth's years how few, age how sure!
> Youth's years how few, age how sure!
> how sure!
> age how sure!
> age how sure!
> how
> sure!

Example 8: Britten, 'The Autumn Wind', *Songs from the Chinese*, bars 61 to end

Meanwhile, more musical rhetoric lurks in Britten's use of another rhetorical device called *palillogia*—the repetition of a melodic fragment at the same pitch. We can see how Dowland's repetition of the word 'farewell' on the note A in Example 9 is very closely replicated by Britten's similar reiteration of the words 'age how sure' on the note E in Example 8. The composers use the technique to emphasize the matter and bring both songs to their respective closures.

Example 9: Dowland, 'Farewell Too Faire'

Britten's use of *reduplicatio* can be further observed in the fifth song 'Depression':

> Turned to Jade are the boy's rosy cheeks;
> To his sick temples the frost of winter clings.
> Do not wonder that my body sinks to decay;
> Though my limbs are old, my heart is older yet.

The technique is utilized to transform

> Though my limbs are old, my heart is older yet.

into

> Though my limbs are old, are old
> my heart is older, older, older, older yet.

Example 10: Britten, 'Depression', *Songs from the Chinese*, bars 9 to end

The use of *reduplicatio* in this section effectively amplifies the meaning in the text. However, another device from the tool kit of musical rhetoric is simultaneously employed here, invoking Dowland yet again. *Synonymia* is the repetition of a musical fragment at different pitch levels.[143] In his song 'Behold A Wonder Here' (Example 11) Dowland employs *synonymia* on the word 'hundred' to emphasize the way love can be blindly persistent. In Example 10, we can see how Britten similarly underscores time and age in his employment of *synonymia* on the word 'older' (bars 11 and 12) and the reiteration of the correlating accompanying fragments, thus demonstrating again that he has

143 'In the language arts, *synonymia* specifies a figure designed to make the sense stronger and more obvious by using words which differ from the preceding one in form or sound but which mean the same.' See Robert Toft, *Tune Thy Musicke To Thy Hart: The Art of Eloquent Singing in England 1597-1622* (Toronto: University of Toronto, 1993), 32.

assimilated specific technical and thematic elements of Dowland's musical idiolect.

Example 11: Dowland, 'Behold A Wonder Here'

As we have noted earlier, 'Dance Song', which concludes the cycle, is a ritualistic poem. Its third verse is extended through the repetition of certain words and phrases, resulting in an outburst that, on each repeat, rises to more extreme heights. This controlled sense of climax hearkens back to the rhetorical devices Dowland brought to bear in his music and which were governed by the understanding that it is a fundamental rule in the delivery of speech 'to begin at the lowest that you the better aspire to the height of amplyficacion'.[144] Dowland exploits this technique of *gradatio* (*climax*) in his song 'Flow My Tears' in a sequence that ascends by degrees, heightening the emotional charge at every step (see also 'Come Again! Sweet Love Doth Now Invite' in Example 7).

---

[144] Francis Pilkington (ca. 1565 – 1638), in Robert Toft, *Tune Thy Musicke To Thy Hart: The Art of Eloquent Singing in England 1597-1622* (Toronto: University of Toronto, 1993), 33-4.

Example 12: Dowland, 'Flow My Tears'

Britten uses the same technique in 'Dance Song' when he repeatedly places the word 'Alas' at a higher rung of the emotional ladder until the third outburst takes the singer to an extremity of expression.

Example 13: Britten, 'Dance Song', *Songs from the Chinese*, vocal part, bars 15 to end

In this section, I have provided evidence that Britten's *Songs from the Chinese* is imbued with Dowland's musical rhetoric. I reiterate that Britten was not deliberately imitating Dowland's compositional style. Indeed, I do not think that he was even conscious in any overt academic sense of the taxonomy of such techniques. If they are employed in Op. 58, it is because Britten naturally understood and absorbed the essential traits of Dowland's musical idiolect: such profound symbiosis was quite likely an unconscious element of his compositional thinking. The extraordinary aspect of this synergy is that, far from undermining his own distinctive voice, the intuitive appropriation of these technical attributes from Dowland's practice actually enhances Britten's 'unfailing ability vividly to translate words into musical terms that seem inevitable'.[145]

A Closer Look at Songs from the Chinese

> '...The Glamour
> Of childish days upon me, my manhood is cast
> Down in the flood of remembrance, I weep like a child of the past.'[146]

> **Colin Smythe:** Did he choose the 'Songs from the Chinese' because of their simplicity?
> **Peter Pears:** Are they so simple?[147]

Britten may be considered as the artisan composer *par excellence* in that he always found inventively practical ways to solve creative challenges. It goes without saying that he was intimately familiar with Pears' voice and so the vocal music that he composed for him is subtly nuanced and discreetly fashioned to the tenor's unique signature as a singer. However, with such an idiosyncratic instrument as the guitar, Britten's capacity to create wholly convincing illuminations of the text in this cycle demonstrates an advanced musical intelligence supported by an impressively practical methodology. Time and again, we will observe that Britten's accompaniment writing for the instrument is both innately guitaristic and eminently suited to the text.

What we see from Op. 58 is that Britten had a tremendous ability to extrapolate numerous narratives, sometimes contradictory, from a given text. This characteristic curiously parallels a basic function of the poetry itself in the form of the imagistic device that we discussed earlier, known as *xing*, in which descriptions of immediate surroundings simultaneously suggest other possible interpretations emerging from broader contexts. Accordingly, with masterfully wrought vocal lines and judiciously formulated accompaniments, Britten weaves from a chosen poem many threads of sub-textual and metaphoric narrativity, enriching and complexifying the song's meanings.

Songs from the Chinese demonstrates that all the armoury of Britten's compositional practice is placed at the service of the 'word': it is a method of composition that I call text-intrinsic. In Chapter Five, I argue that this process is also manifest in *Nocturnal*—an instrumental work, which nonetheless is wholly dependent upon the words set in its

---

145 Graham Johnson, *Britten, Voice & Piano*, 2.

146 D. H. Lawrence, 'The Piano', in *The Complete Poems of D.H. Lawrence* (Hertfordshire: Wordsworth Editions, 1994), 112.

147 Colin Smythe, 'Interview with Peter Pears', in *Trinity News* (1962).

theme as a basis for melodic and harmonic development. Thus, when I use the term text-intrinsic in relation to Op. 58 (and to the *Folksong Arrangements* and the 'Second Lute Song', for that matter), I am not necessarily referring to Britten's self-evident gift for word setting. Rather, I wish to focus on the way he formulates the harmony, rhythms, structures, textures and dynamics of the accompaniment to illuminate the text's meaning. We shall see, for instance, how an irregular rhythmic accompaniment underscores the image of an ox walking unevenly on cobbled stones in 'The Herd-Boy', and observe how the use of guitar glissandi emphasizing the 'dying of a plucked string' effectively draws attention to the theme of death and decay in 'Depression'. What follows is an investigation of Britten's text-intrinsic methods, which will be analysed from numerous technical perspectives. Meanwhile, a preliminary exploration of each poem's background and genus will help contextualize Britten's musical settings.

'The Big Chariot'

> 'The Big Chariot'
> Don't help on the big chariot;[148]
> You will only make yourself dusty.
> Don't think about the sorrows of the world;
> You will only make yourself wretched.
>
> Don't help on the big chariot;
> You won't be able to see for dust.
> Don't think about the sorrows of the world;
> You will never escape from your despair.
>
> Don't help on the big chariot;
> You'll be stifled with dust.
> Don't think about the sorrows of the world;
> You will only load yourself with care.

In his *Chinese Poems*, Arthur Waley tells us that while in the service of the Emperor Chuian, the poet of 'The Big Chariot' was ordered to liaise with soldiers from Lo Yang, a city in the Henan province, and take them a thousand miles away to Nan Hui Yi to gather equipment and artillery for an impending war. The text, therefore, expresses the poet's dislike of the dusty journey while following the chariot every day. As the poem uses the imagistic device *xing* through metaphorical connotations

[148] Arthur Waley, trans., *The Book of Songs* (New York: Grove Press, 1987), 321. The first line of each stanza of this poem is, in fact, translated as: 'Don't escort the big chariot'.

inherent in it, we are invited to contemplate not only the poet's physical trials and tribulations but also broader considerations such as skepticism about philosophizing too much, the fear of being consumed by the negativity and tragedies that life brings, having unrealistic aspirations to change the world, and being merely an insignificant part of a larger, uncaring political or social system. As we have noted, admonitions of this sort often bestow upon poetry a 'moralizing' didactic function. Waley suggests that the 305 poems collected in the *Shī Jīng* were probably chosen from about three thousand, so it is likely that this formula was of a common generic pattern for poems of complaint, forewarning and counsel. The following poem not only provides an interesting example of this poetic formula, it also helps contextualize 'The Big Chariot', to which it is quite similar:

> Do not till too big a field,
> Or weeds will ramp it.
> Do not love a distant man,
> Or heart's pain will chafe you.
>
> Do not till too big a field,
> Or weeds will top it.
> Do not love a distant man,
> Or heart's pain will fret you...[etc.][149]

Waley develops upon the function of these poems stating that they

> expressed directly or allegorically the feelings of the people about their rulers. They vented their grievances or (much more rarely) expressed their satisfaction...This was the Golden Age of poetry, when every poem had a moral or political meaning, and could be used by the rulers of China to guide them in their task.[150]

Thus, 'Don't help on the big chariot' may also be interpreted as a warning against the perils of war—a theme that deeply resonated with Britten. While this contextual information allows us to observe *xing* as a tool for 'unconcealing' hidden meanings in the poem, I now wish to investigate how Britten, through composition, reinforces this process.

'The Big Chariot' provides an excellent example of Britten's desire to build structural and harmonic schemata not as separate 'containers' ready to receive any given text but designed specifically to reflect the poem's formal outline and enhance the text's multiple meanings.

---

149 Ibid., 49.

150 Arthur Waley, *The Life and Times of Po Chü-I* (London: Allen & Unwin, 1949), 108.

Structurally, the song is organized to reflect that each stanza is divided into two groups of two lines—1 and 3, and 2 and 4. Lines 1 and 3 give warnings: 'Don't help on...' and 'Don't think about...', etc., while lines 2 and 4 are philosophical commentaries articulating the consequences if the warnings are not heeded: 'You will only make yourself dusty' and 'You will only make yourself wretched', etc. The second and third stanzas utilize the same structural plan as the first. Britten's structuring of the voice part and guitar accompaniment in a binary fashion skilfully echoes and amplifies the 'cause and effect' stratification inherent within the text. To this end, he has arranged the musical material into two distinguishing sections that correlate with the stanza's couplets:

Figure 5: Stanza division into two couplets

Couplet 1: Don't help on the big chariot;
You will only make yourself dusty.

Couplet 2: Don't think about the sorrows of the world;
You will only make yourself wretched.

Example 14 demonstrates the way Britten has manipulated range and dynamics to provide distinctive characterization for each couplet structure and to musically enhance the text's imagery. For the first couplet, the top staves of the example show the voice placement as relatively high (C^1). The guitar part is divided into two distinct components: a fast melodic figuration below (whose rumblings imitate the heavy wheels of the chariot) and triadic chords above. Both parts have a *forte* dynamic and a musical heading 'Heavy', indicating the oppressive burden the poet's duties are imposing on him.

In contrast, the second couplet shown in the bottom staves place the voice in the lower register (between F♯ and A). Meanwhile, the two components of the guitar accompaniment are reversed: the melodic figuration now takes a higher position, while the triadic chords are played in the lower register. Correspondingly, the dynamics have been reversed from *forte* to *pianissimo* with an instruction to go 'lightly'.

Example 14: Britten, 'The Big Chariot', *Songs from the Chinese*, bars 1-3, and 8-10

This dialectical reversal is repeated in the following two stanzas starting at bars 14 and 27, respectively. As I have intimated, the harmonic structure replicates the stanzaic design: the first stanza opens in F major, the second in G minor and the third in E major. Examples 15 and 16 show that the correlating vocal lines reinforce the harmonic sequence: C at bar 1, D at bar 14 and E at bar 27. Similarly, the vocal parts of the second couplets, which start on bars 8, 21 and 35, respectively, rise in minor 3rds from F♯, to A and then to C. Example 15 shows that the sequential nature of the vocal part forms a structural blueprint that is both incrementally driven to create harmonic movement and cogently framed by C pitches and an F major tonality that provides a rational harmonic design:

Example 15: Trajectory of starting pitches

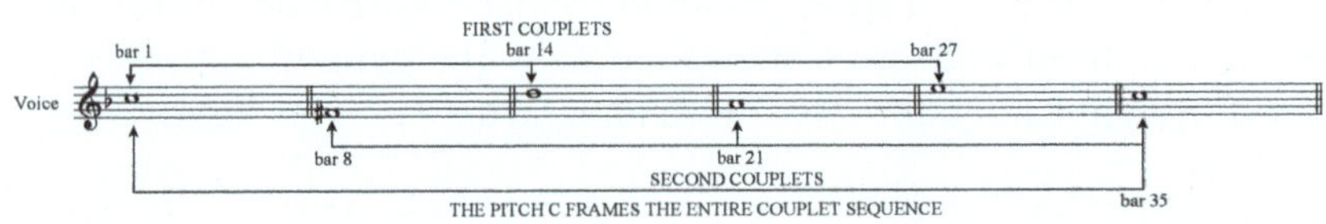

The ingenuity of Britten's harmonic plan lies not in its function as a persuasive and rigorous stand-alone structure, but more pertinently as a generating pattern that musically amplifies the ever-increasing burden the poet experiences as he endeavours to help on the big chariot. Thus, the structural design functions specifically as a text-intrinsic device. Although an F major harmony frames the work, such harmonic and psychological stability in Britten's music is seldom free from elements of anxiety and ambiguity. The established security of the F major tonality at the end of the song is thus rendered unstable when Britten allows the guitar part to continue rising into harmonics that imply an ethereal G minor harmony (see Example 18).

Example 16: Britten, 'The Big Chariot', *Songs from the Chinese*, bars 1, 14 and 27

Example 17: Britten, 'The Big Chariot', *Songs from the Chinese*, bars 8, 21 and 35

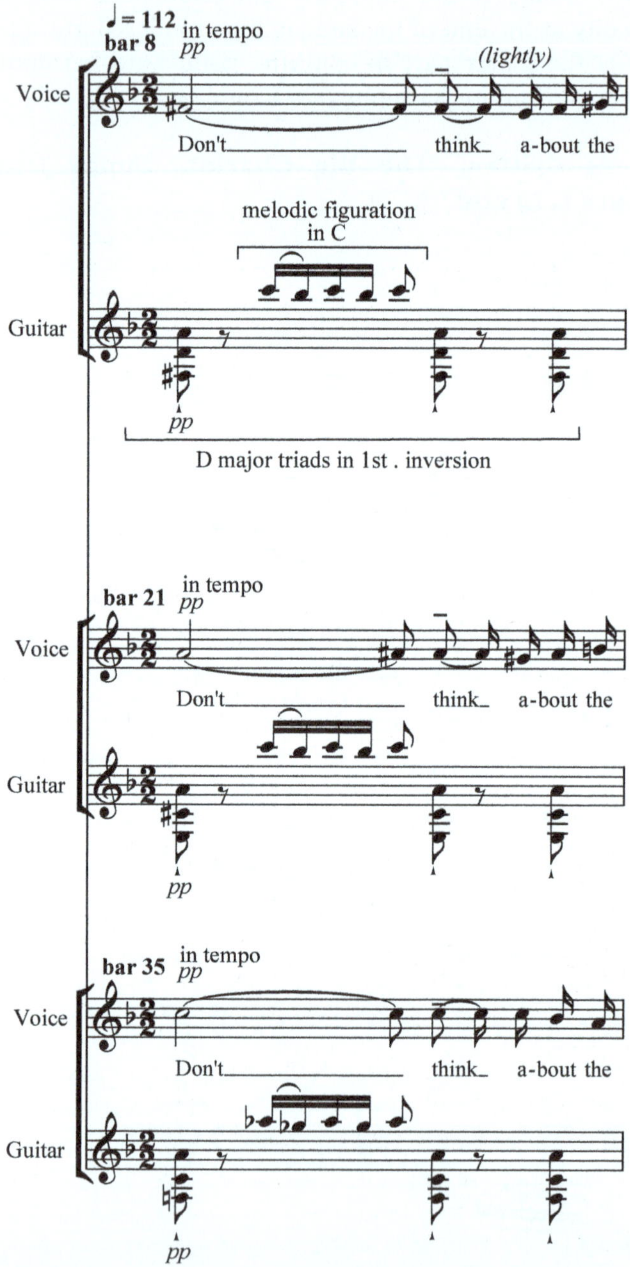

Example 18: Britten, 'The Big Chariot', *Songs from the Chinese*, bars 40 to end

As if replication of the poem's structure through the stratification of the musical instrumentation and formal design were not enough, Britten further underscores the text with a judicious application of bi-tonal elements. The use of bi-tonality is closely allied to the couplet division of the stanza, which influenced the instrumentation and dynamics. As example 16 demonstrates, the opening bars of the first three couplets display unambiguous tonal writing—in F major, G minor and E major, respectively. These explicit tonalities buttress the poet's unequivocal demands: 'Don't help on the big chariot'. However, when we come to the second set of couplets in Example 17, we observe that the guitar accompaniment's two components now occupy separate tonal regions that are frequently juxtaposed. The music from bar 8, for example, superimposes a D major chord (in its 1st inversion) with a melodic line centred on C. The music emerging from bars 21 and 35 also displays similar bi-tonal textures, which enhance the more poignant plea not to 'think about the sorrows of the world'.

While these examples show that Britten integrates his use of bitonality into the formal patterns of the structural design, he also employs the device in more spontaneous ways, which can be seen, for example, at bar 6 on the word 'dusty'. Here, the imprecision of the tonality provides an apt sound image of the dust; and its sharp tonal clash musically underscores the consequences that might ensue if you 'help on the big chariot'. This investigation of the song's formal designs demonstrates one example of Britten's text-intrinsic method. Processes such as these may be used in any context, but in Britten's hands they specifically serve to effectively elaborate the text's meanings.

'The Old Lute'

> **'The Old Lute'**
> Of chord and cassiawood is the lute compounded;
> Within it lie ancient melodies.
> Ancient melodies - weak and savourless,
> Not appealing to present men's taste.
> Light and colour are faded from the jade stops;
> Dust has covered the rose-red strings.
> Decay and ruin came to it long ago,
> But the sound that is left is still cold and clear.
> I do not refuse to play it, if you want me to;
> But even if I play people will not listen.
>
> How did it come to be neglected so?
> Because of the Ch'i-ang flute and the zithern of Ch'in

Arthur Waley believed that Po Chü-i wrote 'The Old Lute' some time between the years 807 and 809. There is little mention of music in his earlier poems, though from 818 there is evidence that he actually played a lute-type instrument. Music was played everywhere in Chinese society at this time; social events and religious ceremonies were accompanied by music, and we have noted that poems from previous epochs (the *Book of Songs*) were in fact originally narrated or sung with musical accompaniment. Furthermore, it was during the reign of Wu-ti between 141 and 87 BCE that the Office of Music (Yüeh fu) was established as part of a policy of imperial expansion and it played an important role in the development and recording of Chinese poetry. Apart from accompanying poetry, music was also thought to have certain magical powers that could even alter the seasons and deflect impending dangers. As Waley points out:

> [Po Chü-i] definitely regarded the introduction of foreign music into Court performances in 755 as the cause of the foreign invasion in 756. Even a Court performance of visiting musicians (the Burmese orchestra that came to Ch'ang-an in 801-802) he describes with disapproval...because such episodes were likely to distract the Emperor from his political duties...The Board which was concerned with the music of the Court Ancestral Sacrifices was, according to Po, much to blame for the decline of traditional music.[151]

This passage provides the socio-political context for 'The Old Lute'. Po Chü-i regrets the trend that chooses 'modern' instruments over the long-established Chinese Ch'in. Barbarian peoples in West China

---

[151] Ibid., 150-151.

brought the novel Ch'iang flute and the Ch'in zither to China during the T'ang Dynasty and the 'brilliant sound of these instruments soon displaced the favourite and traditional Chinese Chin, translated by Waley as "lute"'.[152] The demise of 'The Old Lute' is thus caused by fashionable trends for instruments considered by the poet to be vulgar and foreign. Their popularity also metaphorically represents a breakdown in social mores. This unambiguous exploration of decay and change in 'The Old Lute' must also have resonated deeply with Britten, knowing what we do about his initial ambivalence toward the guitar and his preference for the lute. He must have seen parallels between the poet's concern for the decline of the Chinese Ch'in and his own concern for the neglect of the English lute—an instrument that in his time was completely superseded in popularity by the 'fashionable' and 'foreign' guitar.

The reference in the text to jade is pointed, as it alludes to the frets or perhaps a decorative engraving embedded in the instrument. Furthermore, this ornamental stone is associated with the idea of preciousness; it was once bestowed with a currency function and for thousands of years was a symbol of love, virtue and high status. Its standing as a royal gemstone thus signifies the lofty position the lute once held. Jade also represents the white purity of the virgin, which further suggests that the emergence of more crude and fashionable new instruments is a defilement of sorts.

From a purely technical perspective, 'The Old Lute' could not be more unlike the opening song in the cycle. Its harmonic makeup is radically different in that it shows evidence of the influence of Balinese gamelan music, especially in its similarity to the formation of polyphonic stratifications and an ensuing heterophony characteristic of that genre.[153] Heterophony results when numerous variations of a given scale are heard simultaneously. This type of complex monophony forms the basic harmonic construction in Balinese gamelan music. Based on anhemitonic pentatonic scales, the fragments often occur with longer note values in the lower registers and ever-shortening note values the higher the pitches are placed.[154]

152 Ti-Fei Hse, 'Chinese influence in Four Twentieth Century Song Cycles by Roussel, Carpenter, Griffes and Britten' (PhD diss., American Conservatory of Music, 1988), 97.

153 See Mervyn Cooke, *Britten and the Far East* (Woodbridge: The Boydell Press, 1998) for a study of the influence of Balinese gamelan music on Britten's work.

154 A pentatonic scale has five pitches per octave in contrast to a seven-note heptatonic scale, such as the major scale. Pentatonic scales may be either

As Example 4 above demonstrates, 'The Old Lute' achieves something strikingly similar in its amalgamation of five melodic fragments derived from the Lydian mode (starting on E), which are shared between the voice part and four other strands executed on the guitar. We have noted earlier that this stratification correlates particularly well to Dowland's lute-song constructions. However, Britten's ballet *The Prince of the Pagodas* can also be seen as an influence of equal importance. Completed only one year before *Songs from the Chinese*, *Pagodas* overtly displays elements of gamelan derivation and there is little doubt that the composer carried aspects of this influence through to 'The Old Lute'.

Britten's use of heterophony in the song again demonstrates his aim to place technique at the service of text. In creating a restrictive modal paradigm, the ensuing harmonic system metaphorically reflects the enclosed world of the forgotten lute. The confined nature of each modal fragment constructs a harmonically static environment that gives the song a strictly indwelling perspective. The heading 'Slow and remote' (crotchet = 44) adds to this inert quality and the overall result is a sonic image of a half-forgotten past: 'Dust has covered the rose-red strings'. Thus, the very structure that creates the static harmony intensifies the words' meanings; as in 'The Big Chariot', form itself is text-intrinsic.

'The Autumn Wind'

'The Autumn Wind'
Autumn wind rises;
White clouds fly
Grass and trees wither;
Geese go south.
Orchids all in bloom;
Chrysanthemums smell sweet.
I think of my lovely lady;
I never can forget.
Floating pagoda boat
Crosses Fên River;
Across the mid-stream
White waves rise.
Flute and drum keep time,
To sound of rower's song;
Amidst revel and feasting
Sad thoughts come;
Youth's years how few;
Age how sure!

hemitonic or anhemitonic: the former contains one or more semitones while the latter contains no semitones.

In 'The Autumn Wind', the poet complains about an official journey that requires him to leave his mistress behind in the capital. He and his ministers are seated in an official barge surrounded by their rowers who heave to the repetitive playing of a flute and drum. We have already noted that in Chinese poetry the coming of autumn is a powerful metaphor for the fear of approaching age. 'The Autumn Wind', however, contains additional images that suggest and echo the poet's separation from his lover. The lines 'Autumn wind rises' and 'white clouds fly' actively portray the boat's journey; 'Geese go south' also suggests this, and we have noted that reference to withering grass generally means separation, as each year grass disappears and returns like a traveller. The poet's agitated mood is strikingly underscored by Britten's guitar accompaniment, which is written in swirling semiquavers that rise and fall like the autumn wind and the turbulent white waves.

Example 19: Britten, 'The Autumn Wind', *Songs from the Chinese*, bars 1-6

Anxiety is harmonically wrought by the constant clash of the 2nds between the vocal part on the note C of bar 3 and the upper auxiliary D notes of the guitar accompaniment. It is noteworthy that a description of a rocking boat was a long-established metaphor for a lover's turmoil, as this poem from the *Shī Jīng* demonstrates:

> Tossed is that cypress boat,
> Wave-tossed it floats.
> My heart is in turmoil, I cannot sleep.
> But secret is my grief.[155]

Meanwhile, traces of gamelan influence can be observed in the subtle use of hidden heterophony. My added stave in Example 19 isolates a latent melody within the accompaniment figuration that closely shadows the vocal line: although one is a related variant of the other, they are desynchronized. The turbulent thoughts, the wind and

[155] Arthur Waley, trans., *The Book of Songs*, 71.

high waves are all invoked by the incessant semiquaver movement. However, when the poet stops to think about his 'lovely lady', the guitar breaks out into an arpeggiated flourish followed only by the resonance of the sustaining strings—a web of sound within which the poet inwardly reflects upon love and longing. Yet, this moment of internalized contemplation does not last, as the reality of the 'Flute and drum', which keep time to the 'sound of rower's song', returns the poet unceremoniously to his agitated state.

Example 20: Britten, 'The Autumn Wind', *Songs from the Chinese*, bars 37-42

From bar 38, in a passage demonstrating effective text-intrinsic writing, Britten cleverly imitates the beating drum with the repetitive B-E-B-E ostinato of the lower strings of the guitar. This ostinato is interspersed with a similar though inverted rhythmisc motif in the voice part (C♯-D♮), which operates in contrary and syncopated relation to the guitar part, further adding sonic and rhythmic proof of the lover's unease. Additionally, all the notes of the accompaniment figuration interplay with the vocal line to create the hidden heterophony noted earlier. Indeed, throughout the song, the guitar has been shadowing the vocal line in this manner. Sometimes it does so with its upper figurations, as in bars 3 and 4 of Example 19, sometimes with its lower ones (see bars 8 and 9 of score). But the real implication of the binary construction in the accompaniment is only brought into clear focus near the end of the song where 'the curves of the external climate [the autumn wind] coincide with the curves of the internal climate of the ageing poet'.[156] This synchronicity occurs with the dialectical play on the words 'youth' and 'age' in the line: 'Youth's years how few, age how sure!'

---

[156] Wai-Lim Yip, ed. and trans., *Chinese Poetry* (Durham: Duke University Press, 1997), 16.

Example 21: Britten, 'The Autumn Wind', *Songs from the Chinese*, bars 51-54

Thus, it becomes clear that the passing of youth is the central theme of the song. The ultimate brevity of life and the futility of duties that take one away from the precious moments of being with a lover force the poet towards an undeniable philosophical truth. Example 21 shows how the sung phrase 'Youth's years how few' is followed a demisemiquaver out of synchrony by the accompaniment in mid-register indicating the carefree nature of youth. Its upbeat, syncopated vocal line ends on an upturn suggesting a positive, buoyant quality. In stark contrast, the words 'age how sure' are weighed down with the guitar's lower notes, which do not follow the vocal line closely from behind but underpin it simultaneously with the exact same rhythmic pattern reinforcing the words' incontrovertible argument. The vocal phrase is shaped in contrary motion to the previous one, with its final notes descending with heavy inevitability. More than most, this song underscores Britten's innate understanding of instrumental character. He demonstrates a distinctive ability to extract from the guitar's potentially limiting idiosyncrasies a most effective and text-intrinsic support.

'The Herd Boy'

> **'The Herd Boy'**
> In the southern village the boy who minds the ox
> With his naked feet stands on the ox's back.
> Through the hole in his coat the river wind blows;
> Through his broken hat the mountain rain pours.
> On the long dyke he seemed to be far away;
> In the narrow lane suddenly we were face to face
> The boy is home and the ox is back in its stall;
> And a dark smoke oozes through the thatched roof.

'The Herd-Boy' paints an idealized picture of rural life and can be interpreted as an expression of profound freedom and abandon in nature; a vision that emanates from Yu Lu's personal interpretation of Taoism. The theme of simplicity and innocence was a favourite of the poet's, as can be observed in another poem of his from 1203 that describes a spring festival and which is remarkably similar in tone and content to 'The Herd-Boy':

> ***Festive Rain***[157]
> No time at all since the year began,
> suddenly Spring Festival is upon us.
> Stretching in forever, the grasses' deepening colour;
> hsiao-hsiao, the sound of rain growing shriller;
> steering his plow, ambling the bright water,
> what does he care if straw sandals get soggy?
> Village boys have an even better time,
> barefoot, standing tall on the water ox's back.

However, in addition to the theme of rural idyll, there is another more personal aspect to Britten's setting of 'The Herd-Boy'. When work commenced on Op. 58, Britten and Pears had not long returned from their extended tour of the Far East. There can be little doubt that the composer's memory of seeing boys in various states of work and play offered him a wealth of imagery that fed his eroticizing and idealizing proclivities. Specifically, the memory of young working children in Bali standing on the backs of oxen must have been triggered by the imagery in this poem; in fact, it may very well have been the reason he chose it in the first place. In a letter written on 8 February 1956 to his young friend Roger Duncan (with whom he was very close at this period) Britten reports, 'One thing I forgot to tell you about Bali...is that the animals there are the nicest you ever see, splendid cows, water buffalos (usually with little naked boys riding them)...'[158] The scene that Britten describes in his letter to Duncan is clearly evocative of the one depicted in the song. Thus, his vivid memory of 'naked boys' points to an erotic reading of 'The Herd Boy', which is borne out in the way he sets the text, as I shall demonstrate. In this context, it is worth pointing out that Britten's depiction of a naked boy at work in Bali also recalls another description of young boys whom he heard playing Balinese music. In a letter also written to Duncan, Britten reports:

---

157 Burton Watson, trans., *The Old Man Who Does As He Pleases: Selections from the Poetry and Prose of Lu Yu* (New York: Columbia University Press, 1973), 57.

158 Philip Reed, Mervyn Cooke & Donald Mitchell, eds., *Letters From A Life:* 405.

> I must tell you all about Balinese music when I see you, & perhaps play you some (I am bringing some recordings back with me) but what would have amused you was one Gamelan (the Balinese orchestra), made up of about 30 instruments, gongs, drums, xylophone, glockenspiels of all shapes & sizes – all played by little boys less than 14 years old. Jolly good they were too, & enjoying it like fun.[159]

There seems little doubt that the intoxicating resonance of the gamelan orchestra was associated in Britten's musical imagination with the prepubescent male child.[160] The idea of employing similar sounds in *Death in Venice* to accompany the children's beach games might very well have been planted in his imagination by the scene of the boy musicians in Bali. Indeed, for Britten, the enchanting, metallic timbre of the gamelan orchestra appears to have conflated with the intoxication of concealed desire, as celesta and gong sounds create the trademark music for the pederast Quint in *The Turn of the Screw*. However, the association of the gamelan with boyish innocence actually predates his Far East trip and these operas. In the early 1940s, Britten was a close friend of the composer Colin McPhee (1900-1964) who first introduced him to Balinese music. McPhee also had paedophilic inclinations and his immersion in Balinese music was directly connected to his numerous sexual liaisons with Balinese boys. It is highly likely that Britten appropriated McPhee's conflation of young boys and gamelan music at this time. Prince Ludwig of Hesse, who accompanied Britten on his Far East tour, provides telling reflections on the children's gamelan orchestra and child dancers about which Britten wrote so fervently:

> The whole thing is stimulating and soporific at the same time. Hanging over the bamboo barrier and lying beside it are many sleeping children as young as the dancers. But two priests in white robes with white headbands seem intensely and almost dangerously adult...There is an odd atmosphere in this place. The dancing and the sleeping children and the drugged audience give one the impression that something sinister is going on. Here, the charming and musical tinkling and singing of the gamelan seems to produce these odd and long drawn-out sounds one hears before one is overwhelmed by an anaesthetic.[161]

---

[159] Ibid., 402-403.

[160] For a further discussion on this subject see Mervyn Cooke, *Britten and the Far East* (Woodbridge: The Boydell Press, 1998) and Philip Brett, *Music and Sexuality in Britten*, ed. George E. Haggerty (Berkeley: University of California Press, 2006).

[161] Humphrey Carpenter, *Benjamin Britten: A Biography* (London: Faber and Faber, 1992), 372.

It is unlikely that Britten failed to be seduced by this atmosphere where the adoration of children would seemingly be made easy given the soporific conditions. A conflation between exotic cultures and prepubescent boys seems to have been galvanized in Britten's psyche by the enthralling mix of gamelan music and dance. Although there is no reference to gamelan music in 'The Herd Boy', its use in various guises in a number of the cycle's songs ('The Old Lute' and 'The Autumn Wind' most notably) suggests that where longing is portrayed in the text and music, it may also suggest the sub-textual desire for the unattainable boy. In 'The Herd Boy', the poem's evocation of a boy on an ox's back must have brought into sharp relief Britten's firmly embedded memories of the Far East with all its attendant associations of innocence, sexual desire and the unattainable. These disquieting elements form the basis for an assessment of Britten's setting.

The poem's painting of the southern village, the ox, the boy's naked feet and torn hat has all the appearance of the simplicity and spontaneity of rural life. However, as we have noted regarding the poetic device *xing*, descriptions of nature often act as powerful conduits for the narrator's latent psychological state. On one level the line 'The boy is home and the ox is back in its stall' suggests that all is well. However, Waley explains that it is in contrasting the human world with nature that the darker side of the human condition is exposed:

> Nature goes its accustomed way, only man changes; such is the burden of many songs. The birds and beasts come back to the farm at dusk; but the warrior knows no rest. The kite soars into the clouds, the fish hides in the depths of its pool; but for man there is no escape.[162]

A poem from the *Book of Songs* offers further clarification:

> ...Another day is ending,
> The sheep and cows are coming down.
> My lord is on service;
> How can I not be sad?[163]

In 'The Herd Boy', this psychological unease is presented with typical understated stoicism in the last line where dark smoke 'oozing' from the thatched roof conjures up images of depression, waste and exhaustion. Earlier, the narrator was elated because he came 'face to face' with the boy, but this soon turns to depression because the short encounter simply reminds him of his own free and careless youth that is long past.

---

[162] Arthur Waley, trans, *The Book of Songs*, 14.
[163] Ibid., 92.

Thus, the line telling us that the boy 'seemed to be far away' suggests the poet's own irretrievable distance from youth.

The 'Herd-Boy' takes on greater resonance when we consider that Lu Yu had a lifelong obsession with immortality and with finding a magic elixir that would give him eternal life.[164] There is little doubt that Britten made a deep connection with these themes, which expand upon the previous song's resigned philosophy that youth's years are few and age is sure. The psychological depth of Britten's identification with children is of cardinal importance to understanding his music. His attraction to prepubescent boys has been more openly acknowledged in recent studies as a significant *idée fixe* in both his personal and musical life.[165] If paedophilic desire fed into Britten's greatest operatic works from *The Turn of the Screw* to *Death in Venice*, it should come as no surprise to discover it in more intimate songs such as 'The Herd Boy'.

Structurally, the translated poem is through-composed, but that design is treated differently by Britten who uses its first and last lines to create a frame for the song. Thus the words 'In the southern village the boy who minds the ox' and 'And a dark smoke oozes through the thatched roof', which frame the song, are sung in a free, recitative style over a G minor harmony. Through the careful manipulation of dynamic markings and word setting of the first line, Britten ingeniously directs the awareness towards the main focus of his attention—the boy. The short pause after 'village', followed by the rising minor 6th from F♯ to D¹

164 At a certain period in his life, Lu Yu believed that he had found the magic ingredients for a gold alchemical potion. According to a celebrated elixir manual of the 17th century written by the alchemist Sun Ssu-mo, this potion included equal parts of gold and mercury with twice the amounts each of realgar and orpiment, which made it an extremely poisonous concoction. Lu Yu delayed taking this brew until the end of his life (it is not known whether it killed him or not). See Ho Peng Yoke, Goh Thean Chye and Beda Lim, *Lu Yu, The Poet-Alchemist* (Canberra: Faculty of Asian Studies, Australian National University, 1972).

165 This point should not be underestimated, as Britten surrounded himself with images of youth. In the Red House, for example, one can still see a significant number of paintings depicting boyhood and innocence, such as the portrait of Charles Golding Constable in a Royal Navy uniform (painted by his father John Constable) and the painting entitled *Football on Cookham Moor*, which shows three youths playing football in view of two observing men. Another painting in the Red House is of Roger Duncan, whom Britten and Pears temporarily adopted. According to the Red House tour guides, when he composed, Britten always placed in front of him a statue by Georg Erhlich entitled *Die Bruder*—a study of two youths; one holding the hand of the other. He even took this statue with him when he had to compose away from home. As well as other cited references, see John Bridcut, *Britten's Children* (London: Faber and Faber, 2007).

on the word 'boy' just before the guitar's *forte* on the third of its reiterated G minor chords is masterful in its timing and has more than a hint of swelling, ecstatic sexual desire, before the song's intruding accompaniment brings the narrator back to his senses.

Example 22: Britten, 'The Herd Boy', *Songs from the Chinese*, bars 1-3

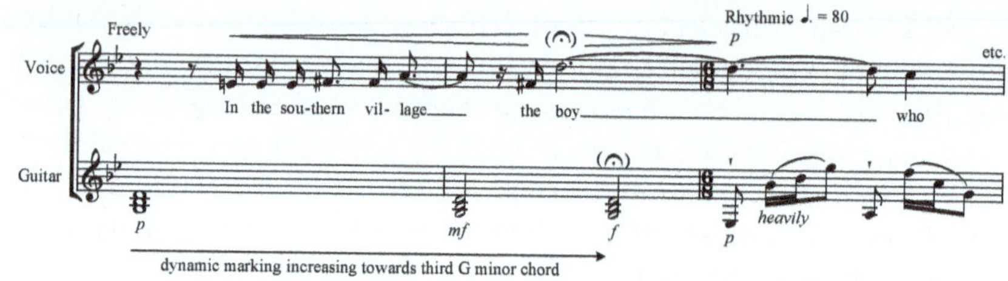

The second of the two lines that frame the song is set over a series of swirling arpeggios performed ad lib., which imitate the swirling smoke oozing from the thatched roof. The music within this frame is given its character by the bouncing 6/8 rhythm of the guitar's accompaniment, as can be seen in bar 3 of Example 22. Example 23 shows that occasionally the pulse loosens its grip when 8/8 and 9/8 time signatures are stumbled upon. The shifting rhythm suggests not only the boy's youth, his freedom from rigid responsibilities and his spontaneous balancing when his naked feet stand on the ox's back but also the slightly lilting gate of the ox itself grappling with the uneven, stony road.

Example 23: Britten, 'The Herd Boy', *Songs from the Chinese*, bars 5-11

The lilting rhythm is further enhanced by the use of the hemiola in some 6/8 bars where three crotchet beats are heard instead of two dotted crotchet beats, as in Example 23 at bars 6 and 9. Despite the song's declared tonality of G minor, Britten is quite happy to exploit the guitar's open strings to 'colour' the harmony. The top staves of Example 24 show that in bar 3 of the song the open sixth and fifth strings of the guitar, E and A respectively, provide the bass harmonies, which clearly undermine an otherwise established G minor tonality.

Example 24: Britten, 'The Herd Boy', *Songs from the Chinese*, bars 2-3, 10-11, 14-15 and 22-23

The song's emotional focal point—'In the narrow lane suddenly we were face to face'—is achieved by a brilliantly controlled use of four sequentially rising pitches in the vocal part. This rising sequence can be traced in Example 24 by following the voice line when it sings four sustained pitches: starting on the word 'boy' with the note D at bar 2; then moving to 'blows' on E♮ at bar 11, rising to F♯ on the word 'pours' and finally reaching its *dénouement* with the word 'face' on a triumphant G♮ at bar 23, the highest pitched note in the entire song. Both the suddenness and the joy of the close encounter with the boy is underscored by an unadulterated G major chord in the accompaniment, the return to the established 6/8 rhythmic feature following two bars of uncertain pulse (8/8 and 9/8 at bars 21 and 22, respectively) and a climactic, unrestrained dynamic marking of *ff*. As the boy represents the unattainable, the ecstasy of the encounter is all too brief—a fact echoed in the last (framing) line 'And a dark smoke oozes through the thatched roof', which, as we have noted, reminds us of the irrefutable fact of impending age and lost youth. The entire formal plan for this song provides yet another example of a structural pattern uniquely designed as a text-intrinsic device, a system by which latent interpretations are rendered 'unconcealed' and brought into disturbing relief.

'Depression'

> 'There is no decrescendo in music like the dying of a plucked string, no more perfect death.'[166]
>
> **'Depression'**
> [I hug my pillow and do not speak a word;
> in my empty room no sound stirs.
> Who knows that, all day a-bed,
> I am not ill and am not even asleep?]
>
> Turned to Jade are the boy's rosy cheeks;
> To his sick temples the frost of winter clings.
> Do not wonder that my body sinks to decay;
> Though my limbs are old, my heart is older yet.

Despite its brief fifteen bars, this song represents the emotional core of the cycle. Songs two, three and four, with their obsessions of youth, age and death, seem to inevitably culminate with 'Depression'. The opening lines of the poem immediately set the tone of lost youth—the image of a boy is lithely carried through from the previous song. The notion of lost youth is thus conflated with the theme of sickness and ageing. The

---

[166] Julian Bream, cited in Malcolm Welter, 'A Conversation with Julian Bream', *Guitar Review* 37 (1972): 12.

coming of winter is invoked in the line 'To his sick temples the frost of winter clings'; an image that signals weakness and decline. The predominant mood of this short poem is governed by the stoic resignation we have observed as a central facet of Chinese poetics; the acquiescence in time's decaying effect is made bearable through the understanding that the heart is older than the body.

Technically, 'Depression' is similar to 'The Old Lute' in that its harmonic character is derived from highly unusual compositional methods. In the latter, we observed that the harmony was an aggregate of superimposed and related modal fragments. 'Depression' finds its harmonic character through the guitar alone; its glissando chords, vibrato sounds and processes of accumulation emerge out of the idiosyncratic nature of the instrument. Although the opening harmony of the accompaniment is built from an F major chord, its 1st inversion position and the constant glissando movement away from any harmonically predominant centre undermine any real sense of established tonality. As the resulting note amalgamations circumvent traditional Western harmonic theory of any period, the music correspondingly evades temporal and geographical boundaries. This text-intrinsic approach creates ethereal harmonies unconnected to any grounded tonal system; thus, the words that speak of decay and death are perfectly represented sonically with disembodied tonalities.

As I have repeatedly argued, Britten masterfully exploits the guitar's unique capacities to find the most perfect solution to the text's challenges. Example 25 shows numerous sets of two chords joined by glissando slurs indicating that only the first is plucked. The second chords of these pairs, whose resonances emerge solely from what remains in sound after the glissando has been executed, are obviously weaker than the first plucked chords. This glissando technique that repeatedly plays on strong and weak resonances is, yet again, so text-intrinsic that it perfectly parallels the poet's stronger, youthful past in comparison to his ailing, ageing present.

Example 25: Britten, 'Depression', *Songs from the Chinese*, bars 9 to end

'Dance Song'

> 'The Unicorn can only win
> The race that she was born to run.
> If hearts are gold, the money's on.'[167]

'Dance Song'
The unicorn's hoofs!
The duke's sons throng,
Alas for the unicorn!

The unicorn's brow!
The duke's kinsmen throng,
Alas for the unicorn!

---

[167] 'A Unicorn Called Ariel', in Paul Keegan, ed., *Ted Hughes: Collected Poems* (London, Faber and Faber, 2003), 833.

The unicorn's horn!
The duke's clansmen throng,
Alas for the unicorn!

With 'Dance Song' we have returned once more to the ancient *Book of Songs* or *Shī Jīng* to provide the final framing song of the cycle. After the emotional nausea of the swirling, glissando chords of 'Depression' and the tragic mood of its meditation, Britten clearly wished to bring *Songs from the Chinese* to some formal and technical conclusion that would further have the function of containing the volatile emotional impact of its central songs. This is successfully achieved with 'Dance Song', a rather odd ceremonial poem, which we have seen is also known as the 'song of the lin hunter' in a different translation. A lin is sometimes referred to as a giraffe, but in this context it really means the mythical lin; one of the three most important mythical animals in Chinese folklore, along with the dragon and the phoenix. In this context, Waley's replacement of a Chinese mythical animal with the Western mythical unicorn is apt. In an effort to provide some sort of contextual understanding of this unusual poem, a commentary by Waley highlights the fact that 'Dance Song' bears a remarkable similarity to another poem in the *Shī Jīng*, which is known to have had a ceremonial function:

Strong grow the reeds;
At one shot I kill five swine.
Alas for the Tsou-yü!

Strong grows the wormwood;
At one shot I kill five hogs.
Alas for the Tsou-yü! [168]

Waley provides more clues in his discussion of this poem, which, because of its close affinity to 'Dance Song', may also be helpful to our understanding of the poem:

> ...it is said [in the *Book of Rites*] that in the pantomime which represented the victory of King Wu of Chou over Shang, at the end of the dance, 'to the left they shoot the Wild Cat's Head and to the right the Tsou-yü,' which was a mythological animal, parallel to the unicorn. Here we have the song that the archers, boasting of their prowess, sing while they 'shoot the Tsou-yü.'[169]

---

[168] Arthur Waley, trans., *The Book of Songs*, 220.
[169] Ibid.

We can therefore surmise that 'Dance Song' was also used as part of a ceremony. 'It takes place at the full moon of the eighth month. Masked dances sometimes end by the chief mask being set up and shot at. That, I think, is what's happening here. The archers shoot away first its hoof, then its brow, then its horn'.[170]

In light of Waley's explanation, we can see from the score's demisemiquaver movement that Britten honed in on the visual image of men riding forth on horses towards a target to the cheers of a crowd and the beating of drums. Other technical features enhance this text-intrinsic setting. For example, the opening vocal lines of the song—'The unicorn's hoof!'—are pitched in open 4^{ths}, like ceremonial trumpets or hunting horns. The following line, 'The duke's sons (kinsmen) throng', suggests a gathering of family members and others to watch the rider charging towards the target. The image is not only evocatively scored in the guitar's busy accompaniment chords but also in its descending arpeggios, which represent the horse looming closer to the target. It might also symbolize the target itself: the spiraling twists of the unicorn's horn (see bars 5 and 6 of Example 26).

Example 26: Britten, 'Dance Song', *Songs from the Chinese*, bars 3-6

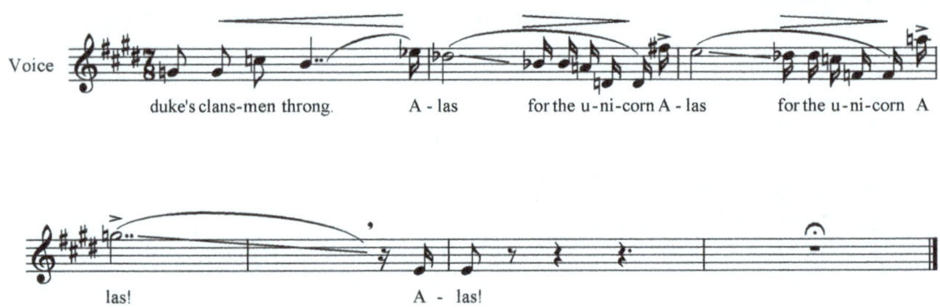

If this is a hunting poem, or even a mock hunting poem, as Waley suggests, then Britten must have leaned toward its broader metaphorical implications. From what we know of his anti-hunting views, it is very unlikely he would have written a song celebrating a hunt, even a simulated one. A rejection of the hunting connotation in this song makes more sense when we consider that hunting in this society was more than a sport; as hunting parties included contingents

170 Ibid., 219.

of drumbeaters, the hunt also served as a war game.[171] Thus, 'Dance Song' represents two practices for which Britten had genuine distaste. Consequently, we have to look elsewhere to understand his decision to set the poem. I believe that this can be found in the mythology surrounding the unicorn itself.

In European folklore and Christian literature, the unicorn has a number of distinctive characteristics: it is an unattainable target, at least for a man; it is impossible to catch; and its horn is said to have magical powers.[172] According to extant woodcarvings and tapestries, some dating back hundreds of years,[173] the hunting party in pursuit of a unicorn never wore camouflaged clothing but rather sported colourful clothes and engaged in much pageantry. It was therefore understood that the unicorn would not be caught, and that the hunt took on the function of a ceremonial activity. Additionally, the special virtues associated with the unicorn and its powerful talismanic horn indicate that one was not hunting an animal as such but rather acting out a ritual in pursuit of perfection. As the purity of youth and its manifestation in the image of the prepubescent boy is a recurring theme in *Songs from the Chinese*, the hunt for the unicorn can be seen as a potent metaphor for the search for perfection. Building on this concept, it is easy to see how Britten might transfer this model to the pursuit of lost innocence. The strong sexual connotation inherent in unicorn mythology and the phallic implications of its horn—the powder ground from it was believed to be a powerful aphrodisiac—further supports the hypothesis of an erotic pursuit of a young boy.[174]

There is yet a further potent subtext for the unicorn that may also have appealed to Britten. The Lion and the Unicorn are symbols that appear in the full Royal coat of arms of the United Kingdom. The lion symbolizes England and the unicorn represents Scotland. Thus, the

---

171 W. Scott Morton and Charlton M. Lewis, *China: Its History and Culture* (New York: McGraw-Hill, 1995), 142.

172 That Britten might seek European or Christian meanings in an emblem from a Chinese poem should not be surprising. Numerous aspects of Buddhist philosophy were replaced with Christian ideology in the final version of the *Curlew River* libretto. It was thought that the unicorn could only be captured when he was lured to seek refuge with his head in the lap of a maiden.

173 *La Dame à la licorne*, a series of six tapestries on display in the Musée du Moyen Age, is one of the finest examples from the European Middle Ages that depicts a unicorn.

174 The final panel of *La Dame à la licorne* shows the unicorn in the garden of delights where each flower represents an aspect of love and fertility. The blood-red juice from the pomegranate tree above drips on his pure white coat (the pomegranate is a potent symbol for both sexuality and holiness).

amalgamation dates back to the accession of James I of England (James VI of Scotland) in 1603. The Poet Laureate, Ted Hughes (1930-1998), underscores this connection in his poem 'The Unicorn' where he conflates the unicorn with the person of the Queen:

> **'The Unicorn'**
> Forty years
> The Unicorn
> Has kept watch.
> Her Lion sleeps
>
> In the people...[175]

Britten's position as a composer of national importance is relevant in this regard. As we have noted, he not only saw himself as the leading figure in the development of 20th-century English song, but also as the reviver and protector of England's 'golden age' of music. *Gloriana*, which celebrated the accession to the throne of Queen Elizabeth II in 1953, certainly elevated him to an important position in the national consciousness. The dedication of *Songs from the Chinese* to 'Peg and Lu', the Prince and Princess of Hesse and the Rhine, adds further weight to this thesis. They were among numerous members of the extended British Royal Family with whom Britten developed close relations from the early 1950s. Peg, the Honorable Margaret Campbell Geddes, was the daughter of Sir Aukland Geddes (later Baron Geddes) and Lu was the head of the House of Rhine. After the war, the Hesses worked steadfastly to re-establish links between the British and German Royal families (the Duke of Edinburgh was a relative to Ludwig). Thus, it would seem most appropriate for Britten to conclude this song cycle with a covert nod to the Royal pedigree of its dedicatees.

Throughout this chapter, we have made repeated reference to *xing*, which functioned as a means of making ambiguous allusions to sensitive political situations and promoted allegorical connotation whereby poems metaphorically connect to broader associations depending on the context of the poet or reader. Britten seems to have understood this intuitively, as the very ambiguity of 'Dance Song' allowed him to conflate three separate readings into his setting of the poem. Firstly, it invokes an ancient ceremonial ritual, secondly, it symbolizes the pursuit, both sexual and spiritual, of youth as

---

175 'The Unicorn', in Paul Keegan, ed., *Ted Hughes: Collected Poems* (London, Faber and Faber, 2003), 832. This is a celebratory poem written for the 40th year of the accession to the throne of Elizabeth II.

manifested in the image of a naked boy, and thirdly, it acts as a celebration of the British monarchy.

'Dance Song' is more than a rousing, throwaway finish to *Songs from the Chinese*. As he so often did elsewhere, Britten used this song to sum up in allegorical gestures many themes of a personal nature. These themes were deeply engrained obsessions—the regret for a lost youth, the sexual desire for a prepubescent boy, the fear of ageing and sickness, the distrust of fashionable trends and perhaps even the celebration of his own roots in the image of royalty. That the song is set in a snappy E major key to the heading 'Gay' suggests a clear audacity that runs contrary to the mood of acquiescence inherent in much of the cycle. The final 'Alas!' is in this regard more defiant than resigned.

Chapter Four: *Folksong Arrangements Volume VI*

Britten's approach to folksong arrangement is unique among English composers in the way in which he illuminates the text through the persuasive dramatizing power of his accompaniments. Before an analysis of his technical methods is undertaken here, a consideration of the cultural and political state of music in England will usefully locate Britten's stance *vis-à-vis* folksong. This cannot be separated from his consciously held attitudes relating to cultural definitions of Englishness at a time when such interpretations were hotly contested. Expanding upon themes already intimated in Chapter One, what follows offers a historical and cultural overview of the musical environment into which Britten arrived as a young composer in the 1930s.

Emerging out of the folksong revival that culminated in Cecil Sharp's formation of the English Folk Dance and Song Society in the 1930s, the movement that became known as the English musical renaissance argued for a national art music based on modes extrapolated from English folksong. As we have seen, Britten held diametrically opposed views about the direction English music should take. In addition to his opinion that modal source material was too restrictive harmonically, he also rejected the established practice of arranging folksongs in simplified settings, since he believed that such arrangements were neither authentic nor musically interesting. Thus, I argue that Britten consciously arranged English folksongs *against* the prevailing attitudes articulated by those of the pastoral school. His methods of folksong setting, long accepted as the purview of Sharp, Vaughan Williams, et al., can be seen as a reinforcement of his radically different compositional aesthetics.

The transient and migratory nature of folksong means that aspects of origin, genre, text, subtext, locus and dialect all play a role in developing a comprehensive understanding of the form. Thus, an anthropological and socio-cultural perspective on 'I will give my love an apple', for example, is gained from an appreciation of the riddle genre to which the song belongs; a discussion of the influence that bagpipes had on Northumberland folksong provides new perspectives on the melodic contours of 'Bonny at Morn'.

As I have suggested, Britten's folksong arrangements are particularly distinguished by the technical and imaginative quality of his accompaniments—he rarely, if at all, interferes with the original melodies; hence the exploration of text-intrinsic devices he uses to amplify narrative elements and to reveal latent psychological depths. Thus, *how* Britten composed his arrangements against the pastoralists becomes a central focus of this chapter. Britten is not interested in attempting to preserve folksong's putative simplicity—an abiding and, it must be said, naive principle of the revivalists. On the contrary, he is intent upon extracting whatever narratives and sub-texts the songs may explicitly or implicitly exhibit. In this regard, Britten relies upon the same skills of musical rhetoric assimilated from Dowland and Purcell that he puts to use in composing original songs, as we have seen in the chapter on *Songs from the Chinese*. I make no overt connection between Dowland's lute songs and Britten's folksongs. I do, however, argue that what Britten learned from Dowland's musical rhetoric is employed through text-intrinsic devices to enliven his arrangements. That Britten was working with folksong as a fixed artifact—a set melody with a set text—his ability to underscore its multi-narrativity points to the consummate control he had over such devices.

English Folksong—The Pastoral School and Britten's Rebellion

As we have noted, one of the leading figures in the English folksong revival was Cecil Sharp. On his death in 1924 he had collected over five thousand songs. He also published a number of songbooks specifically designed for use by teachers and children in schools. The inclusion of folksongs in the school curriculum was a powerful method of cultural encoding and the nurturing of a specifically English pride of place:

> ...remembering that the primary purpose of education is to place the children of the present generation in possession of the cultural achievements of the past so that they may as quickly as possible enter into their racial inheritance, what better form of music or of literature can we give them than the folk-songs and folk-ballads of the race to

which they belong, or of the nation whose language they speak?[176]

In 1911, Sharp founded the English Folk Dance Society, which promoted traditional dance through workshops held nationwide. It subsequently merged with the Folk Song Society in 1932 to form the English Folk Dance and Song Society. At this time, the folk revival movement was at its most powerful. Apart from its success in schools, it enjoyed government patronage, held a national festival annually in the Albert Hall and published numerous journals and pamphlets. Not surprisingly, Sharp's triumph in the promotion of folksong had an extensive influence upon the genre's prestige as a valid source material for the composition of art music. His philosophy of wanting to 'arouse that love of country and pride of race the absence of which we now deplore'[177] had an impact on a growing number of classical composers who started looking to folksong for inspiration. Sharp was at pains to highlight the vast repertoire of songs available to the art composer:

> ...we have scores of melodies which, although cast in scales long since discarded by the art musician, nevertheless throb with the pulse of life and make a strong appeal to modern musical tastes and feeling. Manifestly, such tunes as these cannot be quietly dismissed as mediaeval survivals and relegated, as such, to the lumber room. They reveal, rather, a new species of melody suggesting many possibilities to the composer of the present day.[178]

Classical music that placed English folksong at its core was naturally suited to elements of nationalism; these traits can be seen in the works of composers such as Hubert Parry, Charles Villiers Stanford, Arnold Bax, E. J. Moeran, John Ireland and R.O. Morris. Perhaps the most prominent composer of this movement, Vaughan Williams started collecting folksongs in 1903; over the next ten years he amassed hundreds, becoming after Sharp the leading figure in the promotion of the genre. Later in his life he served as president of the English Folk Dance and Song Society. Works by Vaughan Williams such as *The Lark Ascending*, *Norfolk Rhapsodies*, *On Wenlock Edge* and *An Oxford Elegy* typified a central impetus of the revivalists to invoke a specifically English landscape. His Symphony No. 3—*The Pastoral*—is exemplary of this school:

---

[176] Olive Dame Campbell and Cecil J. Sharp, *Introduction to English Folk Songs from the Appalachians* (New York: G.P. Putnam's Sons, 1917), xx.

[177] Cecil J. Sharp, *English Folksong: Some Conclusions*, ed. Maud Karpeles (Yorkshire: EP Publishing, 1972), 136.

[178] Cecil J. Sharp, ed., *One Hundred English Folksongs* (Boston: Oliver Ditson Company, 1916), xv.

> Even before Vaughan Williams's patenting of the type, hundreds of pieces were produced which overtly celebrated the rural world. A variety of reference points were utilised: actual places marked on the Ordnance Survey; the landscape's physical appearance; the seasons or months of the year. Times of the day, and their elemental atmospheres; folk song- and dance-based pieces; and last but not least, appropriate works of Shakespeare or Housman. In 1922, with Vaughan Williams's A *Pastoral Symphony*, this idiom reached its culminating destiny of fusion with large-scale symphonic utterance.[179]

Many of these works achieved a sense of locale through the incorporation of modal scales into broader chromatic statements typical of the post-romantic period. Folksongs such as *Greensleeves* were fully integrated into scores or were partially quoted; and pentatonic scales vied with more tonally obscure passages. Those who wished to establish a national music based on folksong looked to Vaughan Williams for example and leadership; and he was likewise forthright in his defence of what he saw as the essential attributes of a national musical idiom. In a series of lectures he gave in the US in 1937, he argued that folk music was 'the precious ore from which all good music was wrought' and that it represented 'an imperative foundation of any national music'.[180] Paraphrasing Parry, he further insisted that style was ultimately national. Indeed, adopting Parry's emphasis upon an organic and racial community, arguments he put forward defending his music often employed a rhetoric that could easily be appropriated by sinister forces of the period. In the volatile years leading up to the Second World War, comments stating that 'it is the millstream forcing its way through narrow channels which gathers strength to turn the water wheel' could conveniently be misconstrued or legitimized for political ends, dubious or benign.[181] Indeed, the debate surrounding what should constitute English music became blatantly ideological, as evidenced by the divisive rhetoric of *National Music and Other Essays*, where Vaughan Williams names those whom he considers ideal nationalist composers and castigates those he does not hesitate to derogatorily condemn as 'little Germans or little Frenchmen':

> We have in England today a certain number of composers who have achieved fame. In the older generation, Elgar and Parry, amongst those of middle age Holst and Bax, and of the quite young Walton and Lambert. All these served their apprenticeships at home. There are

[179] Robert Stradling and Meirion Hughes, *The English Musical Renaissance 1860-1940* (London: Routledge, 1993), 159.
[180] Ibid., 194.
[181] Ibid., 162.

> several others who thought that their own country was not good enough for them and went off in the early stages to become little Germans or little Frenchmen. Their names I will not give to you because they are unknown even to their fellow-countrymen.[182]

This passage exposes an unambiguous chasm that separated two camps of English composition whose representatives polemically vied for competing definitions of what English music should be. Vaughan Williams' lack of diplomacy is exposed in his overt criticism of the 'ethnically German' Frederick Delius, arguing that his music represents a 'colourless cosmopolitanism which makes me occasionally despair of England as a musical nation.[183] Naturally, composers who were uncomfortable with narrow definitions of Englishness held this type of rhetoric in deep suspicion, as such views had significant ramifications regarding broader social and cultural attitudes. Leaving aside debates regarding the value of modal material for art composition, Britten would have been rather nervous of the type of social conservatism that accompanied such constricted definitions of Englishness. In the pre-war period, Britten, under the influence of W.H. Auden, was publicly situated on the political left and privately struggled with the heteronormative ethos of society, which would undoubtedly have been upheld by right-leaning viewpoints. His opposition to such thinking thus extended to matters beyond the merely musical.

This socio-cultural and musical divide therefore provides the backdrop to Britten's rejection of the folksong as an important resource for classical music. Even before he came under the cosmopolitan influence of his teacher, Frank Bridge, Britten's diaries demonstrate that he had had strong leanings towards European aesthetic developments in art and music. By the time he was sixteen, for example, he wrote: 'I am thinking much about modernism in art. Debating whether Impressionism, Expressionism, Classicism etc. are right. I have half-decided on Schönberg.'[184] A few months later he is '...getting very fond of Schönberg, especially with study'.[185] Britten's interest in Schoenberg at this time had much to do with his innate musical tendencies and youthful curiosity but was also influenced by a growing dislike, from around the early 1930s, for the homegrown pastoral

182 Vaughan Williams, *National Music and Other Essays* (Oxford: Oxford University Press, 1934), 11.
183 Robert Stradling and Meirion Hughes, 199.
184 John Evans, ed. *Journeying Boy: The Diaries of the Young Benjamin Britten 1928-1938* (London: Faber & Faber, 2009), 27.
185 Ibid., 37.

traditional of which the music of Vaughan Williams was representative. In his diaries, he becomes progressively more averse to the folksong-based school of English music, as this compilation of written fragments clearly indicates:

> 'I am afraid that I don't much like his music, however much I try.'
>
> 'Dan Godrey conducts V. Williams appalling Wasps.'
>
> '...the rest was an anti-climax. V.W. has shown in places an apt use of chorus, in others dreadful disregard of natural movements. The music was full of folk-song. (if you like that sort of thing)...it was dreadful.'
>
> 'Job of Vaughan Williams seemed interminable. There are some nice things in it if you arn't [sic] tired of folk song modalism—but most of it is heavy, dull, imitative & amateurish.'
>
> 'I attempt to listen abit [sic] of V. Williams piano concerto – but it is too bad even for him...I go to bed with a nice (if erotic) taste in my mouth from the Adagietto of M[ahler].'[186]

Significantly, Britten's rebellion against the stance Vaughan Williams and others took relating to the importance of modal music as a compositional resource did not prevent him from addressing English folksong head on.[187] It did, however, impact the way he approached the genre. This apparent anomaly in Britten's thinking has resulted in a number of conflicting views among Britten scholars, as Philip Brett has pointed out.[188] While Peter Evans is at pains to deny his folksong arrangements any significance whatsoever, Donald Mitchell views them as a further example of the composer's cosmopolitanism. Noting that the second volume of folksongs are of French origin, Mitchell keenly pushes the point that 'even in this sphere Britten has to remind us of his

---

[186] Ibid., 130, 140 and 142-3 (discussing the ballad folk-opera *Hugh the Drover, or, Love in the Stocks*), 200 and 359.

[187] Arnold Whittall has explored Britten's relationship to the pastoral school, which is complex and multivalent: 'Although the movement ('Pastoral', from *Serenade*, Op. 31) could be said to be composed out a dismissal of Vaughan Williams-style pastoralism in its avoidance of folkish melody and modal harmony, it might also be thought to adopt a more positive approach by relating to the wider history of the genre in a way the more narrow nationalism that Benjamin Britten so disliked could not.' See Arnold Whittall, 'The Signs of Genre: Britten's Version of Pastoral', in *Sundry sorts of music books: Essays on The British Library Collections*, eds. Chris Banks, Arthur Searle and Malcolm Turner (London: The British Library, 1993), 370.

[188] Philip Brett, *Music and Sexuality in Britten*, ed. George E. Haggerty (Berkeley: University of California Press, 2006), 157.

European outlook'. He nevertheless insists that 'it would...be a mistake to imply that Britten has been influenced much by folk song...since he is far too complex a figure for so simple a musical constituent to be determinant of his style.'[189] Neither of these comments fully explains Britten's engagement with folksong, which I suggest was not only undertaken in direct opposition to the stance held by Sharp, Vaughan Williams, et al., but also as a means to genuinely explore the depth and complexity of a treasured ethnic resource.

As we have seen, Britten largely circumvented the pastoral school, drawing his inspiration from cosmopolitan sources and the music of the Elizabethan and Jacobean periods. It is this combination of influences, and in particular the unique skills that Dowland and Purcell had for the affective employment of musical rhetoric that greatly influenced Britten's approach to folksong arrangement. This accounts for the unusual vitality and complexity of many of his folksong accompaniments and their capacity to act as powerful psychological conduits—an approach to the genre that runs contrary to the English pastoral tradition. Britten rejected that tradition's notion of simple arrangement as a means of capturing the 'true' performance-style of the original because he intuited correctly that once a folksong was transferred from oral to notated media a 'true' performance-style is impossible. Rejecting this enterprise, Britten opted to employ text-intrinsic methods to folksong's raw materials. This approach gave him the opportunity to demonstrate his musical aesthetics through a medium long considered the exclusive preserve of the pastoralists.

Connecting the setting of English folksong to musical rhetoric techniques of older periods might seem implausible. However, we have seen in earlier chapters how Dowland's skill as an expert practitioner of musical rhetoric significantly influenced Britten's compositional signature. We have also learned how he utilized such skills to enhance his guitar accompaniments through text-intrinsic methods. Analysis shows that Britten's approach to folksong setting is similar. Thus, as the connections between Dowland and Britten have been teased out, specifically in relation to works for and with guitar—*Songs from the Chinese*, the 'Second Lute Song' and *Nocturnal* (see Chapter Five)—it is no longer radical to conclude that such Dowland-inspired methods have also been applied to his folksong arrangements with guitar. In this

---

[189] Donald Mitchell and Hans Keller, eds., *Benjamin Britten: A Commentary on his works from a group of specialists* (London: Rockliff, 1952), 47-8; cited in Philip Brett, 'Toeing the line' in *The Musical Times*, Vol. 137, No. 1843 (1996): 7-13.

sense, Britten's settings are not arrangements at all but rather re-compositions that use folksongs for their melodic contours and narrative content.

The efficacy of Britten's approach to folksong can be appreciated when we compare his settings to those that had already been in vogue for many years. For example, his arrangements of 'I will give my love an apple' and 'Sailor-boy' demonstrate a technically complex exploitation of their narrative and psychological elements, which contrasts markedly with the rather unsophisticated approach taken by Vaughan Williams and Sharp, which exemplifies the revivalists' established practice.

Example 27: Cecil Sharp, 'Soldier Boy' ('Sailor-boy')

For example, Sharp insisted that the simplicity of his arrangement of 'Soldier Boy' (the same song as 'Sailor-boy') would allow the folksong to maintain a quality of permanence, remain impervious to the passage of time and satisfy the artistic ideals of every epoch. 'I will give my love an apple' had already been a favourite in England through its well-known arrangement by Vaughan Williams (see Example 28). This followed Sharp's general approach to setting, which was typical of that practised right throughout the Victorian period and well into the 20th century. The right hand of the piano part follows the voice's contour and the accompaniment underscores the melody with conventional academic harmonic procedures lightly spiced with some mild suspended 4ths and simple two-part writing.

Example 28: Vaughan Williams, 'I will give my love an apple'

In stark contrast, Britten's arrangement of 'I will give my love an apple' displays clear evidence of an astute use of text-intrinsic devices, which can be immediately observed in his dreamy accompaniment that nonchalantly crosses bar lines to underscore both the confusing conundrum posed by the words and the fact that the song itself belongs to the 'riddle' genre. The overlapping, resonant guitar phrases produce a euphoric dreamlike state—a harmonic construction that has a desynchronized relationship to the song's melodic contours. Britten rebels against the notion of simplicity in lieu of a sophisticated amplification of the song's inherent psychological elements. Given their predilection for simplicity, it is unlikely that either Sharp or Vaughan Williams would have approved of such modernistic writing with its intricate disorientation and teasing seductiveness.

Example 29: Britten, 'I will give my love an apple'

The notion that Britten arranged folksongs *against* the pastoralists is re-enforced by Philip Brett's provocative question relating to 'I will give my love an apple': he asks whether this 'desiccated setting...[is] further revenge on Vaughan Williams, who collected it?'[190] Britten's comments upon hearing a number of folksong arrangements by Percy Grainger that impressed him do suggest a certain degree of mischievous rivalry when he states that they knocked 'all the V. Williams and R.O. Morris arrangements into a cocked-hat'.[191] Ultimately, it is the technical complexity of Britten's settings that suggests his dissentive attitude. He does more than merely excel in the art of arrangement; the intricate and nuanced achievement of his accompaniments, both technically and allegorically, produces a kind of hybridized song genre. While confined to the melodic and textual restrictions of the original song, Britten fastens attention on the words and dramatizes them to great effect. His gift here lies in his understanding that the essence of the song, or what Walter Benjamin describes as its 'aura', is inevitably lost in the process of arrangement.[192] Thus, if the original is to be touched at all, the only convincing option is to revitalize it, not by reducing it to a simplified academic format but rather by amplifying the narrative, emotive and subjective elements contained therein. In Britten's hands, the folksong is no longer a folksong, but a dramatic and psychological platform for exploring an ancient repository of English consciousness.

A Closer Look at Folksong Arrangements Volume VI

The composition of Britten's folksong arrangements spans a period from 1943 to 1976. There are seven volumes in total, which cover different geographic regions; five for voice and piano, one for voice and harp, and one for voice and guitar. An additional volume of previously unpublished songs appeared in 2001. The collection that concerns us here is *Folksong Arrangements Vol. VI*. Published in 1961, it contains the following songs: 'I will give my love an apple', 'Sailor-boy', 'Master Kilby', 'The Soldier and the Sailor', 'Bonny at Morn' and 'The Shooting of his Dear'.[193]

Tracing a completely accurate performance and recording history of

---

190 Philip Brett, 'Toeing the line': 11.

191 John Evans, ed., *Journeying Boy: The Diaries of the Young Benjamin Britten 1928-1938* (London, Faber & Faber, 2009). The diary excerpt is dated 3 March 1933.

192 See Walter Benjamin, *The Work of Art in the Age of Mechanical Reproduction*, trans. J.A. Underwood (London: Penguin, 2008).

193 Benjamin Britten, *Folksong Arrangements Volume VI: England* (High Voice & Guitar), Boosey & Hawkes, 1961.

these folksongs is impossible due to the haphazard nature of their inclusion in concert programmes and the likelihood that Britten made these arrangements in short periods between larger projects. The individual folksongs contained in *Volume VI* were premiered at different times and venues. Records at the Britten-Pears Library (including the *Aldeburgh Festival Programme Books 1954-1960*) contain contradictory information that makes it difficult to be conclusive in this regard. One source states that 'I will give my love an apple', 'The Soldier and the Sailor' and 'The Shooting of his Dear' were first performed at the Wigmore Hall on 6 May 1956 with Peter Pears and Julian Bream. However, a programme note for the concert on 17 June 1958 at Great Glemham House in which *Songs from the Chinese* received its first performance suggests that 'The Shooting of his dear', 'Master Kilby' and 'The Soldier and the Sailor' were being premiered.[194] Thus, we have no option but to conclude that performances on the day did not necessarily adhere to the published programmes. The radio broadcast premieres of the folksongs have an equally chequered history.[195] Even the 1963 RCA recording of the folksongs by Pears and Bream excludes 'Bonny at Morn'. This chaotic history of performances and recordings indicates that the folksongs were likely to have been arranged at different times in spontaneous response to requests by Pears and Bream for additional music.

Further confusion inheres in the actual title of the collection. *Folksong Arrangements Volume VI* is sub-titled 'England', but this does not offer a completely accurate picture of what the collection contains. According to the score, the following songs originate from different regions of England: 'I will give my love an apple' (Dorset), 'Master Kilby' (Somerset), 'The Soldier and the Sailor' (Oxfordshire), 'Bonny at Morn' (Northumberland) and 'The Shooting of his Dear' (Norfolk). However, 'Sailor-boy' is from Kentucky and was collected by Sharp during a visit to the Appalachian Mountains. Additionally, we will discover that some of the other songs in this 'English' collection may very well have originated in other countries.

---

194 The full programme appears on page 22.

195 The BBC Midland Home Service first broadcast 'The Soldier and the Sailor and 'The Shooting of his Dear' on 28 May 1957, with Pears and Bream. 'Bonny at Morn' was broadcast on 4 January 1966 on the BBC Music Programme from an RCA recording made by the tenor Robert Tear and the guitarist Desmond Dupré. 'I will give my love an apple' and 'Sailor-Boy' was broadcast in June 1966 on the BBC Music Programme from an RCA recording by Pears and Bream; and their RCA recording of 'Master Kilby' was broadcast on 16 December 1966 on the BBC Music Programme.

'Sailor-boy' is published in Sharp's *Seventeen Nursery Songs from the Appalachian Mountains* under the title 'Soldier Boy'. One might legitimately ask why this song, clearly identified as Appalachian, is included in a collection of English folksongs. The answer can be found in another book edited by Sharp entitled *English Folk Songs from the Appalachians*.[196] In its Introduction, he suggests that

> one or other of those English communities that lie scattered in various parts of the world might provide as good a field for the collector as England itself, and yield as bountiful and rich a harvest. The investigation...has proved that at least one such community does in fact exist in the Southern Appalachian Mountains of North America.[197]

At the time of its discovery, *Sailor-boy* was no longer extant in England. The fact that the song had to be rediscovered in its American version and find its way back to England underscores the migratory and transformative nature of the folksong genre.

'I will give my love an apple'

While folksongs such as 'Sailor-boy' demonstrate what might be called a transient anthropology, being carried by diasporic communities to different geographic regions, they still tend to retain their communal roles. For example, 'I will give my love an apple', in its more common version (*I gave my love a cherry*) is thought to have been carried, like 'Sailor-boy', by settlers to the Appalachian Mountains, although it doesn't appear in Sharp's *Appalachians* collection. Despite the song's transient nature—appearing in different versions and geographical regions—both its variants retain their central attributes as riddles—a song genre that operates a number of significant societal functions.

> ***I gave my love a cherry***
> I gave my love a cherry without a stone
> I gave my love a chicken without a bone
>
> I gave my love a ring that had no end
> I gave my love a baby with no crying
> How can there be a cherry that has no stone?
> How can there be a chicken that has no bone?
> How can there be a ring that has no end?
> How can there be a baby with no crying?
> A cherry when it's blooming it has no stone

196 Olive Dame Campbell and Cecil J. Sharp, eds. *English Folk Songs from the Appalachians* (New York: G.P. Putnam's Sons, 1917).

197 Ibid., i.

A chicken when it's piping, it has no bone
A ring while it's rolling, it has no end
A baby when it's sleeping, has no crying

'I will give my love an apple'
I will give my love an apple without e'er a core,
I will give my love a house without e'er a door,
I will give my love a palace wherein she may be,
And she may unlock it without any key.

My head is the apple without e'er a core,
My mind is the house without e'er a door,
My heart is the palace wherein she may be,
And she may unlock it without any key.

Although Britten's score states that 'I will give my love an apple' was 'collected and arranged by H.E.D. Hammond and R. Vaughan Williams', we must assume that the former was the collector and that the latter was the arranger. The song was first documented in July 1906 in Sherborne, Dorset and was notated from a version sung by a J. Burrows.[198] It is a lyrical truncation of a riddling episode found not only in *I gave my love a cherry* but also in a considerable number of similarly constructed ballads. The riddle at the centre of the song is the psychological element upon which Britten focuses in his arrangement. Riddles are considered quite significant in anthropological studies. Ian Hamnett, for example, suggests that by providing a safe conduit for potential social conflict, the riddle 'teaches rules of social conduct, interprets and explains natural phenomena, and permits the discussion of some feared and imminent crisis...[it is a] "conceptualizing mechanism" and thus [an] educative process of considerable indigenous importance'.[199] Craig Williamson explains the riddle's significance as a mode through which the world may be explored metaphorically, suggesting that it makes 'a game of probing the normally shaped and symbolized universe and offer[s] other ways of seeing'.[200]

This understanding of the riddle genre merely emphasizes Britten's clear interest in the latent allegorical potential of 'I will give my love an

---

198 The Roud Folksong Index: (http://library.efdss.org/cgibin/textpage.cgi?file=aboutRoud&access=on). Date sourced: 11 August 2010.

199 See: http://www.era.anthropology.ac.uk/era_resources/era/riddles/hamnet.html. Date sourced: 30 January 2013.

200 Craig Williamson, ed. and trans., *A Feast of Creatures: Anglo-Saxon Riddle-Songs* (Philadelphia: University of Pennsylvania Press, 2011), 33.

apple'. The anthropological importance of the song is made evident not only by the established genre to which it belongs but also because many versions of the same song extend far back into English cultural history; different versions of 'I will give my love an apple', for example, date back to the 15th century.[201]

As the cited anthropological explication of the genre clarifies, the riddle functions so that a series of apparently irrational images are resolved in subsequent verses. Britten's approach to the arrangement of 'I will give my love an apple' is centred upon exploiting the metaphorical elements of the riddle genre. We have seen in Example 29 how the uneven grouping of the quaver-note accompaniment underscores the confusion caused by the song's conundrum. The listener is simply unable to detect a reliable pulse from the rhythmic evidence offered by the note groups of the guitar's accompaniment. The undefined pulse creates an indolent seductiveness that entrances the listener with bell-like, 'campanella'-style arpeggios, which frequently stack 6ths, 7ths and 9ths above standard triadic formations. As Britten's harmonic changes occur at unusual places in the guitar part, the vocal line's harmonic implications are rarely realized at the exact moment in which they would be expected; the melodic and harmonic entities are not accurately synchronized. Such controlled confusion is a text-intrinsic device that draws the listener into a musical riddle that amplifies both the song's theme and genre.

Another example deliberately illuminates the riddle inherent in the words 'And she may unlock it without any key'. The first appearance of this line is scored with a B minor 7th harmony with an added 6th. On its repeat, however, Britten shifts the harmony down to a B♭ major (with an added 6th), which creates a greater gravitational pull towards the ultimate cadence in A. Again, the accompaniment ingeniously invokes the turning of the key with the screw-like diminishment of the note groups—5 quavers, 4 quavers and 3 quavers (see X in Example 30). Additionally, through a text-intrinsic device, it makes an exact musical representation of the words 'without any key', playing on the double meaning of the word 'key'—something with which to unlock a door and the tonality of a piece of music. The vocally established key of A minor is directly undermined by the guitar's A major arpeggio—a process that quite literally leaves the music briefly 'without any key'.

---

201 See Appendix VI for a 15th-century version of *I gave my love a cherry*.

Example 30: Britten, 'I will give my love an apple' (last four bars)

'Sailor-boy'

'Sailor-boy'
We go walking on the green grass, thus, thus, thus.
Come all you pretty fair maids,
Come walk with us.
So pretty and so fair
As you take yourself to be,
I'll choose you for a partner,
Come walk along with me.
We go walking on the green grass, thus, thus, thus.
I would not be a blacksmith
That smuts his nose and chin,
I'd rather be a sailor boy
That sails through the wind.
Sailor boy, sailor boy,
Sailor boy for me,
If ever I get married
A sailor's wife she'll be.
We go walking on the green grass, thus, thus, thus.

As we have noted, 'Sailor-boy' was collected in the Appalachian Mountains by Sharp under the title 'Soldier Boy'.

'Soldier Boy'
I would not marry a doctor,
He's always killing the sick;
I'd rather marry a soldier boy
That marches double quick,
Soldier boy, soldier boy, *etc.*

I would not marry a farmer,
He's always selling grain;
I'd rather marry a soldier boy
That marches through the rain.
Soldier boy, soldier boy, *etc.*

However, its particularly transient history means that it reappears in numerous guises. In yet another version the song is known as *The Railroader*, which, it is recorded, was sung in Missouri by a Mrs. May Kennedy McCord in 1934, and was 'learned from the man who furnished the music for the circle-swing at a picnic near Galena, Missouri in 1897' (see Appendix VI).[202] John Moulden has suggested that this song is probably 'My boy Willie', which is common in Ireland and may have been brought to America by Irish immigrants, many of whom worked on the railways.[203]

For the most part, Britten's setting of 'Sailor-boy' employs a simple, single-line counter-melody on the guitar, which gives the song a rather light and carefree atmosphere. Its characteristic rhythmic jaunt is quite reminiscent of the 'Morris Dance' from his opera *Gloriana*, which may have been a deliberate tactic on Britten's part to re-establish the original English credentials of this itinerant folksong.

Example 31: Britten, 'Sailor-boy' (guitar introduction)—top stave, and the opening of 'Morris Dance' (flute 1 part) from *Gloriana*—bottom stave

The guitar's monodic writing can only give an intimation of the song's harmonic structure. However, the accompaniment's scantiness is compensated for by the sheer vitality of the guitar lines, which interweave the vocal part. Britten's innate sense of textural shading is underscored in the final refrain, 'We go walking on the green grass, thus, thus, thus'; at this point he fills out the accompaniment with syncopated chords and more resonant bass notes that jauntily describe the confident gait of the sailor. It is only now we hear texturally what we have been missing.

202 Source: http://www.mudcat.org/thread.cfm?threadid=53515#824189. Date sourced: 11 August 2010.

203 Source: Email exchange with John Moulden, 11 August 2010.

Example 32: Britten, 'Sailor-boy', 'We go walking on the green grass, thus, thus, thus', bars 21-25

'Master Kilby'

Cecil Sharp and Maud Karpeles collected this song in Curry Rivel, Somerset, on the 6 January 1909, when a Harry Richards sang it. Britten's score states that the 'words and melody [come] from *Folk Songs for Schools*', which explains the exclusion of the final verse. This is one of the damaging modifications that Sharp's project for collection and dissemination of folksongs made to some of the originals. In this case, he extracted the final verse of 'Master Kilby', considering it offensive to the moral codes of Edwardian society: school children, he assumed, were clearly not ready to hear about a woman who 'lay asking for more'. This is a very significant impairment of the song through the expurgation of crucial themes, which include from Kilby's perspective the pursuit of sexual pleasure, and from Nancy's, the notion of female sexual agency. Thus, the censorship of this verse has robbed the song of much of its symbolic function. Moulden's belief that 'Master Kilby' is 'a unique song, so far as I know only once collected' merely amplifies the sense of damage done to a work that uniquely served to articulate a particular taboo within rural English communities.[204]

[204] Ibid.

'Master Kilby' [205]
In the heat of the day
When the sun shines so freely,
There I met Master Kilby,
So fine and so gay.

I pull'd off my hat
And I bowed to the ground
And I said 'Master Kilby
Oh, where are you bound?'

'I am bound for the West,
There in hopes to find rest,
And in Nancy's soft bosom
I will build a new nest

I was the master
Of ten thousand pounds
All in gay gold and silver
Or in king William's crowns.

I would part with it all
With my own heart so freely,
But it's all for the sake
Of my charming Nancy.

She's the fairest of girls,
She's the choice of my own heart,
She is painted like waxwork
In every part

[Oh, I gave her some kisses
It was down on the sea shore
But still she lay asking
Lay asking for more']

The text's apparent simplicity in fact comprises a complex interweaving of three protagonists. The first is the narrator who, at the opening of the song, meets Kilby and asks him where he is going, the second character is Kilby himself and the third is Nancy, the focus of Kilby's expressed desire. This complex layering of *dramatis personae* is ingeniously reflected in the various gradations to the accompaniment that Britten employs. Such nuance is achieved by a number of subtle devices, one of which is a judicious handling of the guitar's register. For example, in the opening two verses, pleasant major 6^{ths} (7^{ths} are very quickly resolved) situated at the centre of the instrument's register are employed, giving the song both the 'graceful' air the musical heading asks for and a 'civilized' atmosphere representative of the refined

---

205 Source: http://www.metrolyrics.com/master-kilby-lyrics-john-wesley-harding.html. Date sourced: 11 August 2010.

society to which the protagonists clearly belong. Again, this is a central *modus operandi* of the original folksong: a civilized encounter between 'gentlemen' is established so that the real and 'shocking' nature of Kilby's pursuit, held back until the final verse, is ultimately revealed in a dramatic *coup de théâtre*. In this light, the final verse's expurgation by Sharp has not only diminished the element of taboo associated with the sexual pursuit of pleasure but has also stripped the song of a technical device structured to deliver an effective *dénouement*.

Example 33: Britten, 'Master Kilby'

The use of the accompaniment to bring latent tensions into relief can be observed at the mention of the name 'Kil-by' in the 4/4 bar of Example 33. The vocal part rises to the high F♯ and resolves on the second syllable with a dotted crotchet E and a quaver D♮. This clashes with the guitar's D♯, which has the effect of pointing attention to the second narrator of the song, Kilby, from whom we are now about to hear. The touch of dissonance added at this point has been employed to cast a shadow over Kilby, perhaps a subtle, dark shading of his character that insinuates his libidinous intentions. This particular interpretation is problematized by the fact that we are not aware if Britten himself knew of the final verse's expurgation. On the other hand, it is fair to suggest that, as Britten was particularly sensitive to hidden codes of sexuality, it is likely that he sensed the erotic undertones of the song in any case and wished to amplify them.

Kilby's sexual intentions are further reinforced by the guitar part when he starts to speak. Gone are the earlier diminishing hairpin dynamics we see in Example 33 that gracefully dissipate the energy in ways that suggest a harmless character. That nonchalance is now replaced by dynamics demanding 'rather f'. The accompaniment now resides in the (masculine?) lower register of the instrument and numerous clashing 2^{nds} add to a subtle but growing sense of increased tension. The pulsing bass notes at the first quaver of every bar are given accents, which suggest a growing physical tension and prowess. Thus, the graceful opening has been expertly replaced by a sexually driven compulsion to seek 'Nancy's soft bosom'. The entire 'orchestration' of the guitar part points to a text-intrinsic amplification of the narrative.

Example 34: Britten, 'Master Kilby' (verse 3)

There are many further examples of the accompaniment's effective dramatization of the text. In the fifth verse, for instance, when Kilby makes the admission that he 'would part with it all with my own heart so freely', the guitar music appropriately softens to reflect his loving thoughts and reinstates the register and intervals that accompanied the first two verses. Additionally, in the final verse where Kilby is listing Nancy's qualities, the accompaniment is elevated to a higher register reflecting his exaltation. The use of *ponticello* to create a brittle sound when Kilby says that 'She's the fairest of girls' accentuates her delicate image. His description of her as 'painted like waxwork' is scored in translucent 3^{rds} and 4^{ths}, which are left suspended until the words, 'in every part' are sung, whereupon the accompaniment fleetingly rises into the higher regions of the instrument. This ascent effectively evokes both a seductive search for 'every part' and a state of rising bliss. The loss of control that inheres in sexual ecstasy is illustrated by the disintegration of the established rhythmic integrity of the accompaniment from the word 'part' to a three-quaver grouping that pulsates to its own irrational trajectory. Freeing itself from the strictures of the ¾ time signature, the music drives to its desired end by way of syncopated gasps until the tension is finally released at the moment the final sustained dotted minim sounds.

Example 35: Britten, 'Master Kilby' (verse 6)

'The Soldier and the Sailor'

Sung by a Shepherd Haden in Bampton, Oxfordshire, this song was collected by Sharp on 21 August 1909.[206]

'The Soldier and the Sailor'
As the soldier and the sailor
Was a-walking one day,
Said the soldier to the sailor:
'I've a mind for to pray'.
'Pray on then', said the sailor,
'Pray on once again,
And whatever you do pray for,
I will answer 'Amen'.
'Now the first thing I'll pray for,
I'll pray for the Queen,
That she have peace and plenty
All the days of her reign,
And where she got one man
I wish she had ten;

[206] Source: The Roud Index: http://library.efdss.org/cgi-bin/query.cgi?index_roud =on&field=9&op=and&query=The%20soldier%20and%20the%20sailor&start=3&output=Record&access=off. Date sourced: 11 August 2010.

And never want for an army'.
Said the sailor, 'Amen'.

'Now the next thing I'll pray for,
I'll pray for the Queen,
That she have peace and plenty
All the days of her reign,
And where she got one ship
I wish she had ten;
And never want for a navy'.
Said the sailor, 'Amen'.

'Now the next thing I'll pray for,
Is a pot of good beer,
For good liquor were sent us
Our spirits to cheer,
And where we got one pot,
I wish we had ten,
And never want for liquor'.
Said the sailor, 'Amen'.

In stark contrast to 'Master Kilby', which we have noted is likely to have been unique, 'The Soldier and the Sailor' has mutated into numerous versions and has turned up in many different regions. Moulden explains that 'The Soldier and the Sailor' 'is a common song with many variants such as "The topman and the afterguard", which turns on a defiant hardening by the sailor of his statement—"and if we have one drink, then let us have ten—let's have a bloody brewery, said the sailor 'Amen'"'.[207] The song is also known in an even more comical version entitled 'The Soldier's Prayer'—a rendering that, judging by the text, would never have passed Sharp's censorial eye (see Appendix VI). In setting Sharp's version, Britten focuses on 'The Soldier and the Sailor' as a drinking song and thus the unrelenting consumption of alcohol is humorously underscored by his shaping of the guitar part. Example 36 demonstrates the effects that increasing intoxication has on the articulation of the accompaniment.

[207] Source: Email exchange with John Moulden, 11 August 2010.

Example 36: Britten, 'The Soldier and the Sailor', guitar accompaniment to verses 1 & 2, verse 3, verse 4, and verse 4 (continued)

The musical instruction here is 'Heavy and rhythmic', which sets the scene for vibrant, robust drinking and general merriment. Executed vigorously in the lower register, the accompaniment tells us that we are in unrefined male company (top stave, Example 36). The juxtaposition of praying and drinking gives the song its essential irreverence, a point further emphasized by the mock-religious quoting of the word 'Amen', which, being rendered in a 4/4 bar, suggests an inebriated inability to keep time:

Example 37: Britten, 'The Soldier and the Sailor', 'And whatever you do pray for, I will answer "Amen"'

The second stave of Example 36 shows that as the 'praying' becomes more fervent the guitar part rises in register, accentuating the escalated spirit of verse 3. Of course, by the time we get to verse 4, we become aware that the real purpose behind all this praying is 'a pot of good beer'. By this stage, however, the soldier and the sailor are slurring their words—a fact made evident in stave three of Example 36 by the ascending glissando runs in the bass part of the accompaniment. This is a musical notation and context that, perhaps uniquely, asks the guitarist to perform in a drunken manner! Later in the verse, the glissandi descend (reversing their previous upbeat orientation) giving an impression that the drink may actually have gotten the better of the two (see Example 36, stave 4). The repeated 'Amen' to finish the song is another example of the musical rhetoric device known as *palillogia*, which we discussed in Chapter Three. The repetition of a melodic fragment at the same pitch is a technique employed to emphasize the matter at hand and bring the song to a decisive close. We have already seen how Dowland employs this in his song 'Farewell Too Faire' and how Britten similarly uses it in 'The Autumn Wind'.

Example 38: Britten, 'The Soldier and the Sailor', '"Amen", "Amen"'

At the end of 'The Soldier and the Sailor', Britten places the first 'Amen' in free time over a plagal cadence in C, for extra mock-religious zeal. The unexpected A♭ major chord that initiates the second 'Amen' and the following melodic figure in that bar ending on E♭ and D♭ further suggest the disorientation of the intoxicated drinkers. The final gesture of ascending 3^rds^ in the guitar part gives the strong impression of beers being raised (and consumed) one last time in salute to the final 'Amen': a highly effective visual rendering in music of the narrative's comic scene. Graham Johnson describes the situation aptly when he suggests that the last eight bars of the song are marked 'Freely', and the guitar's postlude seems to totter unsteadily on its pins as the singer sinks under the table. His final 'Amen' has all the solemnity of those who are well and truly drunk. 'The Soldier and the Sailor' is quite simply the most masterful depiction of gradually deepening inebriation that I know of in the entire song repertoire.[208]

'Bonny at Morn'

'Bonny at Morn' is an attractive Northumbrian lullaby first noted by a pioneer folksong collector called John Bell early in the 19th century; though it had to wait until 1882 to be published in *Northumbrian Minstrelsy*.[209] Northumbria is the only part of England with its own regional music-dialect. Its stock of melodies is stylistically distinct from models anywhere else in the country because many have been influenced by the unique sound and technique of the Northumbrian pipes. The Introduction to *Northumbrian Minstrelsy* explains further:

> The inhabitants of the district lying between the Firth of Forth and the Humber having sprung originally from the same race, or combination of races, have a style of music which is peculiar to themselves. But though the music of the Scottish Lowlands has a general resemblance to that of Northumberland, a delicate ear can observe a difference between the melodies originating north and south of the Tweed. This is probably owing to the fact that for several centuries the two districts formed parts of two kingdoms. The musical instrument most in vogue in ancient Northumbria...was the bagpipes. We seem to have got it from the Romans...At Stanwix, near Carlisle, which was one of the stations of the Roman Wall, a Roman sculpture still exists exhibiting a performer upon the pipes.[210]

In addition to songs influenced by the bagpipes, Northumbria has engendered numerous other unique forms of cultural artistic expression including its own type of dance music, the Rapper Sword Dance, border ballads, one of the strongest broadside collections outside London,[211] and a large number of shanties and Keelmen songs.[212] Britten sourced

---

[208] Graham Johnson, *Britten, Voice & Piano*, 101-103.

[209] J. Collingwood Bruce and John Stokoe, eds., *Northumbrian Minstrelsy* (Newcastle-upon-Tyne: Society of Antiquaries, 1882).

[210] Ibid., iii/iv.

[211] The Rapper Sword Dance is a hilt-and-point sword dance that dates back to at least 1715. Source: Origins and History of Rapper: http://www.rapper.org.uk/history.html. Date sourced: 11 August 2010.

[212] Unique to the Newcastle region, Keelmen were highly skilled boatmen who handled the movement of coal from the riverside to ships on the River Tyne. The Keelmen took their name from their small vessels called keels, which could carry heavy loads of coal.

'Bonny at Morn', one of the finest examples of Northumbria's folksongs, from *North Countrie Folk Songs for Schools*, edited by W.G. Whittaker (reprinted from the *Northumbrian Minstrelsy*).[213]

'Bonny at Morn'
The sheep's in the meadows,
The kye's in the corn,
(Thou's ower lang in thy bed)
Bonny at morn
The sheep's in the meadows,
The kye's in the corn,
(Thou's ower lang in thy bed)
Bonny at morn
Canny at night,
Bonny at morn
(Thou's ower lang in thy bed)
Bonny at morn.

The bird's in the nest,
The trout's in the burn,
Thou hinders thy mother
In many a turn.
The bird's in the nest,
The trout's in the burn,
Thou hinders thy mother
In many a turn.
Canny at night,
Bonny at morn
(Thou's ower lang in thy bed)
Bonny at morn.

We're all laid idle
Wi' keeping the bairn
The lad winnot work
And the lass winnot learn,
We're all laid idle
Wi' keeping the bairn
The lad winnot work
And the lass winnot learn,
Canny at night,
Bonny at morn
(Thou's ower lang in thy bed)
Bonny at morn.

'Bonny at Morn' must have been a favourite of Britten's, as it is the only folksong that he set twice; though both are very different in character and complexity. The later version, which is relatively simple in comparison to the guitar setting, is the fourth of *Eight Folk Song*

213 W.G. Whittaker, ed., *North Countrie Folk Songs for Schools* (Curwen, 1921).

Arrangements (for voice and harp) published in 1976. As this study of text-intrinsic techniques focuses on the accompaniment's role in effectively illuminating narratives, it is to be assumed that different instruments render different types of figuration. Notwithstanding, the harp accompaniment to 'Bonny at Morn' is uncharacteristically subdued. Example 39 demonstrates the limited degree to which the mood develops beyond that established in the opening bars with its dreamy repetitive arpeggios in the left hand and its hint of the song's melody in the right. However, a perusal of all the songs in *Eight Folk Song Arrangements* would appear to indicate that Britten chose to compose to the strengths of the harp rather than to force it to operate beyond its inherent capabilities. *Eight Folk Song Arrangements* was Britten's penultimate composition, completed very close to his death in December 1976, and it is also likely that the unusually restrained nature of the collection reflects the composer's flagging energies.

Example 39: Britten, 'Bonny at Morn', for voice and harp, bars 1-8

In stark contrast to the harp arrangement of 'Bonny at Morn', the guitar version treats each verse differently, utilizing exceptionally vivid accompaniments that closely reflect the dramatic action. Indeed, this approach so effectively scans the trajectory of the narrative that the song almost takes on the structural characteristic of a through-composed work. The accompaniment sets the 'Gently rocking' mood with chords falling on the 2nd and 5th beats of the 6/4 bar (reminiscent of Satie's *Gymnopedies*), which gives the impression of a cot being gently pushed to and fro. However, this apparently simple opening belies a complex vocal line. Moulden has pointed out that north English tunes have surprising intervals and rhythms in comparison with the south. Wide intervallic leaps of this kind stem from the influence of the Northumbrian pipes and it is widely believed that 'Bonny at Morn' was originally a pipe tune before words were set to it.[214] Example 41 exhibits another folksong from the same region called *The Northumberland Pipes* that displays bagpipe-influenced intervallic gaps, which are a feature of 'Bonny at Morn' (see Example 40).[215]

Example 40: Britten, 'Bonny at Morn', bars 9-14

---

[214] Source: Email exchange with John Moulden, 11 August 2010.

[215] W. Gillies Whittaker, ed. and arr., *The Hexhamshire Lass: Ballads and Folk Songs from the North Country* (London: Curwen & Son, 1978), 12-14. The folksong 'Pelton Lonnin' from the same collection is also most likely derivedfrom a pipe tune.

Example 40: 'The Northumberland Pipes', vocal part

Example 41: Britten, 'Bonny at Morn', bars 9-14

Britten's arrangement weaves the accompaniment guitar lines in contrary motion to the vocal part, gradually thickening them so that they become sluggish dyads and triads, nudging around in the depths of the instrument. This suggests a groggy inability to wake up, hence the scorn in bar 13: 'Thou's ower lang in thy bed' [you are oversleeping]. Once this mood is established, however, the guitar part immediately rises into the higher register to accompany the words 'Bonny at morn', thereby underscoring a contradiction inherent in the lines. In order to apprehend the paradox, it must be understood that, in the score, the words contained within brackets are derisively addressed to him who lounges about in bed well into the morning, while the lullaby is affectionately sung to the sleeping child. The increasing agitation of the song reflects the time consumed in caring for the child. Thus, the text works through multi-layers of meanings and moods. I have repeatedly highlighted that Britten's text-intrinsic accompaniments display a highly refined sensitivity to narratives and often underscore sub-texts and metaphoric interpretations. Graham Johnson has gone so far as to place Britten's arrangements on a par with the best of German lieder:

> Almost all the accompaniments are based—as in Schubert's—on a single pianistic motif which somehow encapsulates the mood of the whole, and is capable of infinite modification and expansion in the interest of textual illustration...[216]

Despite its guitar setting, 'Bonny at Morn' is not exempt from Johnson's 'pianistic motif' thesis. From bar 20 ('more agitated'), for example, the accompaniment takes on an increasingly animated character emphasizing the heightened intensity of mood in the unfolding text. It doubles the speed of its twisting lines, and in so doing, manages to conjure up the 'trout's in the burn' with its Schubertian leaps and dips.

[216] Graham Johnson, *Britten, Voice & Piano*, 101-103.

Example 42: Britten, 'Bonny at Morn', bars 20-23

Britten illuminates the increasing agitation of the singer at a climactic point in bar 32 where the chorus, which complains about her inability to work, returns for the third and last time. He achieves a suitably turbulent state in the arpeggiated accompaniment:

Example 43: Britten, 'Bonny at Morn', bars 32-3

Following this hysteria, the chorus returns again but with the tension relieved so that the song reverts to the gentle rocking accompaniment with which it started.

'The Shooting of his Dear'

'The Shooting of his Dear'
O come all you young fellows that carry a gun,
I'd have you get home by the light of the sun,
For young Jimmy was a fowler and a fowling alone,
When he shot his own true love in the room of a swan.

Then home went young Jimmy with his dog and his gun,
Saying, 'Uncle, dear uncle, have you heard what I've done?
Cursed be that old ginsmith that made my old gun,
For I've shot my own true love in the room of a swan.'

Then out came bold uncle with his locks hanging grey,
Saying, 'Jimmy, dear Jimmy, don't you go away
Don't you leave your own country till the trial come on,
For you never will be hanged for the shooting a swan.'

So the trial came on and pretty Polly did appear,
Saying, 'Uncle, dear uncle, let Jimmy go clear,
For my apron was bound round me and he took me for a swan,
And his poor heart lay bleeding for Polly his own.'

According to the published score, 'The Shooting of His Dear' comes from Norfolk, where the composer E.J. Moeran notated it from a performance by his friend Harry Cox—a well-known Norfolk folk singer and farm labourer from Potter Heigham.[217] We have already observed how some folksongs have rather confusing histories and the lineage of 'The Shooting of His Dear' is as perplexing as any. Some commentators have suggested that the song originated in Ireland, possibly Donegal. Jennifer J. O'Connor provides an intriguing background:

> At least eighty-eight oral and printed variants (and 19 fragments) of 'Molly Bawn' or 'The Shooting of His Dear' have been collected around the English-speaking world, eight of them (plus one fragment) in Canada...[though it survives as a broadside ballad: *'Young Molly Bawn,'* J.F. Nugent & Co., Dublin[218]]...others believe its story has a long history in oral tradition... the first known date for a printing of 'Molly Bawn' is generally accepted to be 1799, when Robert Jamieson apparently obtained a copy of the "rude original of 'Peggy Baun'". An examination of eighty-eight variants reveals that in its most complete form, the 'Molly Bawn' plot contains the following elements: as the sun is setting, Molly Ban Lavery makes her way home from her uncle's when a sudden shower of rain comes on. A green bush is her only shelter, and huddling beneath it, Molly covers herself with her white apron. Meanwhile her

[217] E. J. Moeran, arr., *Six Folk Songs from Norfolk* (London: Augener Ltd., 1924), 1.

[218] Source: http://www.csufresno.edu/folklore/ballads/LO36.html. Date sourced: 11 August 2010.

> lover, the squire James Reynolds, has been hunting all day with his dog. Upon returning home with his gun in hand, he is attracted to a patch of whiteness showing among the green leaves of a bush. In the falling darkness he supposes this must be the whiteness of a swan's feathers, or the light colour of a fawn's breast. Jimmy raises his gun and shoots; despite the dimness his aim is true. He runs to claim his quarry when to his horror and great grief he finds only his sweetheart lying dead under the bush.[219]

Surprisingly, the fundamental import of the folksong's story has survived in most cases despite the great number of transformations it has undergone and the distance it has travelled. This might explain why the collector Patrick Weston Joyce (1827-1914) heard it as *Molly Bawn*, 'sung in fine style in the streets of Dublin by a poor woman with a child on her arm'.[220] Discussion about the origins of 'The Shooting of His Dear' simply highlights the fundamental transitory and migratory nature of folksong and further points to how the practice of notated arranging works in direct contradiction to the elemental nomadic spirit of oral traditions. It also points to the ultimate inappropriateness of claiming a song to be indisputably 'English' or 'Irish' or 'Welsh'; despite these attempts, folksong has an uncanny tendency to destabilize constructed narratives.

Running in parallel with the song's mixed lineage is evidence that 'The Shooting of His Dear' has appeared in other music genres. The song seems to have captured E. J. Moeran's imagination. Indeed, it is convincingly argued that its theme is incorporated into his brooding *Symphony in G Minor*. The bleak evocation of landscape and mood in the work has been interpreted as an attempt by Moeran to confront his harrowing first-hand experiences of World War I. Moeran was traumatically injured in that war and he suffered for many years after as a result; indeed, the wounds may even have contributed to his early death in 1950. On the topic of influence, Geoffrey Self has argued that 'The Shooting of His Dear' provides significant melodic motifs for the *Symphony*. Directing attention specifically to the line 'for young Jimmy was a fowler', Self asks: 'Could there not be a loose allegory here of a young soldier—Jack (Moeran) rather than Jim—called by duty to the

---

219 Jennifer J. O'Connor, 'The Irish Origins and Variations of the Ballad "Molly Brown"', in *Canadian Journal for Traditional Music* (1986), Source: http://cjtm.icaap.org/content/14/v14art3.html. Date sourced: 11 August 2010.

220 Source: Website—Mainly Norfolk, English Folk and Other Good Music, http://www.informatik.uni-hamburg.de/~zierke/lloyd/songs/pollyvaughan.html. Date sourced: 18 August 2010.

war, his illusions of military chivalry and nobility to be shattered by the awesome reality of the sordid carnage and its bleak aftermath?'[221]

As a conscientious objector, this is exactly the sort of psychological extraction that Britten would have sought when he made his dramatic arrangement of 'The Shooting of His Dear'. In stark contrast (and despite his use of it in *Symphony in G Minor)*, Moeran avoided any such amplification in his setting for piano and voice, which for the most part is rather sparse and of little dramatic interest. As we have noted, this approach is typical of folksong's treatment by the pastoralists to which group it may be argued Moeran by and large belonged. A comparison between both arrangements will bring to light Britten's unique approach to the genre.

Example 44: Moeran, 'The Shooting of His Dear' (excerpt, from bar 22)

221 Geoffrey Self, *The Music of E. J. Moeran* (London: Toccata Press, 1986); cited in Stephen Banfield, 'Bleak Moeran', review of 'The Music of E.J. Moeran', in *The Musical Times* Vol. 128, No. 1730 (1987): 209-210.

Given the connections Moeran made between this song and his dark symphony, the accompaniment seems all the more perfunctory, providing the most basic harmony to the melody and avoiding any attempt to underscore latent themes or sub-texts of which he must have been aware. In stark contrast, Britten saw much in this song that resonated with many of his most abiding passions. Foremost among these was his abhorrence of hunting, which for him bore close association with a deeply held conviction regarding the futility of war: 'My social feelings are the same as they always have been, I disbelieve profoundly in power and violence.'[222] Thus the shocking violence at the heart of 'The Shooting of His Dear' is manifestly foreshadowed by the detonations of the accompaniment that open the song. Britten blatantly recreates the explosive sounds of a shotgun:

Example 45: Britten, 'The Shooting of His Dear', bars 1-9

In the context of the pastoral school's established practice in folksong setting, Britten's violent opening alone is exceptional. Further examples of text illumination can be observed later in the song when an effective aural representation of the birds to be hunted is created with cascading arpeggios that glide up and down, down and up, giving the impression of flocks suddenly scattering in the midst of gunshot bursts.

[222] Murray Schafer, *British Composers in Interview* (London: Faber and Faber, 1963), 117.

This is also evident visually in the score; the arpeggios actually look like the flapping wings of birds.

Example 46: Britten, 'The Shooting of His Dear', bars 14-24

Following the aggressive opening, Britten magically transforms the atmosphere with the simplest of alterations, converting the gunshots into repeating arpeggio figurations that imitate Jimmy running home 'with his dog and his gun' (see Example 46, bars 23-4). The growing agitation of the story's third verse is perfectly caught in the incessant 'more agitated' repetition of the accompaniment:

Example 47: Britten, 'The Shooting of His Dear', bars 41-44

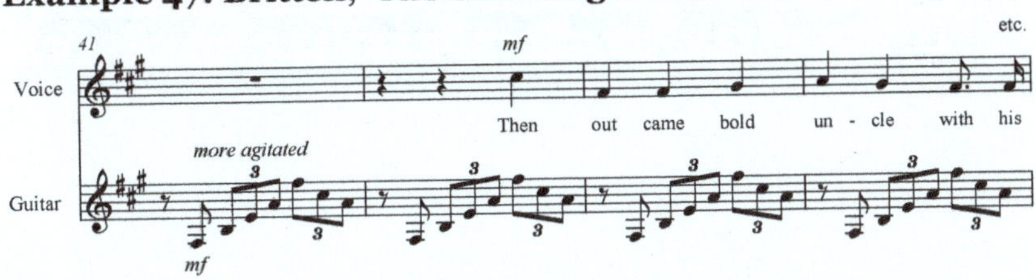

A masterful control of the psychological drama unfolding within the song's narrative is most effectively demonstrated when Polly appears as a spectre at Jimmy's trial. At this point (from bar 61, Example 48), the accompaniment transforms radically, though fluently, from explosive gunshots (which threateningly remind us that Jimmy may be executed for his crime) to an ethereal, incandescent tremolo on the guitar, evoking Polly's mysterious visitation.

Example 48: Britten, 'The Shooting of His Dear', bars 61-69

Never has a folksong been so dramatically rendered in an arrangement. Indeed, a comparison with Moeran's unadventurous setting demonstrates the extraordinary degree to which Britten renovated the practice of English folksong setting. Rather than naively endorse folksong's putative simplicity, through text-intrinsic writing Britten consciously arranged English folksongs *against* the established practices of the pastoral school by placing all his imaginative skill at the service of illuminating the complexity of the genre—its multi-narrativity, its intricacy of text and sub-text, its socio-cultural rationales and its psychological tensions. All these aspects, overt and latent, give to folksong its communal functions, which, as we have noted, serve to educate in rules of behaviour and demeanour, interpret natural phenomena and allow spaces within which taboo subjects may be engaged.

The pastoral school's attempts to preserve the putative simplicity of folksong ignored these functions and undermined folksong's symbolic and cultural agency. Britten intuitively understood that their attempts to 'recover' folksongs neither preserved the originals nor created good music from them. In contrast, Britten's arrangements provided him with an opportunity to use a cultural resource as a means of creating a kind of hybridized genre. A paradox lies at the heart of this project. He did not attempt to capture the 'essence' of the folksong, as he knew that 'aura' could only be preserved through an appropriate oral rendition of it. However, building upon the genre's basic materials, Britten's text-intrinsic arrangements, which resulted in a new type of song, did ingeniously reveal the complexity of English cultural consciousness as it was captured and preserved in its folksong traditions.

Chapter Five: *Nocturnal, after John Dowland*

In Chapter One, I argued that Manual de Falla's *Homenaje, pour le tombeau de Claude Debussy* marks a renaissance in the history of guitar music, being the first work of significance composed for that instrument by a non-guitarist composer. There is an equally strong case to be made for Britten's *Nocturnal*, which also represents a new phase of maturity in the instrument's repertoire. There are of course other earlier works for the guitar that display considerable sophistication—Frank Martin's *Quatre pièces brèves* from 1933 comes to mind. However, it is hard to cite a work composed before 1964 of similar stature to *Nocturnal* with regard to semantic complexity, prolonged musical argument and philosophical depth. This intricately developed 'night fancy',[223] which was at first thought to be almost unplayable, broke completely new ground in guitar composition and performance practice. It led the way for subsequent works conceived from larger, more elaborate musical schemata requiring an enhanced technical prowess and interpretative sophistication, such as Henze's sonatas, Takemitsu's concertos, Ginastera's *Sonata*, Rochberg's *Caprice Variations*, Murail's *Tellur* and Berio's *Sequenza XI*, to name just a few. *Nocturnal* stands not only as an English work of cardinal importance—its enduring shadow hovers darkly over Nicholas Maw's *Music of Memory*—but is arguably the most significant composition in the entire guitar repertoire.

Dowland's influence on *Nocturnal* is of course central; and I have already explored how Elizabethan musical rhetoric impacted *Songs from the Chinese* in Chapter Two. Advancing these ideas, this chapter explores how Britten ingeniously assimilated Dowland's methods of textual-based musical rhetoric into purely instrumental writing in

223 'Night fancy' is the subtitle that Britten wrote on the front page of the MS, which is held at the Britten-Pears Library; it does not appear in the published edition.

Nocturnal. As I have already stated, I do not wish to suggest that Purcell is not of equal importance in relation to Britten's appropriation of musical rhetoric; on the contrary, we will see Purcell's signature profoundly impacting Britten's *Nocturnal*-passacaglia. However, given the practical and symbolic impact that the Britten-Pears-Bream triumvirate had on the revival of Dowland as a major English figure, Britten's guitar works can be viewed as inextricably connected to the Elizabethan. As Dowland's 'Come Heavy Sleep' is the main source of inspiration for *Nocturnal*, a brief introductory analysis of the song's rhetorical devices will naturally be useful in setting the contexts for a more extensive overview of Britten's use of similar methods in Op. 70. Therefore, this analysis, which investigates *Nocturnal* through the lens of musical rhetoric inherited from Dowland, serves a central hypothesis. As in the accompaniment writing for *Songs from the Chinese*, Britten has developed a type of musical idiolect so integrated with Dowland's song, so germane to the words' literal and metaphoric import, that the instrumental music of *Nocturnal* can be said to be wholly text-intrinsic.

If Britten's employment of reverse variation techniques was not actually pioneering, it was decidedly original. He utilized these forms in three important works—*Lachrymae*, Op. 48, *Nocturnal* and *Cello Suite No. 3*, Op. 87. An analysis of all three pieces reveals Britten's genius for renovating established structures. It also encourages a greater appreciation of *Nocturnal* as central to a category of works that employs structural devices specifically to enact processes of distillation of musical material. From a metaphoric perspective, such technical methods of purgation provide a symbolic progression towards the work's central themes of sleep and death—a diminishment of the lived, embodied world. This focus consequently draws attention to the more philosophical implications of the use of reverse variation form as a method of transformative and transcendental agency.

The motif of metaphoric transcendence achieved through technical procedures of distillation is carried forward in Britten's strategic use of passacaglia form in *Nocturnal* as a systematic mechanism of self-destruction. From knowledge of passacaglia's broader historic development, insights regarding the unique methodology employed by Britten in the *Nocturnal*-passacaglia demonstrate his advancement of the form from a Purcellian modal to a new, complex mechanism driven by an apparently illogical conceit that seeks its own functional obliteration. In the context of what we know of Dowland and Britten, however, the symbolic implications of music that strives for its own elimination may be paradoxically affirmative. There is a quasi-Hegelian dialectic here that takes music to a point of negation so that it may manifest a type of transcendence. Thus, the psychological motivations that drive the *Nocturnal*-passacaglia to its ultimate tryst with annihilation and release need to be explored.

Hidden processes of musical rhetoric are not the only components of Britten's music that require 'unconcealment'—to use Heidegger's slogan again. Britten used bi-tonality and other, what I call, 'self-subverting mechanisms' in his instrumental music, as a way of expressing hidden themes and private conflicts. Possible meanings for, and interpretations of, semantically rich but nevertheless non-discursive processes in his instrumental music need to be teased out. Why is *Nocturnal* permeated by such curious tonal ambiguity, constructed out of melodic and harmonic fragments that work in contradistinction to each other and to those that immediately precede or follow them? Theoretical perspectives help unlock the code to Britten's secret idiolect and throw light on the dark machinations that make *Nocturnal* such an intriguing work of concealed encryptions.

Given Britten's prodigious output, it is easy to see how a single work for solo guitar might be overlooked as a significant exemplar of a particular point of style or technique. However, I wish to argue that *Nocturnal* is not only a landmark in guitar repertoire, but that it holds a unique position in Britten's overall output in that it heralds, alongside *Curlew River*, the beginning of his final phase of composition. Indeed, where the church parable marks this stylistic shift in a vocal idiom, *Nocturnal* does so, equally importantly, in an instrumental mode. This gives to Op. 70 an importance that has not yet been fully appreciated.

Locating Dowland's Musical Rhetoric in *Nocturnal*

> Britten's music is itself a kind of wordless language—a characteristic way of presenting and shaping the interplay of essentially musical ideas (themes, rhythms, motives, or keys) within an unfolding discourse. The sounds of music, on this reading, themselves have properties usually ascribed to speech—expression, eloquence, a rhetorical force.[224]

> 'I feel as close to [Dowland] as I do to my youngest contemporary.'[225]

---

224 Philip Rupprecht, *Britten's Musical Language* (Cambridge: Cambridge University Press, 2001), 1.

225 Paul Kildea, ed., *Britten on Music*, 328.

As we have seen in Chapter One, at the time John Dowland published *The First Booke of Songes or Ayres* in 1597, English composers were very much culturally aware of the philosophies underpinning musical rhetoric. I have already shown in Chapter Three that the emergence of the lute song in Dowland's hands represented a dynamic and paradigmatic shift in the level and type of musical expression prevalent at the time. Releasing the performer from the more rigid strictures of the motet and madrigal, the lute song provided a firsthand opportunity for self-expression and personalized interpretation. This newfound freedom made it a superlative medium through which composed rhetorical inventions could be reproduced in powerful and affective performances. Dowland's obsession with darkness, sleep and death, reinforced by his interest in Pessimist Gnosticism, inspired him to compose lute songs with a distinctive musical idiolect manifestly informed by melancholy. Many of these songs thus resonated with Britten who, as we have seen, was almost pathologically obsessed with melancholic themes; and we have noted the uncanny connection between them through their shared belief that death can be ultimately liberating. 'Come Heavy Sleep', the twentieth and penultimate song from Dowland's 1597 compendium, is emblematic of all that obsessed both composers; and Britten's use of it as a theme for a set of nocturnal variations is as natural as it is inspired.

> **'Come Heavy Sleep'**
> Come heavy sleep, the image of true death;
> And close up these my weary weeping eies:
> Whose spring of tears doth stop my vitall breath,
> And tears my hart with sorrows sign swoln cries:
> Come and possess my tired thoughts, worne soule,
> That living dies, till thou on me be stoule.[226]

It is not surprising that Dowland placed 'Come Heavy Sleep' towards the end of his published collection, as it is among the finest in the set. In its craving for escape from the toils of life through sleep, it is effectively elaborated melodically and harmonically through Dowland's expert handling of musical rhetoric. The simplicity of the text follows a standardized poetic convention that allows Dowland to musically

[226] The penultimate line of the first stanza is sometimes rendered as 'Come and possess my tired thoughtworn soul' or 'Come and posses my tired thoughts-worn soul'.

amplify its message. A salient feature of the song (and one that we shall return to often) is the perfect 4th. The importance of this interval can be observed in the opening phrase, 'Come heavy sleep', where the metaphorical weight in the word 'heavy' is expressed musically by the falling 4th on its second syllable.

Example 49: Dowland, 'Come Heavy Sleep' (opening vocal phrase)

The descending perfect 4th provides an exemplary musical correlation to the text's central theme as many numerologists of the period believed that the interval equated to weakness, indecision and ambivalence. This conviction was so widespread that the 4th became known as the 'tear motif'; indeed, Peter Holman describes it as 'a standard emblem of grief'.[227] Other examples of musical rhetoric are worth exploring to place in focus those very features of the song that Britten intuitively seized upon and developed in *Nocturnal*. For example, the use of a type of mirror notation to underscore the line 'the image of true death', where the three descending notes (and their pitch relationships) corresponding to the three syllables of 'the im-age' are quite literally mirrored by the inverted three ascending notes attached to the three syllables contained in 'of true death'. The extended note values correlating to the second half of the phrase further emphasize the longing for release.

Example 50: Dowland, 'Come Heavy Sleep', 'the image of true death'

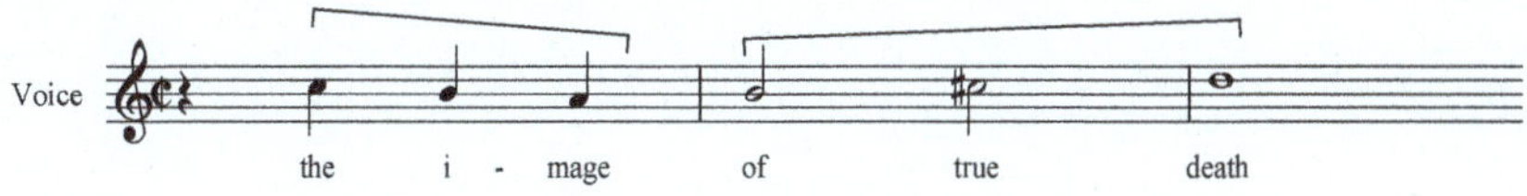

[227] Peter Holman, *Dowland Lachrimae (1604)* (Cambridge: Cambridge University Press, 1999), 40-42.

The composer and theorist Thomas Morley (1557?-1602) insisted that:

> you must have a care that when your matter signifieth 'ascending', 'high', 'heaven', and such like you make your music ascend; and by the contrary where your ditty speaketh 'descending', 'lowness', 'depth', 'hell', and others such, you must make your music descend'.[228]

This cardinal point of musical rhetoric is exemplified by Dowland's shaping of melodic contours to musically amplify the text's meanings. Thus, the words 'And close up' are reflected by four ascending notes the last of which floats on the word 'up' for a considerable period, thereby accentuating its meaning musically. Meanwhile, the staid alliteration of 'weary weeping eies' is astutely reflected in the steady, evenly descending notes, which are laid to rest on the word 'eies', like eyelids heavily closing:

Example 51: Dowland, 'Come Heavy Sleep', 'And close up these my weary weeping eies'

A rhythmic and harmonic language of emotional intensity is effectively created with the sudden harmonic shift Dowland makes on the words 'Come and possess' (from G major to B major)—a musical rhetoric technique known as *mutatio toni*.[229] Rhythmically, the minim/quaver/quaver/crotchet motive mimics the words' spoken rhythms. Meanwhile, the despondent descent of the 4th in the melody from the note B down to F♯ can be interpreted as a metaphoric plunge to the grave.

---

[228] R.A. Harman, ed., 'Morley, A Plaine and Easie Introduction', cited in Peter Holman, *Dowland Lachrimae (1604)* (Cambridge: Cambridge University Press, 1999), 43.

[229] See Dietrich Bartel, *Música Poética: Musical-Rhetorical Figures in German Baroque Music* (Lincoln: University of Nebraska Press, 1997), 334-339.

Example 52: Dowland, 'Come Heavy Sleep', 'Come and posses my tired'

Furthermore, as Diane Poulton has outlined, the last word of 'sorrows sigh swoln cries' ends on a G major chord, which on the lute is played mostly with the open resonating strings. This extra reverberation will support an intense, distressed vocalization from the singer. However, the sudden shift to B major for the next line, 'Come and posses', is more muted, as this chord is executed by playing stopped strings. The singer is almost compelled, therefore, to lower the volume of the voice so that 'the invocation to sleep then take[s] on a kind of hushed urgency'.[230] In relation to theories of musical rhetoric, the physical shift from an 'easy' open chord (G major) to a 'difficult' stopped chord (B major) also had its harmonic implications. As Judy Tarling points out:

> [for] some instruments certain keys are more comfortable to play in than others, and the effect of unequal tunings would oblige composers to select suitable keys for their players, according to whether a sweet or discordant affect was required. Some composers...compiled tables of keys and their likely affects.[231]

Among those composers were Jean-Jacques Rousseau (1712-1778), Marc-Antoine Charpentier (1643-1704), Johann Mattheson (1681-1764) and Jean-Philippe Rameau (1683-1764).[232] When their individual key charts are compared, it can be observed that invariably they affiliate G major with feelings of tenderness, persuasion and seriousness, while B major is understood to embody characteristics of offence, desperation or plaintiveness. In this light, the harmony of G major on the words 'sorrows sigh swoln cries' attempts to persuade with solemn pleading.

[230] Diane Poulton, *John Dowland* (London: Faber and Faber, 1972), 241-2.
[231] Judy Tarling, *The Weapons of Rhetoric*, 76.
[232] Ibid., 77.

The sudden shift to B major on the words 'Come and possess' is altogether more hopeless and despairing, indicating the singer's anguished desolation.

These few illustrations demonstrate Dowland's consummate skill in the use of musical rhetoric as a means to amplify and dramatize textual meaning. Its application was brought to even greater heights in England with Purcell, but it should be remembered that at that time the utilization of rhetoric as a compositional tool was well established throughout the whole of Europe. By the end of the high Baroque, principles of musical rhetoric continued to hold sway and even became a dominant code in the composition of 'independent' music—that is, music composed independently of text, which was growing exponentially in importance. The identification and appraisal of formulations of rhetoric in abstract, instrumental music will deepen our appreciation of Britten's compositional methodologies in *Nocturnal*.

The historical trajectory of musical-rhetoric practice up to the late Baroque, its escalating influence and its spread from text-based music to instrumental composition—forms that jettisoned the semantic 'carriers' of the rhetorical idea (text)—mean that the shifting interrelationships between notes on the one hand and meaning on the other are harder to recognize and assess. In short, the evaluation of musical rhetoric in abstract music is more challenging. This analytical problem is further compounded as 20th-century perspectives on musical rhetoric were shaped considerably by opinions inherited from the 19th century, a period when the principles of musical rhetoric had become all but lost to composers and theorists. The loss of this knowledge as a common reference altered and impaired an appreciation of long-established methodologies in musical thought, but its rediscovery and restoration to active deliberation in more recent times has initiated a re-awakening of compositional and interpretative possibilities. For example, in discussing Purcell's use of *figurae*, Rodney Farnsworthy elucidates the subject and exposes common confusions concerning its application, which persist to this day in some quarters:

> in Purcell's musical rhetoric, the *figurae* consist of unusual configurations of notes that are melismatic—that is, that exist for expression rather than (as is too often thought) for coloratura effect. (For example, a downward run of 16th or 32nd notes may suggest falling

> down). Since musical *figurae* are added to syllabic settings, they seem ornamental; however, *figurae* underscore the verbal text....[233]

He goes on to suggest that much Purcell criticism and performance practice has misunderstood his musical rhetoric practice, stating that his

> *figurae* involved in word-setting [which are described] by such terms as word painting or word coloring...are flattering neither to the words, which are made to seem colorless, nor to the musical figures, which are made to seem to be nothing more than added color, merely contributing a minor detail to the design provided by the words...The librettist and composer of *King Arthur* would have found the term 'ornamental treatment' foreign and incomprehensible.[234]

Carrying this insight forward, we can bring the function of *figurae* as described above to bear upon our understanding of musical rhetoric as applied to instrumental music generally and to Britten's *Nocturnal* in particular. Op. 70 is a piece of purely instrumental music, but it emerges out of a deep meditation upon Dowland's 'Come Heavy Sleep'. I suggest, therefore, that where evidence of compositional extemporization on Dowland's theme exists in *Nocturnal*, it does so not merely as a continuation of the song's textual and musical identities, but emphatically as an extension of the text's rhetorical power as captured in Dowland's melodies, rhythms and harmonies. Thus, *Nocturnal* exhumes from discrete syllables, words and text phrases their original, interred meanings. The work transmits Dowland's musical rhetoric through instrumental *figurae*, or in what we might today call musical figurations—melodic, arpeggiated and harmonic. The original textual meanings contained within Dowland's song come down to us with their rhetorical dynamism intact and amplified in Op. 70's 'Lieder ohne Worte'. Such a perspective allows us to view *Nocturnal* through a musical rhetoric lens—a process that I wish to attempt in what follows.

While investigating a structural blueprint for *Nocturnal*, we shall look in due course at a salient feature of the first variation, namely, that it is not only a deep meditation (*meditativo*) on 'Come Heavy Sleep', but that in fact it *is* the song, though here manifested through Britten's unique musical idiolect. There is hardly greater evidence of Britten's

---

233 Rodney Farnsworthy "'Hither, This Way": A Rhetorical-Musical Analysis of a Scene from Purcell's "King Arthur"', in *The Musical Quarterly*, Vol 74, No. 1 (1990), 84-5.

234 Ibid.

intuitive capturing of Dowland's musical rhetoric than his full reiteration of the song in Variation I of *Nocturnal*. Interestingly, Britten has utilized very specific methods of musical rhetoric. The *Tractatus compositionis augmentatus* (1657?) of the composer and theorist Christoph Bernhard (1628-1692) is illustrative here. In it he states that the musical rhetoric technique of *variatio* 'occurs when, instead of a longer note, numerous shorter ones at various pitches are introduced which rush to the following note'.[235] Wolfgang Printz (1641-1717) helpfully expands upon this definition by explaining that *variatio* refers to 'an artful alteration of a given melodic passage, yet in which the original melody is always noticed'.[236] Many of Britten's melodic figurations in Variation I bear all the hallmarks of *variatio* as defined by these rhetoricians. For example, bars 19 to 24 demonstrate this process clearly: when Britten elaborates upon Dowland's motif 'that living dies' (bar 19), the original melody is 'always noticed'.

Example 53: Dowland, 'that living dies' and Britten, *Nocturnal*, Variation I, bars 19-24

Note that Britten's instruction to accelerate from bar 21 intuitively complies with Bernhard's insistence that the shorter notes should 'rush to the following note'. However, in this passage Britten is merely echoing Dowland's skill in the art of rhetoric, specifically his employment of *subjunctio* (*epizeuxis*): the repetition of certain word phrases. This technique transforms the words

> 'That living dies, till death on me be stole'

into

> 'That living dies, that living dies, that living dies, till death on me be stole.'

[235] Dietrich Bartel, *Música Poética*, 435.
[236] Ibid.

While Dowland rhetorically amplifies the line three times, Britten goes further in his instrumental version by repeating the line five times creating an exponential sense of urgency through the skilful employment of *variatio*. In the same passage, Dowland simultaneously employs *synonymia*—the repetition of a musical fragment at different pitch levels—when the subsequent repeats of 'that living dies' are initiated from different pitch positions (G, D and A, respectively) thereby effectively establishing a binary stratification (see brackets in upper stave, Example 53).[237] Britten similarly exploits this device when he expands the two established strata—three statements at a high register and two at a lower level (see brackets in lower stave, Example 53). A further use of *variatio* is employed in bar 25 of Variation I when the melody that correlates to Dowland's line 'till death on me be stole' is wrought in an even more artful extension. As Farnsworthy reminds us above, *variatio* is not to be confused with mere ornamentation, but is rather at the service of amplifying and illuminating the meaning of the text—a crucial key to understanding the functions underpinning Britten's musical idiolect in *Nocturnal*.

We have seen how Dowland employed the technique of *mutatio toni* to great effect in Example 52 above. In a correlating passage in Variation I, Britten powerfully captures a similarly unexpected harmonic modification shown in Example 54. The intuitive use of *mutatio toni* by Britten occurs when the music moves from an implied harmony (the cadential rest of the previous melodic phrase suggests a C tonality) to an actual key (E major). The abrupt appearance of a chord at this point—the first in the entire work—following a long period of monody further amplifies the affect. The upper melody note F, which immediately follows the chord, demonstrates the technique of *exclamatio* (*ecphonesis*); a rhetorical device called by George Puttenham 'the outcrie'

> because it utters our minde by all such words as do shew [show] any extreme passion, whether it be by way of exclamation or crying out, admiration or wondering, imprecation or cursing, obtestation or taking God and the world to witnes, or any such like as declare an impotent affection...[238]

This note is most effectual as it comes on the off-beat (syncopation is a

---

[237] Robert Toft, *Tune Thy Musicke To Thy Hart: The Art of Eloquent Singing in England 1597-1622* (Toronto: University of Toronto, 1993), 32.

[238] George Puttenham, *The Arte of English Poesie* (1589), ed. Edward Arber (London: Murray & Son, 1869), 221.

typical facet of *exclamatio*) and because it emanates from a different tonal centre (F) to the E major harmony over which it is placed. Without direct reference to the words 'Come and possess', and despite (or because of) the dynamic marking of *ppp*, Britten has very effectively intensified the declamatory significance of the words through the skilful application of bitonality, shifts in registry and the syncopated juxtaposition of melodic and harmonic features.

A further noteworthy utilization of musical rhetoric occurs in Variation I, which has a direct structural affiliation to the theme. 'Come Heavy Sleep' comprises two sections, the latter of which is repeated. In Variation I, Britten's decision to leave the repeat incomplete intuitively employs the technique of rhetoric known as *aposiopesis*: the breaking off in mid-sentence as a representation of emotional distress. Example 6 shows (from bar 16) how Britten accomplishes a complete phrase in the first appearance of this section: 'Come and possess my tired thoughts worn soul'. However, the repeated phrase (from bar 27) is incapable of conclusion, managing at best: 'Come and possess my tired, tired, tired...'.

Example 54: Britten, *Nocturnal*, Variation I, bars 16-18 and 27-29

The effect here is one of a diminished capacity to persist, a loss of conscious orientation such as one may experience when anesthetized, losing consciousness or merely falling asleep. Because of structural affiliation, the use of *aposiopesis* at the end of this variation is replicated in one form or another in all the variations and is thus a salient feature of the work.

The prolonged reflection on 'Come Heavy Sleep' in Variation I is unceremoniously shattered with the explosive arpeggios of Variation II. Given the sheer speed of the figurations and the erratic anarchism of the interjecting chords, Variation II is probably the least 'vocal' movement of the entire work. Yet it paradoxically maintains its essential connection to the song's words and phrases. The music retains a text-intrinsic quality. Example 55 demonstrates how each arpeggio is constructed with phrase contours derived from the song. These phrase fragments are used to ignite the arpeggiated line and are closely modelled upon the phrases pertaining to the following text fragments: 'Come heavy...', 'the image of...', 'And close up these...', 'whose spring of tears...' and 'And tears my heart...', respectively. The arpeggios aggressively develop these initial fragments:

Example 55: Britten, *Nocturnal*, Variation II, 'Very agitated'

In other parts of Variation II, ostensibly chaotic figurations are in fact carefully notated extrapolations of vocal phrases that further evidence the employment of *variatio*. Example 56 is one instance of many in the movement:

Example 56: Dowland, 'that living dies...' and Britten, *Nocturnal*, Variation II, 'Very agitated' (bars 17-18)

Example 57: Dowland, 'till death in me be stole', and Britten, *Nocturnal*, Variation II, 'Very agitated'

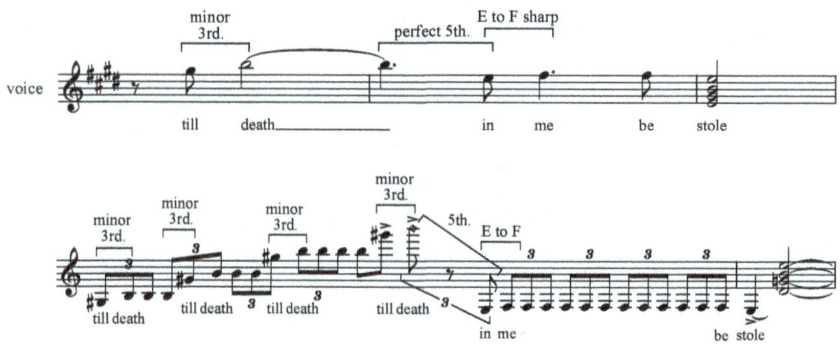

Example 57 demonstrates that even the most instrumentally idiosyncratic and virtuosic figurations are constructed from the song's phrase shapes. We can see here that the 'till death' melodic fragment is transformed into hysterical triplet arpeggios that soar into the highest echelons of the instrument's range, but they preserve the minor 3rd interval that gives the phrase its melodic identity. This has the effect of rhetorical exaggeration and heightened hysteria. The perfect 5th on the words 'death in' is also preserved, although the second note in the guitar version is required to make a desperate plunge from the instrument's highest note into the depths of its lowest, extending the interval to three octaves and a 5th: the rhetorical suggestion of a steep and almost palpable fall to death. Even the relationship of the E to F♯ on the words 'be stole' is manifestly paralleled in the guitar's E to F♮. The text-intrinsic nature of this music guarantees that its rhetorical identity, though wildly distorted, is kept effectively intact.

Variation IV similarly splinters the song's text, and many of its melodic phrases are invoked in the aggressive outbursts that characterize this movement. For example, in the variation's first two bars, the 'Come heavy sleep' phrase is transformed into three explosive fragment derivatives that shatter on the word 'sleep' in a series of repeated notes that dissipate in energy. Example 58 shows how this variation transforms other phrase fragments from the song into disturbing and repetitive paroxysms thereby emitting fragments that are effused with musical rhetoric. These variants in the rhetorical device of *reduplicatio* result in the amplification of the text's meanings.

Example 58: Britten, *Nocturnal*, Variation IV, 'Uneasy'

A particularly persuasive example of Britten's intuitive assimilation of musical rhetoric is to be found in Variation VI. In this movement, a mood of dark indolence only serves to make abstruse a surprisingly obedient affiliation with the theme. The soporific harmony is largely the result of a sophisticated layering of melodic fragments—like half-remembered remnants of 'Come Heavy Sleep'. Sometimes Britten superimposes two melodic fragments from the song within a single phrase; one of these melodic fragments often corresponds to a descending tenor part from the lute accompaniment to the song, which prefigures its use as the ground in the forthcoming Passacaglia. For instance, the first column of the top stave of Example 59 presents the opening phrase of the variation. The second column shows a melody extracted from that music, which is a clear reference to the 'Come heavy sleep' phrase. The third column further shows another extrapolated line, which is evidently a reference to the Passacaglia's ground. Example 59 disentangles many more citations and allusions, which make Variation VI so rich in its association with 'Come Heavy Sleep' despite its sense of disembodied reverie. This is not mere ambient orchestration; here, Britten creates hypnotic harmony by vertically stacking linear fragments of the song, and in so doing, ingeniously renders the musical rhetoric of the phrases into deeply felt harmonic equivalents.

Example 59: Britten, *Nocturnal*, Variation VI (the four phrases)

As example 59 shows, each of these phrases is framed by a four-note chord built on quartal harmony (though a major 3rd forms the upper two notes of the chord). This of course is constructed from the open 2nd, 3rd, 4th and 5th strings of the guitar and thus Britten exploits the 4th's rhetorical significance throughout *Nocturnal* by way of a number of highly idiosyncratic formulae fortuitously compatible with the instrument.

Example 60: Britten, *Nocturnal*, Variation V, accompaniment only

It is to Britten's credit that his reliance upon the instrument's open strings is neither evident (as is often the case in much guitar writing, particularly in the works of Villa-Lobos) nor inhibiting. On the contrary, Britten turns an apparent limitation to his advantage; the first seventeen bars of Variation V, for example, demonstrate a skilful implementation of quartal harmony. In bars 18-20, he further employs a series of parallel chords (executed by placing one finger of the left hand across all four inner strings—2 to 5), which unexpectedly bestows a harmonic dynamism on the accompaniment while retaining its established quartal configuration. Variation VII also demonstrates a prevalent use of quartal harmony, as most of the accompaniment music (in the lower stave) comprises notes using the open strings, the vast majority of which outline the 4th interval (see score). Britten's emphatic use of the perfect 4th, not only melodically but also through the formation of quartal harmonic configurations, intuitively taps into the Elizabethan sensibilities *vis-à-vis* this interval, which we discussed earlier. That interval's melancholic credentials are reaffirmed and realized as foundational to the Op. 70's *modus operandi*.

My exploration of Britten's intuitive cognition of musical rhetoric in *Nocturnal* demonstrates how he imbues abstract figurations with phrase fragments from 'Come Heavy Sleep' charged with musical rhetoric. However, the text-intrinsic hypothesis that has formed the basis of this section is further supported by what we know of Britten's compositional methods. Ronald Duncan reports that Britten admitted that 'he never had a purely musical thought unrelated to a verbal text context. In other words his method of composition was to face himself with a verbal problem and the musical answer emerged simultaneously...'.[239] This makes clear that Britten developed a unique compositional process whereby music carries on from words; where words disappear, music maintains a continuum. Thus, through a singular process of uninterrupted mutation, he captures the rhetorical power encapsulated in the words and music of Dowland's 'Come Heavy Sleep' and infuses it into *Nocturnal.* Britten's realization of abstract music that is nonetheless text-intrinsic is a unique compositional strategy—a process that often renders his instrumental music as 'vocal' as his dramatic work.

Transcendence as a System: Britten's Reverse Variation Form

> Heard melodies are sweet, but those unheard
> Are sweeter; therefore, ye soft pipes, play on;
> Not to the sensual ear, but, more endear'd,
> Pipe to the spirit ditties of no tone...[240]

Benjamin Britten was not at the cutting edge of musical innovation. While the high modernists of 20th-century composition strove to reinvent musical language by restructuring contour, as in Neoclassicism, or through the democratization of pitches, as in Serialism, Britten believed that traditional tonality could still be employed as an intact system. If he brought innovation to music, it was in the way he renovated old, established forms like the passacaglia and the chaconne, elevating them to a central position in 20th-century composition—a status they had enjoyed throughout the Renaissance and Baroque periods but had subsequently lost. Nowhere is Britten's genius for reinventing older forms more striking than in his novel approach to the well-established theme and variation form. There are many examples of his use of its standard layout in works such as *The Young Person's Guide to the Orchestra* or *Variations on a Theme of*

---

[239] Ronald Duncan, *Working with Britten: A Personal Memoir* (Devon: The Rebel Press, 1981), 103-4; cited in Claire Seymour, *The Operas of Benjamin Britten: Expression and Evasion* (Woodbridge: The Boydell Press, 2004), 5.

[240] John Keats, in Augustine Martin, ed., *Soundings* (Dublin: Gill & Macmillan, 1969), 123.

Frank Bridge. However, it is the application of theme and variation as a reverse structure in *Lachrymae, reflections on a song of Dowland*, *Nocturnal, after John Dowland* and *Cello Suite No. 3* that illustrates Britten's dramatically innovative approach to the form. Further to this, he demonstrates particular ingenuity in the unique methods by which he builds his structural schemata. This is achieved in each of the cited works by different means, because the particularity in form and disposition of their respective themes impacts his methodology in different ways.

An interesting facet of Britten's compositional approach, which feeds into our understanding of *Nocturnal*, comes to light in a letter by Julian Bream to the composer.[241] In it, Bream reminds Britten of a discussion they had had some time previously regarding an idea the composer had for a new guitar work, one that was remarkably evolved in terms of both structure and concept. What is intriguing is that, according to Bream, Britten had suggested the use of Dowland's 'Come Heavy Sleep' as a basis for a theme and variations, which would appear in reverse form. The document is also fascinating because we can palpably sense Bream's excitement at the prospect of receiving a solo work from Britten. His fervent invitation to the composer to discover what he calls the guitar's 'secret beauty' not only provides evidence of the guitarist's aspirations for a new work but also his fear that Britten might be distracted from the project—a fear that was clearly not unfounded considering the time it took for the piece to be eventually composed. The letter was written in January 1960, and it discusses a conversation that took place at some undisclosed period previous to that date. *Nocturnal* was not completed until November 1963. Judging by the precision of Bream's 'second-hand' description, this means that Britten's almost fully-formed concept for Op. 70 was held in the cold storage of his mind for at least three years and possibly much longer. As remarkable as this may seem, Britten himself has been unambiguous when commenting on his compositional methodology:

> Usually I have the music complete in my head before putting pencil to paper. That doesn't mean that every note has been composed, perhaps not one has, but I have worked out questions of form, texture, character, and so forth, in a very precise way so that I know exactly what effects I want and how I am going to achieve them.[242]

---

241 Letter from Julian Bream to Benjamin Britten, 12 January 1960. Source: Britten-Pears Library archive.

242 Murray Schafer, *British Composers in Interview* (London: Faber and Faber, 1963), 123.

In relation to *Nocturnal*, Britten's creative decision-making process was likely abetted by the fact that he had had a ready-made template in *Lachrymae*. That both of these works share a reverse variation format (albeit with significant differences) while also being based upon themes by Dowland further indicates their deep connection. In *Nocturnal* and *Lachrymae*, the arrival of the themes at the end, following the fractious journey through the preceding variations, engenders a type of transcendental release—an almost mystical state appealed to by the Gnosticism underpinning Dowland's compositional processes.

The notion that a composition might 'regress' towards the simplicity of its theme rather than 'progress' away from it towards greater complexity sheds significant light on Britten's method. A desire for simplicity marks all his work, in particular from the 1960s onwards; indeed, it became a distinct feature of his late style, of which *Nocturnal* is exemplary. In 1962, Pears remarked in an interview that '[Britten's] utterance is an exceedingly direct one. He always aims at simplicity and lucidity. He wants his music to be clear, but I don't think it necessarily follows that his mind or sensibility is a simple one.'[243] Britten himself makes simplicity a *modus operandi* of his compositional methodology; this passage relating to his views on orchestration sums up his position cogently.

> Generally speaking, I like to think of the smaller combinations of players, and I deplore the tendency of present-day audiences to expect only the luscious 'tutti' effect from an orchestra. I think this has been engendered by a 'Hollywood' method of scoring—both here and abroad—and also by the modern radio sets and electrical gramophones which tend to cut off the upper partials and give the orchestra a constant rounded, booming and 'fat' sound. I've always inclined to the clear and clean—the 'slender' sound of, say, Mozart or Verdi or Mahler—or even Tchaikovsky, if he is played in a restrained, though vital, way.[244]

In light of these comments, we can see how Britten's use of reverse variation reflects his aesthetic sensibilities; and it explains why he returned to this unique system on three occasions. Although his application of this structure was highly original (as I shall demonstrate), it was not strictly pioneering. There is at least one noteworthy precedent: *Istar: Symphonic Variations*, Op. 42, composed in 1896 by Vincent d'Indy. It is not known if Britten was aware of this work, although since it is perhaps d'Indy's most successful composition and his most widely performed, it is possible that Britten was familiar

[243] Colin Smythe, 'Interview with Peter Pears', in *Trinity News* (1962).
[244] Paul Kildea, ed., *Britten on Music*, 43.

with it. *Symphonic Variations* is a programmatic work based on the *Epic of Izdubar*—a story that describes the descent of Istar (the goddess of love, war and sexuality) into the Assyrian 'abode of the dead' leaving, with each step, pieces of her clothing behind. Such a programmatic scheme provided d'Indy with the perfect blueprint for a reversed series of variations progressively diminishing in intricacy towards the ultimate simplicity of the theme—a process intended to imply Istar's eventual nudity. D'Indy himself comments that he

> proceeded from the complex to the simple, causing the chief theme to be born little by little, as if emerging from the special harmony presented in the first version. Thus the theme denudes itself successively of all the ornaments which veil it, and appears in simplicity only at the conclusion...as did Istar in the legend, after putting off her seven veils.[245]

It is also possible that *Symphony No. 2* by Arthur Honegger provided a model for Britten. The work's finale displays something comparable to a reverse variation form when the trumpet at the end highlights a chorale tune the harmonic and melodic attributes of which have been discreetly prepared by previously heard material. While speculations regarding Britten's knowledge or otherwise of these precedents can never be conclusive, it is likely that at least one of these works provided a general model for him. He nonetheless made the reverse variation his own with three imaginative renovations in Opp. 48, 70 and 87.

Composed for the Russian cellist, Mstislav Rostropovich, *Cello Suite No. 3* differs from the other two works that concern us here in that it uses as a basis for variation no less than four Russian themes: three folksongs ('Mourning Song', 'Autumn' and 'Street Song', based on arrangements by Tchaikovsky), and the well-known hymn used in the Russian Orthodox Church, the *Kontakion*. Into the texture of the work's musical material, Britten interlaces melodic fragments from the four themes allowing them to emerge fully in simple succession only in the final movement. In his adaptation, the *Kontakion*—deeply symbolic of Russian identity (it was also used by Rachmaninov in his *Vespers* and by Tchaikovsky in his *Pathétique* Symphony)—incorporates Shostakovich's famous DSCH moniker.[246] Therefore, just as *Lachrymae*

---

245 W.R. Anderson, 'Wireless Notes', in *The Musical Times* Vol. 79, No. 1139 (1938): 31.

246 The DSCH motif is derived from the German transliteration of his name: **D**imitri **SCH**ostakovich—D, E♭, C and B♭.

and *Nocturnal* can be seen as tributes to John Dowland, the violist William Primrose (for whom Op. 48 was written) and Julian Bream, the employment of the Russian folk tunes and the Slavonic hymn at the very end of *Cello Suite No. 3* is a clear tribute to Shostakovich and Rostropovich, both of whom were close friends of Britten from the early 1960s.

If *Cello Suite No. 3* presented Britten at his most Russian, *Lachrymae* served to strengthen his connection to England's Elizabethan music. The theme used for Op. 48 comprises the first eight bars of Dowland's 'If My Complaints Could Passions Move', the fourth song from *The First Booke of Songes or Ayres*.

Example 61: Dowland, 'If My Complaints Could Passions Move' (vocal part), bars 1-8

The vocal part of these eight bars serves as the basis for the ensuing variations, as they do for the tremulous 'lento' Introduction. The first clear reference to the theme, however, only appears in the piano's bass part at bar 9.

Example 62: Britten, *Lachrymae*, bars 9-16

From this we can see that Britten preferred to fashion the variations as undelineated 'reflections'; he clearly wished to avoid declarative allusions to the theme. However, just as the unfolding variations allow the theme to insinuate itself into the listener's consciousness, Britten introduces an unexpected element in Variation VI: another Dowland song 'Flow My Tears', which in its instrumental version is known as the *Lachrymae antiquae*, hence the work's title.[247]

247 'Flow My Tears' became Dowland's most popular lute song. He himself published a series of seven pavans, each based on themes derived from its melody: *Lachrimae, or Seaven Teares, Figured in Seaven Passionate Pavans*, for five viols and lute. It became one of the best-known collections of consort music in his time. His pavan *Lachrymae antiquae* was also extremely popular in the 17th century and was used by many composers as a theme for variations.

Example 63: Britten, *Lachrymae*, first 15 bars of Variation VI

The inclusion of 'Flow My Tears' at this point has the skilful effect of renovating the work without in the least undermining its harmonic and melodic integrity. Variations VII-X return to the original eight-bar theme as a source. However, after the urgent tremolos of Variation X have reached their climax and the music begins to recede towards the work's peaceful conclusion, Britten, with an ingenious twist, replaces the original theme with the second half of Dowland's 'If My Complaints Could Passions Move'—a very beautiful part of the song that we have not heard until now.

Example 64: Dowland, 'If My Complaints Could Passions Move' (vocal part, second section)

Example 65: Britten, *Lachrymae*, final 16 bars

With startling *legerdemain*, Britten draws us unwittingly, in Graham Johnson's words, to the 'almost miraculous unveiling of something we had not realised we were waiting for'.[248] This is the moment towards which the entire work aspires; and yet the surprise on hearing the second part of the song, new material but patiently, inconspicuously primed, is a highly effective moment that captures the transcendental quality that Dowland himself strove for in his music. Such sublimity is underpinned, engendered indeed, by directional forces accruing from the unique physiognomy of its reverse variation structure:

Table 1: Structural Plan of *Lachrymae*

Section	Source
Introduction	Based on the **first 8 bars** of 'If My Complaints Could Passions Move'
Variation 1	as above
Variation 2	as above
Variation 3	as above
Variation 4	as above
Variation 5	as above
Variation 6	Based on 'Flow My Tears'

248 Graham Johnson, *Britten, Voice & Piano*, 109-117.

Variation 7	Based on the **first 8 bars** of 'If My Complaints Could Passions Move'
Variation 8	as above
Variation 9	as above
Variation 10	as above
Theme	Based on the **Second Part** of 'If My Complaints Could Passions Move'

Analysis of the reverse variation structures of Opp. 48 and 87 helps contextualize Britten's use of the method in *Nocturnal*, which is yet again employed with great originality. I would like to present an analytical reading that contains both a structural outline and a sub-structural interpretation. A straightforward overview of the formal contour of *Nocturnal* reveals seven variations, a passacaglia and the concluding theme, 'Come Heavy Sleep'.

Table 2: Structural outline of *Nocturnal*

Var	Var	Var	Var	Var	Var	Var		**Dowland**
I	**II**	**III**	**IV**	**V**	**VI**	**VII**	**Passacaglia**	***Come Heavy Sleep***

However, closer observation reveals that Britten may have conceived the work upon a different sub-structural concept. The variations demonstrate that the treatment of thematic material in most cases is intentionally disconnected, incomplete and incoherent, reflecting the subject matter of the work. The overall effect is one of intentional dislocation and inchoate articulation, which is in keeping with a key aspect of Britten's language—the inability to coherently express inner thoughts and desires. However, there is one variation for which such fragmentation is most certainly not the case, one variation where Britten's instrumental writing is so coherent and oratorical in its linear though melismatic writing that it assumes the quality of an independent vocal part. Variation I is so closely affiliated to 'Come Heavy Sleep' that the song is effectively replicated almost in full, albeit in Britten's inimitable voice. This close structural and melodic correlation means that the text of 'Come Heavy Sleep' can convincingly be sung to all the instrumental lines of Variation I.

Example 66: Britten, *Nocturnal*, Variation I[249]

249 The word setting here is just one of a number of possible variants.

There is little doubt, therefore, that Britten intended Variation I to be a complete representation of the Dowland's song, a kind of 20th-century version of it made manifest in *his* compositional idiolect. This argument points to a complete psychological union with the musical persona of Dowland. The seamless, osmotic transformation of Dowland's 'Come Heavy Sleep' into Britten's rendering of it represents a comprehensive intellective and musical interiorization of one composer's personality by another. Britten himself makes the connection when he tells us that

> ...*Nocturnal*...has some very, to me, disturbing images in it...inspired by this—the Dowland song, which of course itself has very strange undertones in it. Dowland was a person who perhaps even consciously realized the importance of dreams.[250]

The symbolic amalgamation revealed in Variation I evidences Britten's profound musical and psychological affiliation to Dowland's world, and his embedded sense of inheritance of the Elizabethan vocal style. In the context of the structural assessment undertaken here, this new understanding thus suggests a radically altered reading. If it is accepted that Op. 70 both opens with 'Come Heavy Sleep' and closes with it, the structure of the entire work consequently takes on a framed form:

Table 3: New Structural Reading of *Nocturnal*

Britten	Var	Var	Var	Var	Var	Var		**Dowland**
Come Heavy Sleep	**II**	**III**	**IV**	**V**	**VI**	**VII**	**Passa-caglia**	***Come Heavy Sleep***

Where does this leave the framed material? Closer observation reveals Britten's innate sense of structural balance. Of the six remaining variations, two (II and V) are fast, energetic and aggressive. These are followed by variations constrained by more subjective dispositions: passive and introspective movements particularly resonant of dream and sleep.[251] This assortment of dynamic, extroverted music on the one

250 Christopher Palmer, ed., *The Britten Companion* (London: Faber & Faber, 1984), 93.

251 Variation IV does exhibit some aspects of invigorated angularity but its highly fragmentary nature does not quite achieve the sustained level of energized movement that Variations II and V generate.

hand, and reflective, introverted music on the other, implies a further stratification of the remaining six variations. Additionally, the rest marks at the opening of Variations II and V (the only such markings employed in all the variations) provide visual signs that indicate some sort of intended compartmentalization sub-dividing the six variations into two groups of three.

Table 4: Further Structural Reading of *Nocturnal*

[REST] Fast	Slow	Slow	[REST] Fast	Slow	Slow
Var II	Var III	Var IV	Var V	Var VI	Var VII

The passacaglia, for its part, clearly divides into three sections—a grouping made evident by the headings Britten gives to each: 1) *measured* 2) *lively* and 3) *starting broadly*. This latest sub-division thus offers a similar structural format to the two groupings we have observed for the six variations. As a result, the overall picture for the entire work takes on a remarkably balanced profile—three groups each containing three sub-sections framed on either side by the song, 'Come Heavy Sleep'.

Table 5: A sub-structural interpretation of *Nocturnal*

Britten's	Variations I-IV	Variations V - VII	Passacaglia	Dowland's
Come Heavy Sleep	I) Very agitated	V) March-like	*measured*	*Come Heavy Sleep*
	II) Restless	VI) Dreaming	*lively*	
	III) Uneasy	VII) Gently rocking	*starting broadly*	

While this sub-structural interpretation provides a radical revision of a standard reading of Op. 70's formal design, it *is* consistent with various types of framing devices Britten often uses for his works including *Serenade* Op. 31 and *Songs from the Chinese*, to mention just two.[252] Such a revision allows for a more sophisticated reading of Britten's approach to structure; it suggests an alternative lens through which to observe his innate attraction to simplicity, not just in terms of content but also of formal design as a malleable, dynamic organization and not simply as a fixed repository. Indeed, an important facet of Britten's compositional practice from Op. 70 onwards is a growing desire for musical clarity; this is often paralleled by quasi-aleatoric notation and, occasionally, a less rigorous formal control. As we shall see, preliminary compositional kernels observable in *Nocturnal* that evidence this new malleability germinate into fuller stylistic traits in *Curlew River* and subsequent works.[253]

While the particularly close affiliation of the two Dowland-inspired works would seem to leave *Cello Suite No. 3* somewhat isolated, further examination of Op. 87 reveals a greater connection with them than one might suspect; especially if we view them as having a shared preoccupation with death and the search for innocence. Firstly, it should be remembered that the *Kontakion*, with which the suite finishes, is a hymn for the dead.[254] Secondly, the first of the three folksongs used in the work, 'Mourning Song', laments a dying boy. In addition, there is evidence to suggest that some musical material and certain narratives from *Cello Suite No. 3* resurface in Britten's final opera, *Death in Venice*, written directly after it. For example, the theme of the suite's third folksong, 'Street Song', is a pentatonic tune in A major. This detail would be inconsequential were it not for the fact that Britten frequently employs Balinese-style pentatonic music (often in A major) when exploring themes of innocence and the desire for the perfection of youth, both sexual and spiritual—a subject we have already encountered in the chapter on *Songs from the Chinese*. In *Death in Venice*, Aschenbach's object of desire, the youthful Tadzio, is frequently represented by gamelan-derived pentatonic music in A major. The opera's *dénouement* sees Aschenbach die in a paroxysm of desire. Thus, an inevitable drive towards death is paralleled in *Cello*

[252] The horn music that comprises the 'Prologue' and 'Epilogue' of *Serenade* exemplifies this framing technique. The same device in *Songs from the Chinese* relates to Britten's choice of texts. For the first and final songs, he chose poems from *The Book of Songs*. These anonymous and rather declamatory texts date from between 7th and 10th centuries BCE and frame the four central poems written by poets from a much later period. Britten used the framing device to create a kind of protective shield for the more emotional poems placed within. See Chapter Three.

[253] This point is further developed in the section of Chapter Five entitled, Nocturnal: Receptions and Assessments.

[254] See Appendix VII.

Suite No. 3 not only in its use of pentatonic scales in A major, but also with the concluding hymn for the departed. The work's valedictory quality is further heightened by the knowledge that Britten was already critically ill by the time its premiere took place in 1974.

This penetrative reading of *Cello Suite No. 3* brings it back into a closer relationship with the other two reverse-variation works. It is clear that apart from imaginatively renovating an old form, Britten specifically employs reverse variation to address themes of sleep, dreams, death, the unattainable perfection of youth and the transcendent. As I will discuss in due course, he also employs the passacaglia repeatedly in close narrative association with death. It comes as no surprise therefore that the passacaglia is recruited by Britten to work alongside reverse variation in two of the three works under scrutiny here. However, I want to argue that *Lachrymae*, *Nocturnal* and *Cello Suite No. 3* do not merely occupy similar thematic ground, but more pertinently employ specific technical schemata to engender the music with metaphysical import. These works utilize complex reverse variation procedures to mechanistically and systematically distill the musical material and allow it to 'unconceal' its transcendental simplicity.

'Incomprehensible Repose'—Britten's *Nocturnal*-passacaglia

Considering the inherent limitations of the guitar, the passacaglia of Britten's *Nocturnal* is a *tour de force* of technical writing; it represents one of the most sustained, sophisticated and complex musical arguments in the instrument's repertoire. This alone makes it worthy of special attention. Additionally, Britten returned repeatedly to the passacaglia and a number of his innovations to this form are featured in the *Nocturnal*-passacaglia. An assessment of the latter thus requires a contextual reading of the passacaglia and how Britten helped revitalized it as an important 20th-century form.

A standard dictionary definition of the passacaglia states that it is 'an instrumental musical composition consisting of variations usually in a ground in moderately slow triple time'.[255] Though this single-sentence definition can hardly be expected to sufficiently describe a genre spanning hundreds of years, it does refer to what may be the passacaglia's defining attribute—'variations over a ground'. Donald Tovey's definition of a 'ground' is still valuable: 'the constant repetition

[255] Merriam-Webster's Collegiate Dictionary, Eleventh Edition (Merriam-Webster, 2004), 905.

of a single sentence in the bass, which provides a rigid principle, immediately intelligible and capable of indefinite extension and fine cumulative effect.'[256] The ground, however, has been a standard feature of numerously specified genres throughout the ages, as Wilfrid Greenhouse Allt explains:

> A thirteenth and fourteenth century *pes* is referred to by historians as a *ground-bass* or *basso ostinato*. The plainsong, secular tune, hexachord or other device which, like a scaffolding, supports the melodious interweaving of other voices in the fifteenth and sixteenth century Masses and Motets, is called a *ground*. Sixteenth century airs have a personal name attached—*My Ladye Nevel's Grownde*, or the name of a dance—*Galliard Grounde*. One part in a consort of lutes is often *A Ground*. The violinist who extemporised divisions in the seventeenth century, did so to a ground in the bass. In the eighteenth century a ground-bass is sometimes named after the composer, such as *Dr. Pepusch's Ground*, and a reference to compositions as 'in the Purcell manner,' sometimes implies 'on a ground'.[257]

Notwithstanding this *combinatoire* of usage and practice, the application of the phrase 'in the Purcell manner' indicates both the extent to which the ground, or passacaglia, was ubiquitously established as a compositional practice by the late 17th century and the degree to which Henry Purcell's signature as a composer had come to embody that device.[258] Brought to its pinnacle in England with Purcell and later in Germany with Bach and Handel, the passacaglia fell out of favour for most of the 19th century—Beethoven's *32 Variations* for piano and the finale of Brahms's *Fourth Symphony* represent two major exceptions—only to tentatively re-emerge in 1906 with Max Reger's *Introduction, Passacaglia and Fugue for Two Pianos*. Whilst Reger's work developed from a close association with the long tradition of Germanic contrapuntalism, it was the two major revolutionary systems in musical language that took hold in the early 20th century—Serialism and Neoclassicism—that truly instigated the reintroduction of the

---

256 Donald Francis Tovey, *Essays in Musical Analysis* (London, Oxford University Press, 1944), 9.

257 Wilfrid Greenhouse Allt, *Treatment of Ground* (London: Taylor & Francis, 1945/6), 73.

258 The evidence for this can be readily seen in works such as 'May Her Blest Example' from *Ode for Queen Mary*, 1690; the Chaconne and Passacaglia from the masque *King Arthur* of 1691; 'O Let Me Weep' from *The Fairy Queen* and 'Wondrous Machine!' from *Hail! Bright Cecilia*, both from 1692; 'A Prince of Glorious Race Descended' from *Ode on the Duke of Gloucester's Birthday*, 1695; and 'When I Am Laid To Earth' or 'Dido's Lament' from *Dido and Aeneas* of 1688, which for many is exemplary of the form.

passacaglia.

For composers in both camps, it was a simple device that helped bring a 'rigid principle' back into formal structure. Schoenberg displayed a particular attachment to it while Stravinsky and Hindemith obviously found its ostinato attribute a beneficially controlling influence. Although Britten's use of the passacaglia allowed him to resonate with these broader European trends, his embracement of the device had more to do with his desire to inherit the 'Purcellian manner'. Purcell's innate skill at handling the ground and his expertise in musical rhetoric became very important touchstones for Britten. Indeed, apart from Hindemith, he is the composer who, more than most, adopted the passacaglia as a distinguishing feature of his music. In more recent years, György Ligeti developed an equally strong affiliation to the form with his signature *lamentoso* ground. Ezra Pound's early 20th-century imperative to 'make it new' is robustly answered by Britten and Ligeti who, building on the early modernists, took a quintessential Renaissance and Baroque form and made it into a central, vital feature of mid- to late 20th-century compositional practice.

Britten's innovation of the passacaglia is formulated in the way he consciously works against the restrictions imposed by prescriptive formulae. Indeed, it is in the torsions between the disciplining, controlling ground, which acts as a harmonic determinant, and the expressive material that seeks to extricate itself from this ground that Britten creates some of his most dynamic and dramatic music.[259] This is why he locates passacaglias at crucial points in his operas and song-cycles; they lead to the dramatic apogee of a scene or cycle. Similarly, its arrival in *Nocturnal*, following the deep psychological investigations of the seven preceding variations, is designed to carry the weight of that experience to its dramatic *dénouement*. Britten's ability to procure highly emotive results from the passacaglia explains his frequent use of it. Among the major works that employ the passacaglia or the chaconne are the *Piano Concerto*, the *Violin Concerto*, *Serenade*, *Passacaglia from Peter Grimes*, the *Holy Sonnets of John Donne*, *The Rape of Lucretia*, *Nocturnal* and the second and third string quartets and cello suites.

The imminent, impending character of the passacaglia's repeating

---

[259] This dialectical process foreshadows Ligeti's similarly anarchic relationship to ostinati; see Benjamin Dwyer, 'Transformational Ostinati in György Ligeti's Sonatas for Solo Cello and Solo Viola', in *György Ligeti: Of Foreign Lands and Strange Sounds*, eds Louise Duchesneau and Wolfgang Marx (Woodbridge: Boydell & Brewer, 2011), 19-50.

ground is the likely reason Britten frequently equates the form with themes of death and darkness. Not surprisingly, these appear most effectively in the dramatic works. Among the most well-known examples is the passacaglia interlude in *Peter Grimes*—an instrumental lament that portrays Grimes' insanity and prefigures his looming death. After Lucretia's suicide in the *Rape of Lucretia*, Britten employs an increasingly agitated passacaglia that climaxes in the death of Miles. The ground is worked *against* death in the *Holy Sonnets of John Donne*—'death shall be no more; Death, thou shalt die'. In this context, the use of the passacaglia in *Nocturnal*, with its ruminations on darkness, sleep, dream and death, reinforces a long-established practice in Britten's music.

In technical terms, Britten's essays in passacaglia form are concerned with more than the absorption of 17th-century musical rhetoric as manifest in the works of Purcell. His innovation of the form emerges from an inventive combination of two traditions; he establishes the rhetorically-infused ground as a launching pad for the exposition of dialectical material in the form of fugato style with its attendant subjects and argumentative counter-subjects. Darrell Handel puts this innovation into context:

> Britten's most significant and original contribution to the art of the passacaglia is his abandonment of the traditional monothematic approach. His method of featuring, against the ground, contrasting thematic material of equal importance, and maintaining with masterly skill a fluctuating polarity between the two, are what give his passacaglias their remarkable expressive force and vitality...[260]

Britten's striking combination of these two technical devices is pertinently captured in the 'Dirge' from *Serenade*, Op. 31. The structural modifications exemplified by the 'Dirge' have particular significance for the *Nocturnal*-passacaglia where Britten achieves something rather similar, though in a more concisely constructed way and with some distinguishing modifications. While one might expect the ground of a passacaglia to be in the bass part (as Donald Tovey instructs us), Britten, in the 'Dirge', characteristically renovates the form by giving it to the voice. The ground repeats nine times. Britten introduces a fugato subject in the cellos and double basses at bar 6: one bar before the ground's second outing. When a new fugato subject is

---

260 Darrell Handel, 'Britten's Use of the Passacaglia', in *Tempo, New Series* No. 94 (1970): 6.

presented in bar 10, its counter-subject enters underneath it.[261]

Example 67: Britten, 'Dirge', passacaglia 'ground', fugato theme, and fugato counter-melody

These three strands of music represent the essential building blocks of the entire movement. As expected, the ground does not alter, but running throughout its nine repetitions, Britten creates complex polythematic interlacing of fugato subject and counter-subject that builds upon and theatrically dramatizes the chilling message of the 'Dirge'. This stands as a perfect model by which to study the *Nocturnal*-passacaglia, which evidences the composer's advanced skills in the device. The result is not only technically assured but also distinctively innovative in three ways: firstly, in its fundamental structural format; secondly, in the absorption of musical rhetoric into both the ground and its contrasting material; and thirdly, in its radical modification of the ground itself. I now want to focus on these renovations of passacaglia form.

261 The vertical relationship between the ground, fugato subject and counter-subject is not treated as sacrosanct by Britten at subsequent entries. Sometimes the fugato-subject arrives a bar before the ground commences, sometimes a bar after.

As I have indicated, the passacaglia from *Nocturnal* is pivotally placed between seven variations and the theme, 'Come Heavy Sleep'. The passacaglia itself is divided into three sections: 1) *measured* 2) *lively*, and 3) *starting broadly*. Its ground derives from an inner voice of the lute accompaniment to the theme (or the tenor part in its consort version).

Example 68: Britten, *Nocturnal*, Passacaglia 'ground' and its source

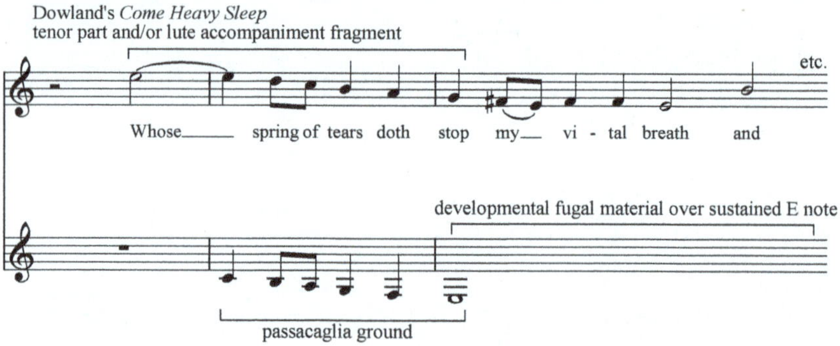

As the lower stave of Example 68 demonstrates, the *Nocturnal*-passacaglia has a unique structural outline. Rather than placing the contrasting material directly over and thus simultaneously with the entire ground, as would normally be the case, Britten activates the contrasting material only when the last note of the ground has been sounded. This 'innovation' is employed as a direct result of the guitar's idiosyncratic nature. Holding back the exposition of material until the point when the open, low E string resonates, frees the guitarist's hands to execute more complex figurations. Typical of Britten's remarkable ability to turn a liability into an asset, the temporal separation of the 'rigid principle' (the ground) and the contrasting thematic material, which leads to an alternating 'call and response', only adds to the dialectic tension that is already a distinguishing feature of his passacaglias (see Example 69).

While the contrasting material that appears above the ground is what creates the fugal structure, as it is derived from fragments of the song, it brings with it a potent rhetorical agency. The passacaglia is thus both an example of contrapuntal architecture and a *bricolage* of rhetorically fused fragments. Thus, Britten's innovative model for the passacaglia as exemplified by the *dirge* is developed a stage further in the *Nocturnal*-passacaglia. The polarization of Darrell Handel's argument (already cited) that Britten's method of featuring 'against the ground, contrasting thematic material'—a musical rhetoric ground and a 'European' fugato style—now requires modification because both ground and developing material, call and response, are infused with a Dowland-inspired musical rhetoric. Example 69 demonstrates how Britten patiently builds his fugal constructions. Every phrase of this material appears once the descending ground has been stated. On each return, phrase lengths are extended to suggest the unconscious piecing together of half-remembered song fragments.

Example 69: Britten, *Nocturnal*, Passacaglia, structural plan of fugal subjects and counter-subjects

The top stave shows how Britten forms the fugal subject through the prolongation of the initial two-note fragment—F♯, B. This unfolding of the fugal material continues for five refrains of the ground. Then, at bar 6, the counter-subject is introduced (centre stave) under the fugal subject, which now resides a minor 3rd higher than before (starting on the notes A, D). This initiates a further prolongation of the fugal and counter-subject material. As the music unfolds, the rhetorical potential of the text is considerably dramatized by the increasingly extended material, which becomes progressively more complex. This continues for another four rotations of the ground until, at bar 9, an additional counter-subject is introduced (bottom stave) below the fugal subject, which again enters a major 3rd higher than previously on the notes C♯ and F♯.

From this point, the first section of the passacaglia—*measured*—continues to expand the fugal material but in a more extemporized fashion. The architectonic, sequential system that constructed the fugal subjects and counter-subjects in three measured phases is now jettisoned for more improvisatory figurations. Unfolding in apparently chaotic gestures, a complex arpeggiated texture ensues, which on closer inspection, demonstrates embedded *figurae* emanating from Dowland. Example 70 shows these extended arpeggios from bar 17 to bar 20 (page 11 of the score).

Example 70: Britten, *Nocturnal*, Passacaglia, from bar 17

The notation here implies two strata. If the upper voice is extrapolated from these busy flourishes and then inverted, we see that this passage surreptitiously emits *figurae* that closely correspond to a number of text fragments from 'Come Heavy Sleep'. The infusion into abstract music of melodic figurations potent with rhetorical agency gives the music a text-intrinsic quality.

In light of further structural innovations in the *Nocturnal*-passacaglia that we will presently observe, Darrell Handel's point that Britten's use of passacaglia is relatively conservative needs to be reconsidered:

> ...in the degree of alteration which he has introduced into the repetitions of the ground itself...those in *Peter Grimes, The Rape of Lucretia* and *Serenade* are completely strict, and only slight modifications appear in those in *The Turn of the Screw* and the *Cello Symphony*; the diversity and importance of the thematic material which is unfolded over the rotations of the ground make any change in the ground itself superfluous...The strictness of Britten's grounds also means that the sense of forward movement lies entirely in the added material.[262]

Although this may be the case for the works cited by Handel, the *Nocturnal*-passacaglia does not easily fit into such classification. In its first section (*measured*), the ground does indeed function as a strictly stable scaffold, with no alterations to its metric contour. In this regard, it complies with Handel's thesis that Britten's passacaglias work by juxtaposing 'against the ground, contrasting thematic material' and, pertinently, that any 'sense of forward movement lies entirely with the added material'. However, from the second section (*lively*) onwards, and running through the third section (*starting broadly*), the ground begins to take on new qualities that markedly alter the function Britten previously delegated to it. From this point onwards, the scaffolding itself comes under constant attack from the contrasting material's interjections; the previously rigorous ground allows itself to be implicated in the emotional argument it had heretofore been attempting to contain. The long established and previously stable rhythmic identity of the ground becomes increasingly distorted as it continues to be more actively involved in the impulsive drive of the dramatic narrative.

Therefore, it can be said that from this point onwards the beneficial polarization of the two distinct compositional opponents at play here—the stable ground and the contrasting material above it—has broken

---

262 Darrell Handel, 'Britten's Use of the Passacaglia', in *Tempo, New Series* No. 94 (1970): 2-3.

down. The intense gravitational pull of the dramatic imperative has engulfed all the musical material of the passacaglia into its drive towards a fatal *dénouement*.

Example 71: Britten, *Nocturnal*, Passacaglia ground, bars 25-34

Because of its quickening pace, thickening textures, more incessant reiteration and increasingly neurotic repetitions, the ground becomes an equal source for the escalating emotional intensity of the passacaglia. Indeed, it soon outflanks the contrasting material and cannibalizes its own function as a stabilizing foundation by becoming a generator of unrestrained dynamism and drama. Out of control, the ground ultimately becomes the driving force behind its own termination; the formally reliable 'rigid principle' actively participates in its own final disintegration.

Example 72 outlines the ground's final gestures and its ultimate fragmentation as it scatters in multiple directions. The entire passage, headed 'with force' (*con forza*), from bar 36 to 42 comprises a series of rapid scales initially played *ff*, which are violently interrupted by explosive arpeggios in E major. At this point, the *Nocturnal*-passacaglia speaks to an irrevocable fate.

Example 72: Britten, *Nocturnal*, Passacaglia, from bar 36 'with force' to bar 42

This entire section comprises 19 six-note scales that correlate exactly to the pitch relationship of the ground. These ground samples do not always appear in a neatly arranged order, but are sometimes grouped together to make longer scales, or they overlap and take off in contrary motion to previous ones. The interjecting E major arpeggios, though aggressive at first, eventually become more calm and ultimately have the effect of dissipating the energy of the entire passage until such time that an E major tonal centre is established. The 19th and final sample has returned in register to the original ground—C, B, A, G, F, E—which for the last time brings the music, in a moment of transcendent beauty, slowly towards the theme for which we have been waiting so long: 'Come Heavy Sleep'.

The *Nocturnal*-passacaglia's blind advance towards its own destruction has more than a touch of tragedy to it—just like the dramatic movement towards the *peripeteia* in Greek tragedy; that point beyond which things will never be the same. The driven nature of the passacaglia, its mechanical *reductio ad absurdum* of hope, fits within the rubric of tragic drama's essential sense of catastrophe—Oedipus's hubris immediately comes to mind. This is a characteristic that remains beyond the grasp of rational understanding. It also has all the hallmarks of a futile death wish. In this regard, Britten's *Nocturnal*-passacaglia pre-empts some of those mechanico-rhythmic *Études* by Ligeti that seem to insist on self-destruction or Jean Tinguely's collapsing sculptures that shake and gyrate themselves to rubble in a humorous, postmodern 'bowing out'. Britten is no postmodernist, however, and explanations need to be found for such apparent negativity. George Steiner outlines certain fundamental attributes of Greek tragedy to which I think Britten would intuitively relate: 'Tragedies such as *Oedipus* and [*King*] *Lear* do show a kind of progress toward self-knowledge. But it is achieved at the price of ruin. Tragic personages are educated by calamity and they reach their fulfilment in death.[263] Britten's employment of the passacaglia certainly resonates with this sentiment as the 'Dirge' from *Serenade* and the *Passacaglia from Peter Grimes* both indicate. However, when Britten composes a complex and troubling passacaglia that ultimately leads to a simplified, innocent theme, a more subtle reading is required. Again, Steiner provides a way forward:

> Tragic drama tells us that the spheres of reason, order, and justice are terribly limited and that no progress in our science or technical resources will enlarge their relevance. Outside and within man is l'autre, the 'otherness' of the world. Call it what you will: a hidden or malevolent God, blind fate, the solicitations of hell, or the brute fury of our animal blood. It waits for us in ambush at the crossroads. It mocks us and destroys us. In certain rare instances, it leads us after destruction to some incomprehensible repose.[264]

This reading of tragedy fundamentally differs from those works of Ligeti and Tinguely whose self-destructive devices may be interpreted as essentially nihilistic. Although Britten's *Nocturnal*-passacaglia has all the manic drive to take itself to an ultimate end game and the blind impulse to push the limits of a desire for death to its final point of imminent annihilation, the arrival of the theme at the end of such a

---

263 George Steiner, *The Death of Tragedy* (London, Faber and Faber, 1961), 169.
264 Ibid., 9.

self-destructing ground brings some strange appeasement. Dowland's 'Come Heavy Sleep', in light of *Nocturnal*-passacaglia's terrible struggle, serves as both the work's 'fulfilment in death' and a type of 'incomprehensible repose'.

The Perfect Lie: Tonal Ambiguities and Subversive Forces in *Nocturnal*

> The lie, the perfect lie, about people whom we know, about the relations that we have had with them, about our motive for some action, a motive which we express in totally different terms, the lie as to what we are, whom we love, what we feel with regard to the person who loves us...that lie is one of the only things in the world that can open a window for us upon what is novel, unknown, that can awaken in us sleeping senses to the contemplation of universes that otherwise we should never have known.[265]

During my analysis of *Songs from the Chinese*, I posited a number of more or less unambiguous readings. I expounded, for example, upon Britten's eroticization and idealization of youth in 'The Herd Boy'. Although commentaries by other critics may differ, there is certainly some solid data to support my interpretation. This mainly pertains to private commentaries Britten made in letters, which allows a reasonable degree of certainty on the matter. However, it is somewhat more problematic to arrive at decisive conclusions about extra-musical meaning with regard to instrumental music. Notwithstanding this dilemma, within defined social and artistic boundaries, general music scholarship has come to accept that music may have implications beyond its non-denotative and abstract condition. In the case of Britten scholarship, I am not alone in identifying the composer's strategies for both concealing and expressing his sexuality through music. These tactics include his use of bi-tonal structures, harmonic symbolism and the employment of melodic, harmonic and rhythmic entities for subversive purposes. Many specialists have explored these processes in detail.[266] I, on the other hand, wish to broadly contextualize this

265 Marcel Proust, *Remembrance of Things Past*, trans. Scott Moncrieff (London: Wordsworth Editions, 2006), 622-3.

266 See Philip Brett, *Music and Sexuality in Britten*, ed. George E. Haggerty (Berkeley: University of California Press, 2006); Claire Seymour, *The Operas of Benjamin Britten: Expression and Evasion* (Woodbridge: The Boydell Press, 2004); Phillip Brett, 'Eros and Orientalism in Britten's Operas', in *Queering the Pitch: The New Gay and Lesbian Musicology*, eds Philip Brett, Elizabeth Wood and Gary C. Thomas (New York: Routledge, 1994) 235-56; Mervyn Cooke, *Britten and the Far East* (Woodbridge: Boydell Press, 2009);

analysis of *Nocturnal* by referring generally to these strategies in order to widen the work's interpretative potential.

In relation to the exploration of latent meaning in instrumental music, *Nocturnal* represents a hybrid case, as it is in fact clearly associated with quite definable themes such as sleep, darkness, death and melancholy. It also deliberates upon a text and its musical setting by Dowland from which motivic quotations, though purely instrumental, may with some perseverance be identified and interpreted; indeed I have argued for Op. 70's text-intrinsic qualities. However, there are numerous elements in *Nocturnal* that cannot be so readily attributed to its dominant themes or Dowland's source material. Such features are cultivated in processes of tonal ambiguity, musical components that are self-subversive, manufactured binaries and the juxtaposition of musical arguments that are often simultaneously contradictory. In *Nocturnal*, there are musical phenomena that we hear for which no specific analytical explanation can be offered. This is where Britten's music functions symbolically: its messages are experienced but cannot be elucidated with empirical certainty.

Many musicologists, particularly those working in more recent years, have explored what could be described as Britten's secret designs—musical constructions representing a private world of feeling but which are not intended to be rendered explicitly. We have seen that from a very early age Britten addressed weighty subjects such as dreams, violence, loss and death. However, it would appear that certain themes were more successfully kept under wraps; Britten's homosexuality and his fascination with youthful innocence, including the more troubling implications of that desire, are central among these. It is true that as the years went on, Britten did 'come out' to a certain extent. Although his operatic themes always tended toward the non-heteronormative, the writing of *Death in Venice* in the early 1970s was certainly something of an 'open letter'. However, despite the increasing liberalism of British society, Britten, in contrast to many of his contemporaries in a similar position, felt unable to fully declare his sexual identity, and this conflict may be seen as a central cause for much of the torment and anguish that can be heard in his music.

A painting that can still be seen in the Red House provides some

---

Lloyd Whitesell, 'Britten's Dubious Trysts', in *Journal of the American Musicological Society* Vol. 56, No. 3 (2003): 637-694; and Mervyn Cooke: 'Britten's "Prophetic Song": tonal symbolism in *Billy Budd*', in *Benjamin Britten Billy Budd*, eds Mervyn Cooke and Philip Reed. (Cambridge: Cambridge University Press, 1993), 85-110.

evidence of Britten's tortured feelings around sexual identity and openness. Apparently, in its first complete version, the artist depicted Britten and Pears sitting side by side with one of Pears's arms leaning affectionately on Britten's shoulders. The scene was so discomfiting for Britten, however, that he demanded that the embrace be painted out of the scene. The result is a rather stultifying portrait that gives the impression that an arm is somehow missing. This is a painting that Britten and Pears commissioned for the privacy of their own home and yet the composer nonetheless felt that the open display of physical affection was too much to bear. Though purely anecdotal, this story encapsulates Britten's inability to outwardly express his innermost feelings. It also offers some explanation for his aversion to the broader gay community and reveals the contradiction he felt as a homosexual who was in certain core respects ashamed of homosexuality. Philip Brett argues that

> some estimation of the damage [Britten's] self-image sustained can be gained from his later attitude to his sexuality and from his hostility to the gay movement and to homosexual life-styles other than his own. According to [Ronald] Duncan 'he remained a reluctant homosexual' and Pears has said, 'the word "gay" was not in his vocabulary..."the gay life," he resented that'.[267]

From our current perspective it is hard to appreciate just how difficult it was for somebody like Britten to declare his hand in the years up to the 1960s. Contemporary society's broadly liberal stance towards the display of sexually ambiguous identities obscures our understanding of the oppressive, puritanical and 'moral' restrictions in place in the mid-20th century.[268] For example, until 1958 all reference to homosexuality was totally prohibited in theatrical presentations. British theatres had to be licensed by the Lord Chamberlain until as late as 1968—a rule that copper-fastened censorship. Throughout the 1950s, British society witnessed a number of high profile purges on homosexuals following the Guy Burgess and Donald McClean spy scandals; homosexual government agents were considered to be highly vulnerable to Soviet manipulation. Perhaps one of the most notorious examples of establishment censure of homosexuals was the Alan Turing

267 Philip Brett, *Music and Sexuality in Britten*, ed. George E. Haggerty (Berkeley: University of California Press, 2006), 25.

268 By no means do I wish to imply that all is well in relation to the discrimination in contemporary societies against non-heteronormative sexual practice. I merely wish to point to the relative difficulties experienced by mid-20th century non-heteronormative members of society.

case. Turing was a well-known mathematician and computer scientist who worked for the British Government's code-breaking centre. He was awarded an OBE (Order of the British Empire) for his groundbreaking cryptanalysis work and for his contribution to national security. However, this was not enough to save him from being convicted of gross indecency and given a choice between imprisonment on the one hand and probation, conditional on his agreement to undergo chemical castration, on the other. His conviction led to the removal of his security clearance and barred him from continuing work for Government Communications Headquarters. Speculation on whether his death in 1954 was a result of suicide or something more sinister is still rife. The British Government belatedly pardoned Turing in 2014.

The Turing case provides a troubling context for Britten's internalized conflicts relating to homosexuality. Britten's fears were real and justified. There is some evidence in fact that he also came under official scrutiny, as it is claimed that Scotland Yard interviewed him during an anti-homosexual drive by the then Home Secretary, David Maxwell-Fyffe.[269] Although British society was gradually liberalizing, it wasn't until ten years after the appearance of the *Wolfenden Report* in 1967 that consensual sex between homosexuals was made legal in England and Wales. Extraordinarily, it took the rest of the United Kingdom many years to implement a change in the law: Scotland did so in 1980, Guernsey in 1983, Jersey in 1990 and the Isle of Man in 1992.[270]

Under such external pressures, it might be argued that Britten could have composed outside the paradigm of his personal experience, to write, as Stravinsky disingenuously proposed, purely abstract and objective music. This was not something, however, that Britten was capable of doing; compositional practice of this kind would have mitigated the need to compose in the first place. Britten thus embedded those feelings that could not be articulated freely into concealed regions of his musical language by devising a number of technical processes that served as metaphors for the contradictory complexity of the private homosexual in a hostile heteronormative environment.

In his text-settings and operatic works, Britten's musical subterfuge

---

[269] 'In a letter to Lord Beaverbrook, the Evening Standard's editor wrote that Scotland Yard was stepping up its action against homosexuals, that Benjamin Britten had been interviewed, and that Cecil Beaton was on the list'; see Kathleen Tynan, *The Life of Kenneth Tynan* (London: Methuen, 1988), 110.

[270] http://www.nationalarchives.gov.uk/cabinetpapers/themes/before-after-wolfenden-report.htm.

is shrewdly applied. For English-speaking audiences the evocation of male beauty and erotic joy expressed in his *Les Illuminations* of 1939 was submerged in Rimbaud's original French.[271] Similarly, Britten intentionally moderated the impact of the homoerotic declarations in *Seven Sonnets of Michelangelo*, dedicated to Pears, by having them sung in Italian. As we have seen, in *Songs from the Chinese* the setting of poetry that is cryptically epigrammatic and evasive of direct statement continues this practice of open concealment. *Canticle I*, for tenor and piano, provides a particularly fascinating example of Britten's covert manner. In this setting of a poem by Francis Quarles, which is based on verses from the *Song of Solomon*, the text encloses within a devout entreaty to God an equally forthright expression of love for 'the beloved':

> So I my best beloved's am; so he is mine.
> Ev'n so we met, and after long pursuit,
> Ev'n so we joined; we both became entire.
> No need for either to renew a suit,
> For I was flax, and he was flames of fire.
> Our firm-united soul did more than twine;
> So I my best beloved's am; so he is mine.

This is a classic example of 'the perfect lie'. Using the protective veil of a Biblical text delivered through the heightened language of a 17th-century metaphysical poet, Britten (to paraphrase Proust) contemplated universes that would otherwise not have been available to him. Britten came to excel at this masking of deeply personal and vulnerable themes in music with ostensibly and radically different agendas. The necessity to liberate through concealment his most personal concerns and anxieties shaped him into a subversive composer of secret codes. In those works where texts are absent, this subversion manifests itself in processes that reflect confluences of desire and distress. Leonard Bernstein recognizes this inner torsion:

> Benjamin Britten was a man at odds with the world. It's strange because on the surface, Britten's music would seem to be decorative, positive, charming, and it's so much more than that. When you hear Britten's music—if you really hear it, not just listen to it superficially—you become aware of something very dark—there are gears that are grinding and not quite meshing, and they make a great pain.[272]

---

271 The work is dedicated to Wulff Scherchen, who was then a close friend of Britten.

272 Tony Palmer, *Benjamin Britten: A Time There Was*, DVD Video (1979; Isolde Films: New Jersey, Kultur).

Bernstein's descriptions of inner conflict point to self-subversive agencies at play in Britten's music, compositional processes that articulate implicitly what has to be denied explicitly. This dichotomy could only be realized through the cultivation of ambiguity, subversion and contradiction. Of course, many 20th-century composers explore bi-tonal processes and harmonically ambiguous music. However, in Britten's case, the stark dichotomy between his private and public selves, the pervasive psychological dread endured in having to constantly express himself in deceptive and cryptic ways was so great that it forced a dualism and ambiguity to enter into the very core of his musical idiolect.

It is not my intention to insist that a work as complex and multi-faceted as *Nocturnal* should be reduced to one reading. If I suggest that the use of bi-tonal structures in Variation I, for example, serves as an allegory for sexual ambiguity or the need for the covert expression of a condemned private desire, I must also submit that it might not do so. No one can be unequivocal on this point. A reading of Op. 70 as an exclusively homo-affirmative expression, would add little to our understanding of a work of such multilayered richness. However, given the arguments I have outlined relating to Britten's sexuality, the censorious period in which he lived and the resourceful strategies he employed to secretly express what was most central to his personality, it is fair to surmise that these aspects are likely to have had a profound impact on his abstract musical discourse. As a result, harmonic ambiguity in Britten's work takes on a deeper, more complex significance.

There are few Britten works in which bi-tonality is so consistently a central feature as in *Nocturnal*. From the very opening, figurations that display subversive attributes shape the melodic contours. The three-bar melodic phrase at bars 10-13, for example, frequently contorts and undermines its own stability. The implicit harmonic inference established by the two D♭ notes in the descending segments of the phrase is negated by the following two D♮ notes in the ascending segments (Example 73). Likewise, the sudden appearance of the F♯ in bar 12 nullifies the tonal implications of the two established F♮ notes (the final notes of bar 10 and 11). Not surprisingly, similar chromatic manipulations of melody may be observed in Dowland's exploitation of momentary dissonance: 'Suspensions, false relations, and the clash of parts moving against each other at temporarily discordant intervals are combined in a musical texture expressive of extraordinary emotional intensity.'[273] An example of this can be seen in the phrase, 'the image of true death'. Its false relations—the C♯ quickly negates the C♮ that precedes it—provide exemplary models of self-subversion for Britten.

Example 73: Dowland, 'the image of true death', and Britten, *Nocturnal*, Variation I, Musingly, bars 10-12

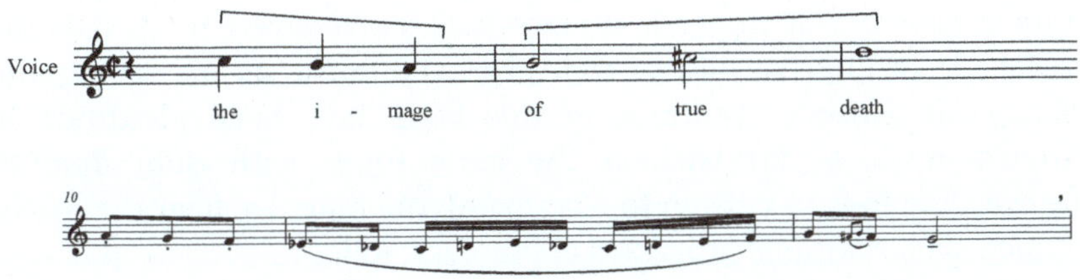

Processes of melodic self-subversion are reflected harmonically for the first time at bars 16-18 and 27-29. An E major triad provides the harmonic basis that is disturbed by a melodic phrase tonally centred in F minor.

Example 74: Britten, *Nocturnal*, Variation I, Musingly, bars 16-18

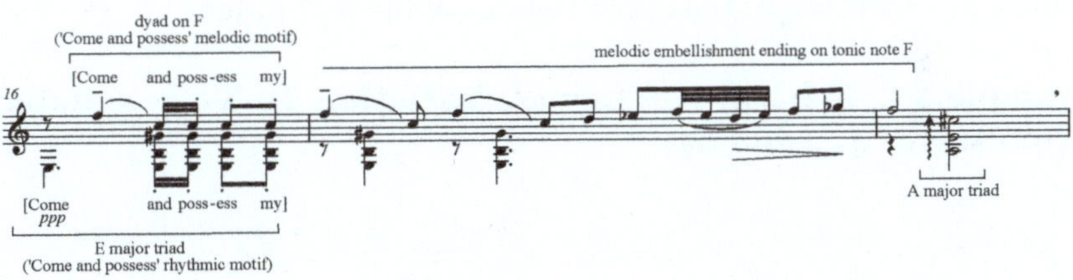

For bar 16, Stephan Goss has argued for a 'perfect symmetry' in the way that the notes G♯ (the 3rd pitch of the E major triad) and A♭ (the 3rd pitch of the F minor scale in its melodic ascending variant), being enharmonic equivalents, act as a 'fulcrum between the two tonalities': E-B-**G**♯ on the bottom and **G**♯ **[A**♭**]**-C-F on top.[274] However, the notion of a fulcrum holding the centre between two tonalities that are 'fused together', as if they were equally weighted, needs to be problematized.

[273] Diane Poulton, *John Dowland* (London: Faber and Faber, 1972), 347.
[274] Stephen Goss, 'Come Heavy Sleep: motive and metaphor in Britten's Nocturnal, opus 70', in *Guitar Forum*, No. 1 (Autumn 2001): 67.

While the simple application of bi-tonal components, of a 'fusion of keys' is accurate enough in its analysis, it fails to account for the self-subversive tendencies I have presented as a central feature of Britten's musical idiolect. Thus, the 'perfect symmetry'-concept of a unifying fulcrum may be misleading, as it would appear that the passage functions on a somewhat different relationship whereby the previously established and stable E major tonality is not met on equal terms by the F minor melody but rather is undermined subversively by it. It is the sinister act of internal dissent that gives the music its disturbing and melancholic attitude. Features of this kind have been identified in Britten's music as far back as the early 1950s with *Billy Budd*.[275] However, the more we listen to *Nocturnal*, the more we hear the extent to which such seditious processes are integral to it.

Variation II provides another superlative example. In the 4th and 5th staves of the movement, a descending F minor arpeggio thwarts the rising E major arpeggio that precedes it. Immediately thereafter, a similar sequence is directly repeated up a minor 3rd. The rising A♭ arpeggio is instantly nullified by the descending A minor arpeggio that follows it. Britten initiates a third sequence with a rising arpeggio in C major (yet again, a sequential figure starting a minor 3rd above the previous one), which is answered by what might have been another descending arpeggio in C♯ minor (though here written enharmonically as D♭). This final gesture, however, breaks away from the sequential pattern to veer towards the upper regions of the instrument.

Example 75: Britten, *Nocturnal*, Variation II, Very agitated (from staves 4, 5 and 6)

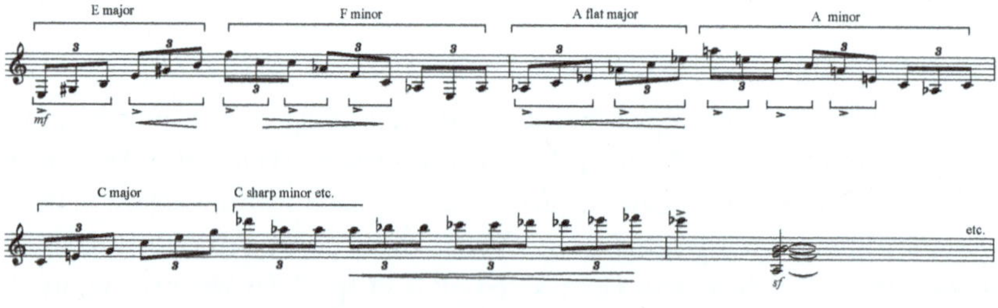

Thus, insurgent forces in minor keys—F minor, A minor and C♯ minor—immediately undermine the established tonal centres in major

[275] Philip Rupprecht, 'Tonal Stratification and Uncertainty in Britten's Music', in *Journal of Music Theory*, Vol. 40, No. 2 (1996), 311-346.

keys—E major, A♭ major and C major. The usurpation of major keys by minor ones brings with it a long-established symbolic implication of light being eclipsed by dark. Such factious tendencies are further emphasized by altered rhythmic groupings. The established rhythmic pattern set up in the ascending arpeggios, that is, two groups of three quavers, is undermined by their descending counterparts, which fall into three groups of two quavers. This is not made obvious by the notation and thus interpretations will differ on this point. However, in practice, the repeat of the C note in the descending F minor arpeggio strongly suggests a division of the notes into three groups of two. Therefore, both the established major keys and their triplet patterns are destabilized. This is what creates the 'very agitated' mood of Variation II and further points to a deeply ingrained self-negating tendency in Britten's musical language.

The angular, anti-vocal character of Variation II is emphasized by the extremity of its range. The musical argument in stave 7 shifts from the highest note of the instrument to its lowest in rapid succession. This acute adjustment in register is designed to amplify, yet again, a destabilizing pressure that the repeated Fs have on the established E major tonality.

Example 76: Britten, *Nocturnal*, Variation II, Very agitated (from staves 7 and 8)

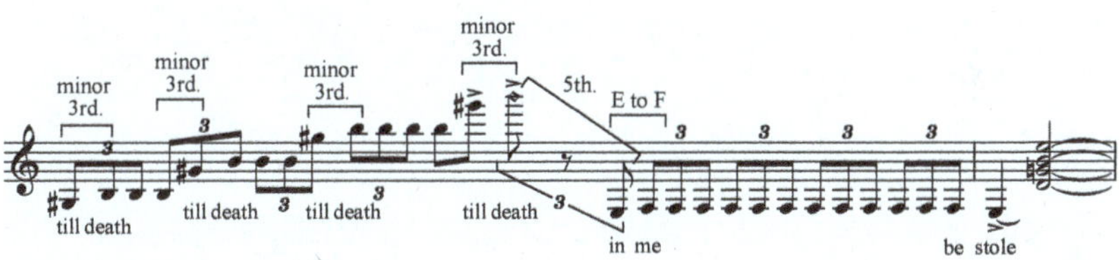

Structured agitation inheres in Variation III's intricate layering of seemingly incompatible material. Here, the prominent conflicting elements are rhythmic. Britten constructs three separate strata that unfold simultaneously: a rather chromatic accompaniment in 3/4 that mediates between two 'vocal' lines in 4/4; the entire assemblage is structured antiphonally.[276] With a concern for sustained polyphonic

[276] Antiphonal works are those in which an ensemble (usually a choir) is divided into two or more distinct groups performing in alternation and together. Antiphonal music reached its apogee with composers such as Giovani

Example 77: Britten: *Nocturnal*, Variation III, Restless (*inquieto*)

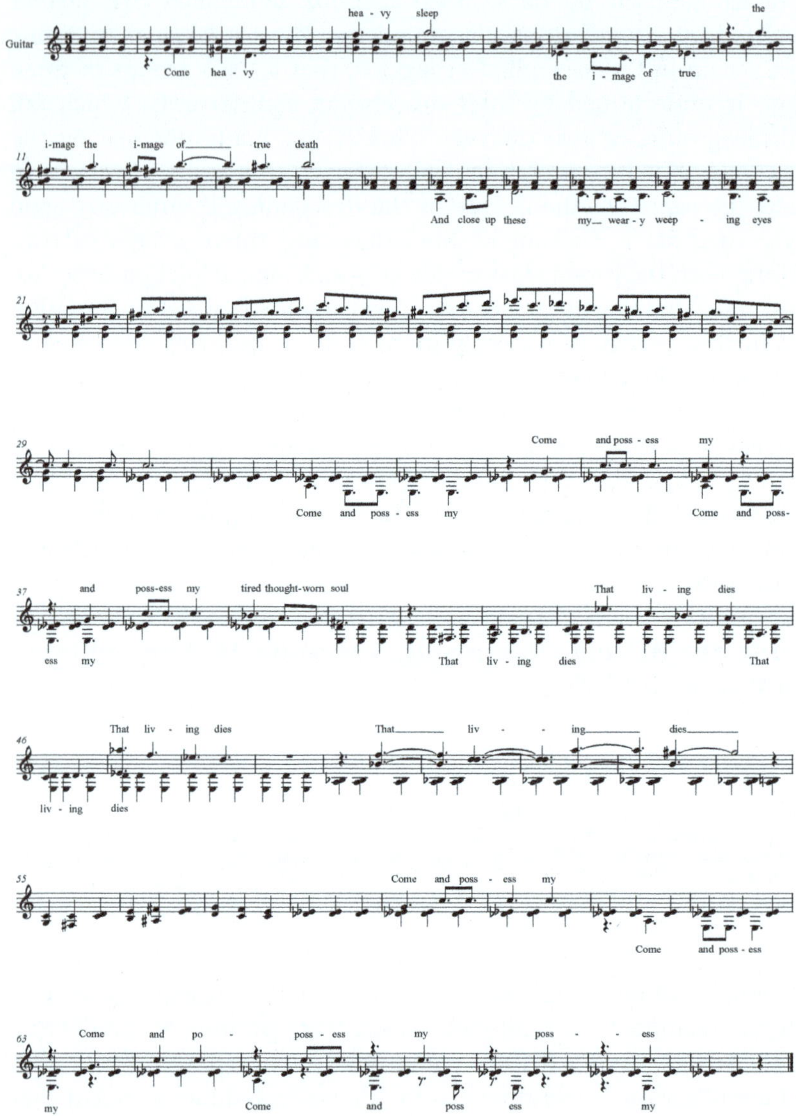

Gabrieli (c. 1554-1612) who was principal organist at San Marco de Venezia. Gabrieli took full advantage of the unusual architectural layout of St. Mark's Basilica with its two choir lofts facing each other to create striking spatial effects.

complexity that contrasts strongly with the previous variation, the melodic lines extract phrase fragments from 'Come Heavy Sleep' and unfold them with deceptive ease around the accompaniment, first below it, then above it.It is only between bars 20 and 30, where the melodic line above the accompaniment soars into the higher register of the instrument, that distinctly recognizable elements of the song are jettisoned, although the quasi-improvised melismas clearly demonstrate melodic relationships to previously established material. Naturally, the tension in this movement lies in the unease with which melodic and accompaniment lines interlace each other. The attendant 'restlessness' is generated because the ear is unable to settle on one defining meter and pulse. This temporal ambiguity finds correlative resonance with the fluctuating chromatic notes that refuse to settle on any one distinct tonal centre long enough to establish a harmonic *terra firma*.

Since *Nocturnal* occupies a peripheral position within Britten's entire *oeuvre*, evidence that Shostakovich may have influenced the work has gone unnoticed to date. Op. 70, however, was written in 1964, only four years after the composers first met and it appears that Britten considered his tonal language to be coterminous with that of Shostakovich. While he states that his music is 'so very different' from the Russian's, it is nonetheless 'conceived...in the same period' and both composers are 'children of similar fathers, and with many of the same aims'.[277] This comment directs our attention to an elemental similarity, heretofore unobserved, between the 'March-like' music of *Nocturnal* and numerous marches by Shostakovich. The comparison is both valid and relevant because, similarly to Britten, Shostakovich was forced to compose in a concealing manner. Though Britten's socio-political environment was by no means as perilous as that of Shostakovich, both composers were conflicted by a need to maintain a public persona and a private integrity in the face of oppression, real or perceived.

The somewhat sinister tone of Britten's 'March-like' has all the attributes of that distinctive Russian propensity to employ official language ambiguously to critique the very forces of oppression that use and admire it. Mikhail Bakhtin's theory of 'carnival' (extrapolated from his study of Rabelais) provides a useful framework within which to

---

[277] Britten's tribute to Shostakovich was written in 1966 and subsequently appeared in a Russian collection of essays on Shostakovich (Moscow: *Sovetskii kompozitor*, 1967). It is cited in Cameron Pyke, 'Shostakovich's Fourteenth Symphony: A Response to War Requiem?', in *Benjamin Britten: New Perspectives on His Life and Work*, ed. Lucy Walker (Woodbridge: The Boydell Press, 2009), 27-45.

consider this. As a counter-ideology to Soviet totalitarianism, he suggests that carnival laughter 'builds its own world in opposition to the official world, its own church versus the official church, its own state versus the official state'.[278] Bakhtin himself used ambiguity as a tool for criticism, employing Bolshevik catch phrases only to expose the weaknesses behind them. The key to his theory lies in the statement that 'the more unofficial and familiar the speech, the less distinct is the line dividing praise and abuse'.[279] We can observe this ambiguous play of praise and criticism in Shostakovich's 'familiar' marches (in particular those of Symphonies Nos. 5 and 7).[280]

Similarly, Britten's fifth variation, 'March-like', exhibits deceptive and cryptic language, as two opposing arguments are convincingly merged. Interlacing content and contexts, Britten presents the plaintive 'Come Heavy Sleep' within the framework of an increasingly threatening march through contradictory materials with astutely chosen instructions. Created from the sinister 'and posses my' rhythmic motive, the accompaniment is given the rather apt instruction *staccato e pesante* (detached and heavy), making it a menacing presence throughout the movement. Meanwhile, the 'melody' of the variation is given the radically opposing direction *singing (cantabile)* Thus, we encounter again separate entities within Britten's musical idiolect, one of which acts seditiously against the other. In this case, the plaintive character of the melody is aggressively undermined by the ominous accompaniment; whatever repose the singing melody offers is taken back by the belligerent march that endeavours to overpower it. This remarkable juxtaposition of conflicting signals within a single musical entity is matched only by Berg in his conflation of the religious and the sensual, using the markings *amoroso* and *religioso* in the same bar at

---

278 Katarina Clark and Michael Holquist, *Mikail Bakhtin* (Cambridge: Harvard University Press, 1984), 308.

279 Ibid., 319.

280 *Symphony No. 7* is often interpreted as a critique of the German invasion of the Soviet Union. Shostakovich's quote from 'Da geh' ich zu Maxim' from Franz Lehar's *The Merry Widow* in the first movement is considered by many critics to have served as a caricature of the Nazis. However, other commentators have argued that the score is also a memorial to the city that 'Stalin destroyed and Hitler merely finished off'. See Solomon Volkov, *Testimony* (New York: Harper & Row, 1979), 156. In relation to *Symphony No. 5*, there has been considerable debate as to the sincerity of the music's so-called 'reply to just criticism', as many of the Symphony's marches appear more akin to Bakhtinian parodies and forced rejoicing than genuine admiration for the Soviet's regime.

the end of his *Violin Concerto* (bar 222), or by C.P.E. Bach's Sonata *Sanguinius und Melancholicus*—a musico-rhetorical conversation between 'Sanguine' and 'Melancholy'.

Example 78: Britten: *Nocturnal*, Variation V (with suggested word setting)

Elements of self-subversion and contradiction are also pervasive in Variation VII. This is immediately made evident by the employment of two staves that operate within distinct harmonic paradigms. Although the movement is in 6/8, the phrasing does not correspond to that time signature's metric requirement. The melody hovering above it falls into patterns of shifting five-quaver, four-quaver, three-quaver, two-quaver and two+two-quaver groups, which constantly undermine the two dotted-crotchet pattern a 6/8 time signature would wish to impose on the music.

Example 79: Britten: *Nocturnal*, Variation VII, 'Gently rocking'

It becomes clear that nothing in Variation VII complies with expectations. The high celestial murmurings of the tremolo eventually fall in register. At about the point where the upper stave changes its key signature, the tremolo line begins to fall below the previously supporting accompaniment, which now begins to rise. By the end of the variation, there has been a complete modification of roles: the tremolo now burrows into the lowest region of the instrument while the bell-like accompaniment notes rise ethereally as harmonics into the higher echelons. The musical rhetoric symbolism would suggest that as the body is taken towards the ground (grave) the spirit rises into celestial bliss. However, this can also be read as an exemplar of ambiguity: tonal uncertainty, conflicting rhythmic pulses and constantly shifting textures conflate to suggest a deep ambivalence that is both disquieting and ominous—a private and damaged world turned upside-down.

Example 80: Britten, *Nocturnal*, associative segues between all variations and the theme

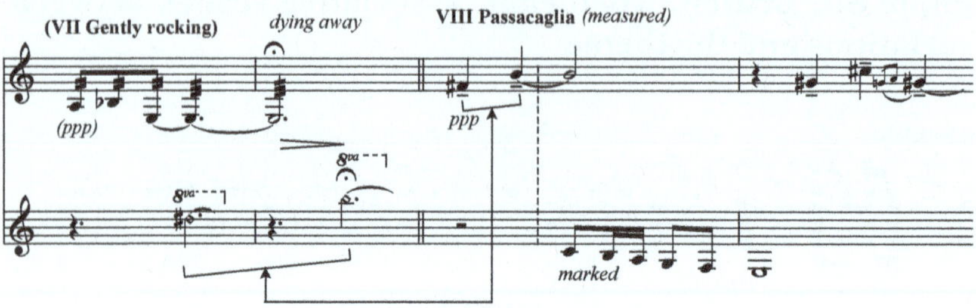

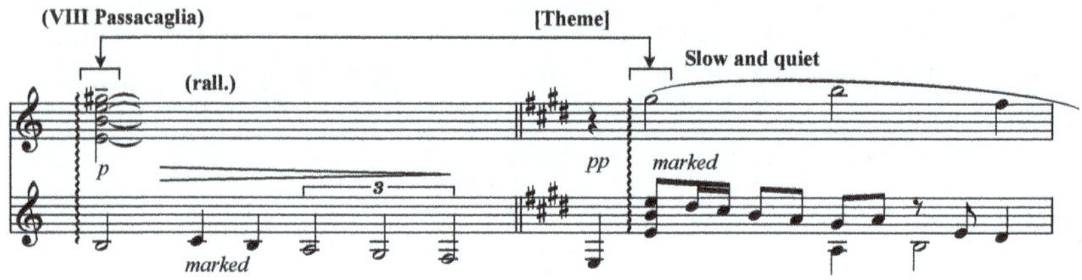

Finally, embedded within the structure of *Nocturnal* is a system of metamorphosis that occurs between each variation. A seamless shifting from one movement to another is achieved through what I call 'associative segue'. This technique uses harmonic, melodic and rhythmic formulae to create smooth and subliminal transitions between sections. We are reminded here that Britten chose not to explicitly employ the term 'variations' for Op. 70's title; he clearly wished to facilitate smooth transitions between the various psychological states the variations explore. Though technical devices, associative segues shrewdly transport the listener unknowingly into the successive variations' different psychological spaces; the listener's constant undetected conveyance from one emotional state to another is both undermining and disturbing.

In this study, I have tried to provide contexts and meanings for certain purely musical phenomena in *Nocturnal.* I have put forward plausible motifs for disturbing aspects in the work that technical processes such as bi-tonality, self-subversive harmonic entities, rhythmic incongruities and associative segues create. As I have been at pains to uphold, nobody can be unequivocal about specific meaning in abstract music. Nevertheless, Britten was a product of a *début de siècle* Europe, a time when new 'identities' were being forged through advancing philosophical and cultural rationales. To long-established gender classifications such as male and female, for example, came new socially constructed categories:

> What was new from the turn of the century was the world-mapping by which every given person, just as he or she was necessarily assignable to a male or a female gender, was now considered necessarily assignable to homo- or a hetero-sexuality, a binarized identity that was full of implications...It was this new development that left no space in the culture exempt from the potent incoherence of homo/heterosexual definition.[281]

This statement captures the nexus of Britten's dilemma. As a new, socially constructed 'species',[282] the homosexual had to negotiate the confusion of being simultaneously within and without society. Britten's failure to negotiate this well

> had it roots in his personal experience as a homosexual—an experience which became central to his art but which he himself could never discuss or even mention in public...His homosexual nature found expression in the lifelong relationship with Pears, which society could accept because its basis was ostensibly professional. But it also resulted in an equally lifelong sense of unworthiness and alienation...Prevented from any open discourse by the self-imposed silence on the matter of sexuality which he shared with most prominent homosexual men of his generation...covert treatment of the issues of sexuality in his music may have offered itself as a personally effective remedy.[283]

Music, therefore, became Britten's outlet and a very significant psychological release. As we have seen, this was more clearly manifest in his text settings and works for stage. However, judging by the intensity of his particular neurosis, music without text, music that functioned free from the 'avarice of logic', offered Britten an even greater freedom to tell, with no impunity at all, the perfect lie.[284]

---

281 Eve Kosofsky Sedgwick, *Epistemology of the Closet* (Berkeley: University of California Press, 1990), 2.

282 Michel Foucault, *The Will to Knowledge: The History of Sexuality I* (London: Penguin, 1976), 101.

283 Philip Brett, *Music and Sexuality in Britten*, 110.

284 George Steiner, *Errata: An Examined Life* (Guernsey: Phoenix, 1998), 66; '[...] verbal discourse remains linear, sequential in time. It is hand cuffed to the avarice of logic...'.

Nocturnal: Receptions and Assessments

Nocturnal received its first performance by Julian Bream in the Jubilee Hall at the Aldeburgh Festival on 12 June 1964.[285] Although an auspicious début of a major new work for the guitar, *Nocturnal* was somewhat overshadowed by the near-simultaneous premieres of two other important works by Britten at the festival—*Curlew River*, Op. 71 and *Cello Symphony*, Op. 68, in its first UK performance.[286]

Figure 6: Programme for Aldeburgh Festival concert, 12 June 1964

Robert de Visée	*Suite in D minor*
Sylvius Leopold Weiss:	*Tombeau sur la mort de M. Comte d'Logy* *Fantasie*
Johann Sebastian Bach:	*Chaconne* (from *Partita No. 2* in D minor, BWV 1004)
Niccolò Paganini:	*Sonata in A Major*
INTERVAL	
Benjamin Britten:	Nocturnal, after John Dowland, Op. 70
Manuel de Falla:	*Homenaje, pour le tombeau de Claude Debussy*
Manuel de Falla:	*Song of the Jack-o-Lantern* (from *Al Amor Brujo*) *The Miller's Dance* (from *The Three-Cornered Hat*)

Contemporary reviews and articles help gauge initial responses to *Nocturnal* by furnishing interesting commentaries on Bream's performance of the work and by providing some insight into the atmosphere of the seventeenth Aldeburgh Festival. For this reason, I have included a number of reviews in some detail. I do so because even a cursory perusal indicates that the 1964 festival actually marked a new phase in Britten's compositional output:

[285] Source: Britten-Pears Library archive.

[286] Rostropovich premiered *Cello Symphony* on 12 March 1964 at the Great Hall, Moscow Conservatory of Music with the Moscow Philharmonic Orchestra conducted by Britten. The British performance took place on 18 June 1964 in Blythburgh Church during the Aldeburgh Festival with Britten conducting the English Chamber Orchestra. *Curlew River* was premiered on 12 June 1964.

> Britten himself sprang the biggest surprise, however, with new works that showed his musical imagination striking out in fresh directions. Not for him a comfortably settled idiom now that he is 50, an idiom made familiar by numerous works leading up to *A Midsummer Night's Dream* and the *War Requiem*, which may perhaps later be seen to mark the end of a phase in his career. Even the new *Nocturnal* for guitar, the fulfillment of a promise made years ago to Julian Bream, is no mere pendant to the several 'sleep' pieces that have stirred his imagination (and haunted ours) in recent years. It is both a marvelously wrought demonstration of the guitar's capabilities under Bream's fingers, and what *The Times* aptly called a 'creative analysis' of a song by Dowland that Bream has helped bring back to favour.
>
> As with Stravinsky and the Bach chorale that forms the basis of his Canonic Variations, Britten has transformed the elements of Dowland's song, *Come, heavy sleep*, into something peculiarly his own. Fragments of the song's melody and harmony in turn stimulate Britten to inventive ideas of a fresh nature, to new harmonic implications and rhythmic processes. They assume a completely different individuality and character in the various sections of the *Nocturnal*, and suddenly fall back into their original form when, near the end, the strains of Dowland's song are ingeniously worked into the fabric of the new piece. I run the risk of making it sound like a somewhat contrived piece, whereas the effect in performance is just the opposite—spontaneous and absorbing.[287]

An interesting review by another commentator provides an atmospheric picture of the concert alongside astute reflections on the pioneering reach of *Nocturnal*. It is particularly curious to observe that the notion of a 'full length solo recital' for guitar was still a relatively unusual affair, which provides some indication of how far things have come in the guitar world since 1964.

> The Aldeburgh Festival this year brings three new works by Benjamin Britten, the first of which, an extended work for solo guitar, was heard last night in Julian Bream's recital at the Jubilee Hall... It is a work of great beauty that valuably enriches the modern literature of the guitar—still surprisingly scanty considering what fine artists of the instrument there are today. As was to be expected Britten keeps clear of conventional guitar figuration, and devises varieties of textures that go far beyond anything that we normally hear in recitals of guitar music.
>
> Each variation is distinguished by some terse, striking invention, developed with great concentration. They encompass a far greater range of expression than the guitar is normally allowed to attempt, from the quietly introspective introduction, marked 'musing', through a sequence marked agitated, restless and uneasy, to a march whose jauntiness has a

[287] Noel Goodwin, 'Britten's Advance', in *Music and Musicians* (1964). Source: Britten-Pears Library archive.

> note of whistling in the dark, and thence to three more peaceful variations, marked dreaming, gently rocking and measured—the last a passacaglia of a serenity that is not perhaps what many dreams lead to, whether they end in sleep or in wakefulness, but satisfyingly rounds off this absorbing sequence of nocturnal mood-pictures.
>
> Julian Beam was playing superlatively. With him the guitar never seems an instrument too limited in its technical and tonal possibilities for a full length solo recital, and if this is partly due to his admirable programme planning it is no less due to his marvelous playing, which can, and last night did, make even a Paganini Sonata a worthwhile musical experience.[288]

This previously cited *Times* review by an unidentified author recognizes the profound nature of Op. 70 suggesting that it is the most penetrating of all Britten's 'sleep'-inspired works and an insightful 'reading' of Dowland's idiom.

> Britten's Nocturnal is, as its title and movement headings (Musing, Agitated, Restless...Dreaming, Gently Rocking) suggest, one of his going-to-sleep pieces... This Nocturnal is a lucid creative analysis of Dowland's song, isolating its materials, explaining their implications and finally demonstrating their coherence. All this may sound painfully didactic, but because the Nocturnal also involves variegated instrumental effects and a fascinating musical portrait gallery under the guise of variations, it holds the attention at many levels, and strikes deeper than at any one of them.[289]

An insightful review/article by Jeremy Noble from August 1964 opens the debate around the importance of *Nocturnal* in relation to Britten's broader output—a topic upon which I will focus in this chapter:

> Quantitatively the slightest of the three Britten novelties, the *Nocturnal upon a song of John Dowland* [sic] for solo guitar, op 70, was naturally a bit overshadowed by *Curlew River* and the *Cello Symphony*. All the same, my own first impression was that in its spare intensity it has a great deal in common with the former, and that it is a more deeply felt and closely reasoned piece than the latter.[290]

Today, guitarists worldwide are fully persuaded of the importance of *Nocturnal*; indeed, it is widely considered the *magnum opus* of the

---

[288] Colin Mason, 'New Britten Work for Guitar', in *The Guardian*, 13 June 1964. Source: The Britten-Pears Library archive.

[289] 'Britten's Going-to-Sleep Piece,' in *The Times*, June 15 1964. Source: Britten-Pears Library archive.

[290] Jeremy Noble, 'Britten's Nocturnal', in *The Musical Times* Vol. 105, No. 1458 (1964): 592-594.

entire repertoire. In sharp contrast, Britten scholars have, on the whole, underestimated the work, presumably because the guitar still largely resides on the periphery of classical music. Stephen Goss rightly wonders if these commentators are 'ignoring the music or the medium?'—a pointed question that hints at the reason why *Nocturnal* has been consistently overlooked when it comes to assessments of Britten's broader output and the various phases of his compositional practice.[291] Despite the generally positive assessment of *Nocturnal* in the above reviews, many commentators have chosen not to critique the work within the context of Britten's entire *oeuvre*. This is evidenced by the cursory sentences that Op. 70 has garnered in numerous publications that overview Britten's corpus. For instance, the commentary below makes important observations about technical innovations pertinent to Britten's emerging late style in *Curlew River*, while equally vital signposts discernible in Op. 70 are not identified:

> The [*Curlew River*] score reveals that in fact [Britten] has succeeded in widening the application of his new manner—so convincingly that its relevance to other areas of his work may be expected to appear in future scores; so far, only the regulation by the 'curlew' sign of independent temporal strata in the Blake songs [Op. 74, 1965] and the *Voices for Today* [Op. 75, 1965] has given a hint of this development.[292]

An analysis of two reviews by Edmund Tracey for *The Observer* places my argument in further relief. One critiques *Nocturnal* in a way that clearly argues for its importance as an intrinsic work in and of itself. However, though Op. 70 receives considerable praise, Tracey offers no suggestion that it is a significant indicator of Britten's new direction:

> [The] first Britten novelty of the Festival [Aldeburgh] came on Friday when Julian Bream introduced the *Nocturnal After John Dowland*, a work for solo guitar written specially for him. As always when Britten explores a new instrumental path, he solves the technical problems with the adroitness and the imagination of a great professional: the colours and contours of this music suit the guitar exactly. There is plenty of contrast—arpeggiated melodies, abrupt exclamations, various types of accompaniment, elaborate part-writing including a complex final passacaglia; but these contrasts are all contained in the unity of the central poetic idea.

---

291 Stephen Goss, 'Come Heavy Sleep: motive and metaphor in Britten's Nocturnal, opus 70', in *Guitar Forum* No. 1 (2001): 53.

292 Peter Evans, 'Britten's New Church Opera', in *The Listener*, June 16, 1966. Source: The Britten-Pears Library archive.

> And, of course, it is this two-fold accomplishment—poetic genius hand in hand with technical mastery—that makes Britten such a rewarding composer. He had obviously enjoyed rising to the special challenge of a piece for solo guitar; but the technical means were interesting only insofar as they served expressive ends. The whole piece is shot through with that melancholy—now meditative, now sharply anguished, now openly death-wishing—which we find in so many of Dowland's songs and dance tunes and which is also a part of Britten's own creative personality. I eagerly look forward to hearing it again.[293]

Despite the positive nature of this review, *Nocturnal* is not included in the shortlist of alleged 'important works'. This is made abundantly clear in Tracey's next review for *The Observer* entitled 'Britten takes a new path'. Numerous technical features in Op. 70 evidence Britten's 'new path' as indicated by the reviewer; however, no reference is made to *Nocturnal*.

> ...when the musical history of this period comes to be written objectively and from a distance, the two major works that Britten introduced during the course of this festival will be seen to herald a new strength and mettle in his creative output...both the new works show a toughness in their intellectual control, a new spartan robustness in their spare bony frames. In two years Britten has travelled a long way from the warm-hearted, grandiose War Requiem...The music [*Curlew River*] is extremely simple and austere: declamation and melody flow together and merge—the second being an extension of the first and not in any way appliqué or self-centred...these spare, expressive phrases do seem both to adumbrate the musical material and finally sum it up.[294]

Op. 70's exclusion from the 'major works that Britten introduced during the course of this festival' is indicative of a general perception that the guitar simply cannot occupy seminal ground in any broad assessment of a composer's work. While this attitude merely reflects the instrument's peripheral position in the world of classical music, its exclusion is I believe myopic and obstructive to a thorough assessment of Britten's music. Despite this broad failure, there have been some perceptive observations of *Nocturnal*. While Arnold Whittall expresses some misgivings about what he sees as certain technical deficits, he nevertheless suggests that Op. 70 holds an important place within Britten's overall output and that it is significant as a model of change in his compositional method:

---

[293] Edmund Tracey, *The Observer*, 14 June 1964. Source: The Britten-Pears Library archive.

[294] Edmund Tracey, 'Britten takes a new path', in *The Observer*, 21 June 1964. Source: The Britten-Pears Library archive.

> With the freer approach to metre, its less insistent use of triadic harmony, coupled with an increased intensity of thematic manipulation, *Nocturnal* adumbrates many of the elements of the 'late Britten' style which are more fully set out in *Curlew River*.[295]

I now want to elucidate how these general comparisons are evidenced in the scores. There are numerous technical procedures that both works share. I outlined previously that *Cello Suite No. 3* foreshadows a number of technical and narrative methods that appear fully elaborated in *Death in Venice*—the work that was composed immediately after it. Similarly, as *Nocturnal* was written in, or around, the time of *Curlew River*, I suggest that it can be seen as exemplary of Britten's new musical idiolect—a kind of shorthand musical draft that finds broader embellishment in the church parable. Indeed, the degree to which certain technical aspects of *Nocturnal* parallel those of *Curlew River* is remarkable. Even in simple renovations of the bar line, both scores make use of the dotted type as a subsidiary of the solid version—a system that does not necessarily insist upon a specific number of beats. For example, at Figure 1 of the *Curlew River* score, Britten creates the following 'open' use of bar lines (both dotted and solid).[296]

Example 81: Britten, *Curlew River*, the use of a dotted bar line as a subsidiary form of the solid bar line in *Curlew River* (Figure 1)

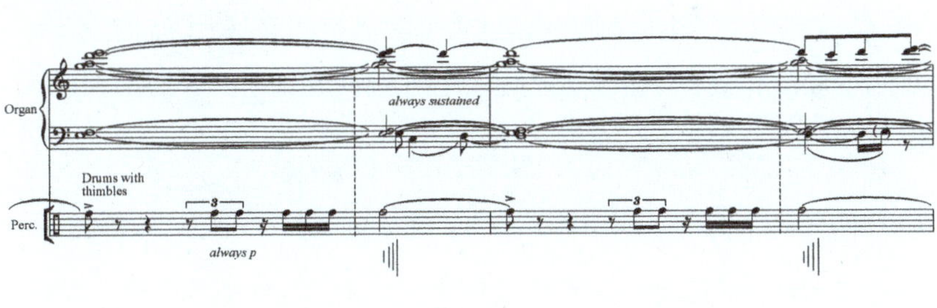

[295] Arnold Whittall, *The Music of Britten and Tippett: Studies in themes and techniques* (Cambridge: Cambridge University Press, 1982), 210.

[296] Note that the score of *Curlew River* is marked throughout by numbered figures and not bar lines, a system that offers the necessary flexibility to accommodate the aleatoric nature of the score.

Example 82: Britten, *Nocturnal*, Passacaglia (opening bars including dotted bar lines)

Imogen Holst's Introduction to the score of *Curlew River* states that

> the word 'measured' at fig. 1 is enough to show that after the freedom of the plainsong the music now moves with a pulse and time patterns. A time signature in brackets shows the unit for counting in, but the actual number of units may vary from bar to bar.[297]

Other examples of the use of 'open' bars in both scores can be seen at Figure 29 of *Curlew River* and the sixth variation of *Nocturnal*. The 'own tempo' of the former offers a similar freedom to that which the free writing and unprescribed barring offers in the latter.

Example 83: Britten, *Curlew River*, Figure 29

---

[297] Benjamin Britten, *Curlew River*, Op. 71, Faber Music Limited: London, 1964/5 [edition: 1983], ix.

Example 84: Britten, *Nocturnal*: Variation VI, 'Dreaming' (first three staves)

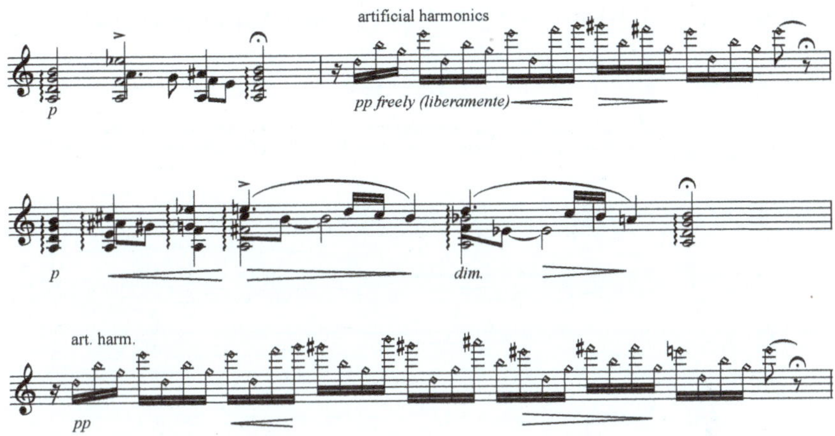

Freedom in rhythmic approach is not the only point of convergence between compositional practices in both scores. There are also remarkable similarities in melodic construction. As I have noted, processes of self-negation are often written into melodic or arpeggiated passages. In Variation IV, note how the descending F♮ has immediately undermined the effect of the ascending F♯ preceding it.

Example 85: Britten, *Nocturnal*, Variation IV, 'Uneasy' (stave three)

The same applies later on in the passage when the falling B♭ of the fourth group immediately overrules the rising B♮ of the third. A number of melodic constructions in *Curlew River* follow an identical procedure. Indeed, the passage (from Figure 54+2, on page 54 of the score) where a solo horn has a free, melismatic and intertwining line is uncannily similar in mood, freedom and melodic function to the guitar example above. Notice how the D and B♭ notes of the third crotchet group immediately undermine the B and D notes of the second. Similarly, the descending F♮ and E♭ notes of the fourth crotchet group also deny the E♮ and F♯ notes of the same group. The acute resemblance of these two passages almost makes them interchangeable between both works.

Example 86: Britten, *Curlew River*, Figure 54+2 [p. 54]

In postulating *Nocturnal* as a pivotal work in Britten's late style, it is worth keeping in mind his innate gift for understanding the peculiar idiosyncrasies of a given instrument. Britten's use of the harp in *Curlew River*, as discussed by Robin Holloway, is remarkably analogous to his use of the guitar.

> And no one since its emancipation from mere arpeggios and glissandi has understood the genius of this instrument as Britten, who makes its technical character so influence his compositional thought that the music grows directly out of what the instrument can and cannot do...Such narrow limits exactly suit an ear exceptionally sensitized to every inflection of every note...[298]

Guitarists will surely recognize this attribute, but more importantly, Holloway's shrewd observations help us gauge the instrument's significance as a suitable agent of Britten's newly emerging style, as a mode of incisive and succinct musical language. Just as the chromatic limitations of the harp embolden Britten to create a new 'fundamental' harmony for *Curlew River*, the guitar's idiosyncratic tuning, its limited range, its harmonic potential restricted to a maximum of six notes and its unsustaining sound force Britten into circumscribed areas that actually suite his late style. Turning a deficit into an asset, the guitar allows Britten to seek the path of least resistance. Thus, from the 1960s

[298] Robin Holloway, 'The Church Parables (II): Limits and Renewals', in *The Britten Companion*, ed. Christopher Palmer (London: Faber and Faber, 1984), 215-226.

onwards, this new phase engenders a purified, concentrated and essential language; this is why Holloway calls this late phase a 'return to the source' and a 'new start'.[299] In an interview that Britten gave just months before, or possibly during, the composition of *Nocturnal*, he had this to say:

> Music for me is clarification; I try to clarify, to refine, to sensitise. Stravinsky once said that one must work perpetually at one's technique. But what is technique? Schoenberg's technique is often a tremendous elaboration. My technique is to tear all the waste away; to achieve perfect clarity of expression. That is my aim.[300]

The characteristic intimacy and relative limitation of the guitar made it a perfect conduit to explore new ideas of regeneration and reduction. In this context, there is hardly a more apposite description (again analogous) of Op. 70 than Holloway's as he attempts to get close to what *Curlew River* and Britten's new perspective represents: '[Britten's *Church Parables*] render unending time and imply vast space and place, by dissolving the bounds of harmony and rhythm until it seems that music itself will drain away leaving nothing behind.'[301] This could be a summary of Op. 70's *raison d'être*, and highlights the level to which *Nocturnal* is coterminous with *Curlew River*—a point evidenced by shared technical methods. For example, both works utilize rhythmic procedures that are designed to bring music to a point of dissolution. The small bells at Figure 88-1 (in *Curlew River*) dissipate in a free rhythmic decline, a kind of rhythmic cadence that invokes silence as an essential structural component within their ever-lengthening sonorities.

Example 87: Britten, *Curlew River*, Figure 88-1 [p. 112]

This technique is almost an *idée fixe* within *Nocturnal*, as all the variations, the passacaglia and even the theme at the end fade out to nothingness. The procedure is exemplified in the music ending

299 Ibid., 216.

300 Murray Schafer, 'British Composers in Interview', in Alan Blyth, *Remembering Britten* (London: Hutchinson, 1981), 66.

301 Robin Holloway, The Church Parables (II), 218.

Variation IV, which is remarkably similar to the 'small bells' music of *Curlew River* above.

Example 88: Britten, *Nocturnal*, Variation IV, final bar

These examples demonstrate that *Nocturnal* shares considerable common ground with *Curlew River*. Both scores employ comparable notational schemata, a quasi-aleatoric freedom, self-subversive melodic constructions and musical devices whose *raisons d'être* are the ultimate attainment of silence. It is not known which score was completed first; given the fact that dramaturgical works often require substantial periods of composition and revision, it is quite plausible that *Nocturnal* was written before *Curlew River* or during some period of delay or alteration to it. This hypothesis is strongly supported by the degree of technical and musical cross-fertilization discernible in the two works. Opp. 70 and 71 additionally share a broad formal design, being variations on a theme: a lute song connects the guitar to a distant English cousin; plainsong connects the church parable to its religious sub-text. I wish to argue that if *Curlew River* represents in a vocal idiom the inauguration of Britten's latest stylistic phase, *Nocturnal* is that style's instrumental marker. In its strategic positioning and in its technical and symbolic representation of his late style, *Nocturnal* thus deserves a greater prestige within the broader context of Britten's *corpus*.

Finally, in a manner both poignant and plausible, *Nocturnal* presides metaphorically over Britten's final period. Op. 70 marks the beginning of Britten's late style epitomized not only by the 'mild notational indeterminacy of the Parables, which quickly made its way into other genres, but in the sparse textures now employed, and the smaller forces required to articulate these new musical arguments'.[302] Those smaller forces are exemplified by *Nocturnal*, which demonstrate Britten's compulsion for a semantic minimalism, perhaps even, as I have been arguing throughout this study, for the ultimate emancipation of music itself—a final and silent transcendence.

Just before he died, Britten wrote a new version of his *Lachrymae*,

[302] Paul Kildea, ed., *Britten on Music*, 288.

reflections on a song of John Dowland.[303] It was to be the last piece he composed. If *Nocturnal* is a profound meditation on Dowland, then the Elizabethan presides over Britten's final years in a shared musical idiolect and deep affiliation, with *Nocturnal* marking the beginning of his final journey and *Lachrymae* marking the end. Such a perspective eerily parallels the very structure I have proposed for Op. 70 with Dowland's song 'Come Heavy Sleep' bookending the work. Thus, the framing structure of *Nocturnal* is analogous to Britten's final compositional phase—a period dominated by a desire for simplicity and transcendence, enclosed and fostered by the consoling presence of Dowland.

303 This is his Op. 48b for solo viola and strings.

Bibliography

Addison, Thomas. *The Spectator* No. 70 May 21, 1711.

Adler, Jeremy, ed. and Michael Hamburger, trans. *Friedrich Hölderlin: Selected Poems and Fragments*. London: Penguin Group, 1994.

Allt, Wilfrid Greenhouse. *Treatment of Ground*. London: Taylor & Francis, 1946.

Anderson, W.R. 'Wireless Notes.' *The Musical Times* Vol. 79, No. 1139 (1938): 30-32.

Attwater, Donald. 'English Folk-Song.' *Music & Letters* Vol. 9, No. 2 (April 1928): 129-139.

Auden, W.H. *The Dance of Death*. London: Faber & Faber, 1935.

Banks, Chris, Arthur Searle and Malcolm Turner, eds. *Sundry sorts of music books: Essays on The British Library Collections*. London: The British Library, 1993.

Banks, Paul, ed. *Britten's Gloriana: Essays and Sources*. Woodbridge: Boydell/Britten-Pears Library, 1993.

Bartel, Dietrich. *Música Poética: Musical-Rhetorical Figures in German Baroque Music*. Nebraska: University of Nebraska Press, 1997.

Benjamin, Walter. 'The Work of Art in the Age of Mechanical Reproduction,' *Illuminations*. New York: Schocken Books, 1969.

Blyth, Alan. *Remembering Britten*. London: Hutchinson, 1981.

Bohlman, Philip V. *The Study of Folk Music in the Modern World*. Indiana: Indiana University Press, 1988.

Bose, Mishtooni. 'Humanism, English Music and the Rhetoric of Criticism.' *Music and Letters* Vol. 77, No. 1 (1996): 1-21.

Brett, Philip Elizabeth Wood and Gary C. Thomas, eds. *Queering the Pitch*. New York: Routledge, 2006.

Brett, Philip. 'Toeing the line.' *The Musical Times* Vol. 137, No. 1843 (1996): 7-13.

Brett, Philip, George E. Haggerty, ed. *Music and Sexuality in Britten*. Berkeley: University of California Press, 2006.

Bridcut, John. *Britten's Children*. London: Faber and Faber, 2007.

Britten, Benjamin. *On Receiving the Aspen Award*. London: Faber and Faber, 1964.

Britten, Benjamin and Donald Mitchell. *Owen Wingrave* (unpublished transcription of a BBC broadcast given in April 1971).

Burton, Robert. *The Anatomy of Melancholy*. Oxford: Lichfield, Short and Cripps, 1621/Da Capo Press, 1971.

Bynner, Witter, trans. *The Jade Mountain*. New York: Doubleday, 1964.

Camus, Albert, Justin O'Brien, trans. *The Myth of Sysiphus, and other essays*. New York: Vintage Books, 1991.

Campbell, Olive Dame and Cecil J. Sharp. *Introduction* to *English Folk Songs from the Appalachians*. New York: G.P. Putnam's Sons, 1917.

Carpenter, Humphrey. *Benjamin Britten: A Biography*. London: Faber and Faber, 1992.

Ch'Eng-En, Wu. *Monkey*. Arthur Waley, trans. Harmonsworth: Penguin Books, 1961.

Ch'ü, T'ung-tsu. *Han Social Structure*. Seattle: University of Washington Press, 1972.

Clark, Katarina and Michael Holquist. *Mikail Bakhtin*. Cambridge: Harvard University Press, 1984.

Collingwood, Bruce, J. and John Stokoe, eds. *Northumbrian Minstrelsy*. Newcastle-upon-Tyne: Society of Antiquaries, 1882.

Cooke, Mervyn. *Britten and the Far East*. Woodbridge: Boydell Press, 2009.

Cooke, Mervyn and Philip Reed. *Benjamin Britten: Billy Budd*. Cambridge: Cambridge University Press, 1993.

Dicaire, David. *The Early Years of Folk Music: Fifty Founders of the Tradition*. North Carolina: McFarland, 1963.

Duncan, Ronald. *Working with Britten: A Personal Memoir*. Devon: The Rebel Press, 1981.

Duchesneau, Louise and Wolfgang Marx, eds. *György Ligeti: Of Foreign Lands and Strange Sounds*. Woodbridge: Boydell & Brewer, 2011.

Elliot, Graham. *Benjamin Britten: The Spiritual Dimension*. Oxford: Oxford University Press, 2006.

Evans, John, ed. *Journeying Boy: The Diaries of the Young Benjamin Britten* 1928-1938. London: Faber and Faber, 2009.

Evans, Peter. *The Music of Benjamin Britten*. London: J.M. Dent, 1979.

Farnsworth, Rodney. "'Hither, This Way": A Rhetorical-Musical Analysis of a Scene from Purcell's "King Arthur"'. *The Musical Quarterly* Vol. 74, No. 1 (1990): 83-97.

Ford, Boris, ed. *Benjamin Britten's Poets - The Poetry He Set to Music.* Manchester: Carcanet Press, 1994.

Foucault, Michel. *The Will to Knowledge: The History of Sexuality I.* London: Penguin, 1976.

Goodwin, Noel. 'Britten's Advance.' *Music and Musicians* (1964).

Goss, Stephen. 'Come Heavy Sleep: motive and metaphor in Britten's *Nocturnal*, opus 70.' *Guitar Forum* No. 1 (2001): 53-75.

Green, Paul. *The Common Glory*. Connecticut: Greenwood Press, 1973.

Green, Roland, et al. *The Princeton Encyclopedia of Poetry & Poetics* (Fourth Edition) Princeton: Princeton University Press, 2012.

Gregor, David. *Victorian Songhunters: The Recovery and Editing of English Vernacular Ballads and Folk Lyrics, 1820-1883*. Oxford: The Scarecrow Press, 2006.

Guignon, Charles B., ed. *The Cambridge Companion to Heidegger*. New York: Cambridge University Press, 2006.

Handel, Darrell. 'Britten's Use of the Passacaglia.' *Tempo, New Series* No. 94 (1970): 2-6.

Hardy, Grant and Behnke Kinney. *The Establishment of the Han Empire and Imperial China*. Connecticut: Greenwood Press, 2005.

Hart, Henry H. *The Hundred Names: A Short Introduction to the Study of Chinese Poetry with Illustrative Translations*. Berkeley: University of California Press, 1933.

Headington, Christopher. *Peter Pears: A Biography*. London: Faber and Faber, 1992.

Headlam Wells, Robin. *Elizabethan Mythologies: studies in poetry, drama and music*. Cambridge: Cambridge University Press, 1994.

---. 'John Dowland and Elizabethan Melancholy.' *Early Music Vol.* 13, No. 4 (1985).

Holbrook, David, ed. *Plucking the Rushes*. London: Heinemann, 1968.

Holman, Peter. *Dowland Lachrimae* (1604). Cambridge: Cambridge University Press, 1999.

Howes, F. *Journal of the English Folk Dance and Song Society* Vol. 1, No. 1 (1932).

Hsu, Cho-yun. *Han Agriculture*. Seattle: University of Washington Press, 1980.

Huckvale, David. *James Bernard, Composer to Count Dracula: A Critical Biography*. Carolina: McFarland, 2006.

Hudson, Richard. 'The Ripresa, the Ritornello, and the Passacaglia.' *Journal of the American Musicological Society* Vol. 24, No. 3 (1971): 364-394.

Hughes, Ted. *Collected Poems*. Paul Keegan, ed. London: Faber and Faber, 2003.

Johnson, Graham. *Britten, Voice & Piano: Lectures on the Vocal Music of Benjamin Britten*. London: The Guildhall School of Music & Drama and Ashgate Publishing Limited, 2003.

Kennedy, Michael. *Portrait of Walton*. Oxford: Oxford University Press, 1989.

Kidson, Frank and Mary Neal. *English Folk-Song and Dance*. New Jersey: Rowman and Littlefield, 1972.

Kildea, Paul, ed. *Britten on Music*. Oxford: Oxford University Press, 2003.

Lambert, Constant. *Music Ho!: A Study of Music in Decline*. London: Hogarth Press, 1934.

Lascelles, George, and Earl of Harwood. *The Tongs and Bones: The Memoirs of Lord Harewood*. London: Weidenfeld & Nicholson, 1981.

Lawrence, D. H. *The Complete Poems of D.H. Lawrence*. Hertfordshire: Wordsworth Editions, 1994.

Loewe, Michael. *Crisis and Conflict in Han China 104 BC to AD 9*. London: Allen & Unwin, 1974.

Mark, Christopher. *Early Benjamin Britten: A Study of Stylistic and Technical Evolution*. New York: Garland Publishing, 1995.

Martin, Augustine, ed. *Soundings*. Dublin: Gill & Macmillan, 1969.

May, Steven W. 'The poems of Edward de Vere, 17th Earl of Oxford and Robert Devereux, 2nd Earl of Essex.' *Studies in Philology* 77 (1980): 5 118.

Mellers, W. H. *Music and Society*. London: Dobson, 1950.

Merriam-Webster's Collegiate Dictionary, Eleventh Edition. Merriam-Webster, 2004.

Mitchell, Donald. 'Catching on to the technique in Pagoda-Land.' *Tempo, New Series* No. 146 (1983): 13-24.

Mitchell, Donald and Hans Keller, eds. *Benjamin Britten: A Commentary on his works from a group of specialists*. London: Rockliff, 1952.

Morton, Scott and Charlton M. Lewis. *China: Its History and Culture*. New York: McGraw-Hill, 1995

Moulden, John. 'The Great Folk Heresy.' *Fortnight* No. 35 (1972): 19-20.

Noble, Jeremy. 'Britten's Nocturnal.' *The Musical Times* Vol. 105, No. 1458 (1964): 592-594.

Palmer, Christopher, ed. *The Britten Companion*. London: Faber & Faber, 1984.

Palmer, Tony. *Julian Bream: A Life on the Road*. London: MacDonald & Co, 1982.

Patrides, C. A. and R.B. Waddington, eds. *The Age of Milton: Backgrounds to Seventh-Century Literature*. Manchester: Manchester University Press, 1980.

Pollard, Michael. *Discovering English Folksong*. Aylesbury: Shire Publications, 1982.

Poulton, Diane. *John Dowland*. London: Faber and Faber, 1972.

Pound, Ezra. *The Translations of Ezra Pound*. London: Faber & Faber, 1953.

Preminger, Alex and T.V.F. Brogan, eds. *The New Princeton Encyclopedia of Poetry and Poetics*. New Jersey: Princeton University Press, 1993.

Proust, Marcel. *Remembrance of Things Past*. Scott Moncrieff, trans. London: Wordsworth Editions, 2006.

Puttenham George. *The Arte of English Poesie* (1589). Edward Arber, ed. London: Murray & Son, 1869.

Reed, Philip, Mervyn Cooke and Donald Mitchell, eds. *Letters From A Life: The Selected Letters of Benjamin Britten* Volume IV 1952-1957. Woodbridge: Boydell Press, 2008.

Richardson, John. *Heidegger*. New York: Routledge, 2012.

Rooley, Anthony. 'New Light on John Dowland's Songs of Darkness.' *Early Music* Vol. 11, No. 12 (1983): 6-21.

Rupprecht, Philip. *Britten's Musical Language*. Cambridge: Cambridge University Press, 2001.

---. 'Tonal Stratification and Uncertainty in Britten's Music.' *Journal of Music Theory* Vol. 40, No. 2 (1996): 311-346.

Schafer, Murray. *British Composers in Interview*. London: Faber & Faber, 1963.

Schmitz, Oscar A. H. *Das Land ohne Musik. Englische Gesellschaftsprobleme*. G. Müller, 1914.

Sedgwick, Eve Kosofsky. *Epistemology of the Closet*. Berkeley: University of California Press, 1990.

Self, Geoffrey. *The Music of E. J. Moeran*. London: Toccata Press, 1986.

Seymour, Claire. *The Operas of Benjamin Britten: Expression and Evasion*. Woodbridge: The Boydell Press, 2004.

Sharp, Cecil J. and Maud Karpeles, eds. *English Folksong: Some Conclusions*. Yorkshire: EP Publishing, 1972.
---. eds. *English Folksong: Some Conclusions*. London: Novello, 1936.
Sharp, Cecil J. and R. Vaughan Williams, eds. *Selection of Collected Folk- Songs*, Volume 1. London: Novello, 1921.
Sharp, Cecil J. ed. *One Hundred English Folksongs*. Boston: Oliver Ditson Company, 1916.
---. arr. *Seventeen Nursery Songs from the Appalachian Mountains*. London: Novello, 1921.
Smythe, Colin. 'Interview with Peter Pears.' *Trinity News* (1962).
Stein, Leon. 'The Passacaglia in the Twentieth Century.' *Music & Letters* Vol. 40, No. 2 (1959): 150-153.
Steiner, George. *Errata: An Examined Life*. Guernsey: Phoenix, 1998.
---. *Martin Heidegger*. Chicago: University of Chicago Press, 1978.
---. *The Death of Tragedy*. London, Faber & Faber, 1961.
Stewart, Bob. *Pagan Imagery in English Folksong*. New Jersey: Humanities Press, 1977.
Strachey, Lytton. *Elizabeth and Essex: A Tragic History*. London: Chatto, 1928.
Stradling, Robert and Meirion Hughes. *The English Musical Renaissance 1860-1940*. London: Routledge, 1993.
Strassberg, Richard E. *Inscribed Landscapes: Travel Writing from Imperial China*. Berkeley: University of California Press, 1994.
Stukrad, Kocku von. *Locations of Knowledge in Medieval and Early Modern Europe: Esoteric Discourse and Western Identities*. Leiden: Brill, 2010.
Tarling, Judy. *The Weapons of Rhetoric: A Guide for Musicians and Audiences*. Hertfordshire: Corda Music, 2004.
Toft, Robert. *Tune Thy Musicke To Thy Hart: The Art of Eloquent Singing in England 1597-1622*. Toronto: University of Toronto, 1993.
Tovey, Donald Francis. *Essays in Musical Analysis*. London: Oxford University Press, 1944.
Tyler, James and Paul Sparks. *The Guitar and its Music*. Oxford: Oxford University Press, 2002.
Tynan, Kathleen. *The Life of Kenneth Tynan*. London: Methuen, 1988.
Volkov, Solomon. *Testimony*. New York: Harper & Row, 1979.
Wade, Graham. *The Art of Julian Bream*. Blaydon on Tyne: Ashley Mark Publishing Company, 2008.
Waley, Arthur, trans. *One Hundred & Seventy Chinese Poems*. London: Constable & Co. Ltd., 1918.
---. trans. *The Book of Songs*. New York: Grove Press, 1987.

---. trans. *The Book of Songs*. London: Allen & Unwin, 1937.
---. trans. *Poems from the Chinese*. London: Ernest Benn, 1925.
---. *The Nō Plays of Japan*. London: Allen & Unwin, 1921.
---. *The Life and Times of Po Chü-i*. London: Allen & Unwin, 1949.
---. *Ballads and Stories from Tun-huang*. London: Allen and Unwin, 1960.
Walker, Lucy, ed. *Benjamin Britten: New Perspectives on His Life and Work*. Woodbridge: Boydell Press, 2009.
Watson, Burton, trans. *Po Chü-i: Selected Poems*. New York: Columbia University Press, 2000.
Watson, Burton, trans. *The Old Man Who Does As He Pleases: Selections from the Poetry and Prose of Lu Yu*. New York: Columbia University Press, 1973.
Watson, Philip. *Grand Canal, Great River*. London: Frances Lincoln Limited, 2007.
Welter, Malcolm. 'A Conversation with Julian Bream.' *Guitar Review* 37 (1972): 12.
Whitesell, Lloyd. 'Britten's Dubious Trysts.' *Journal of the American Musicological Society* Vol. 56, No. 3 (2003): 637-694.
Williamson, Craig, ed. and trans. *A Feast of Creatures: Anglo-Saxon Riddle- Songs*. Philadelphia: University of Pennsylvania Press, 2011.
Wintle, Christopher. *All the Gods: Benjamin Britten's* Night-piece *in Context*. Julian Littlewood, ed. King's Lynn: Plumbago, 2006.
Whittall, Arnold. *The Music of Britten and Tippett: Studies in themes and techniques*. Cambridge: Cambridge University Press, 1982.
Vaughan Williams, Ralph. *National Music and Other Essays*. Oxford: Oxford University Press, 1934.
Xuanmin, Luo and He Yuanjian. *Translating China*. Bristol: MPG Books, 2009.
Yip, Wai-Lim, ed. and trans. *Chinese Poetry*. Durham (U.S.): Duke University Press, 1997.
Yoke, Ho Peng, Goh Thean Chye and Beda Lim. *Lu Yu, The Poet-Alchemist*. Canberra: Faculty of Asian Studies, Australian National University, 1972.
Zoete, Beryl de and Walter Spies. *Dance and Drama in Bali*. London: Faber and Faber, 1938.

Scores

Britten, Benjamin. *Curlew River*, Op. 71. Faber Music Limited, London, 1964/5 [edition: 1983].

---. *Eight Folk Song Arrangements* (1976) Faber Music, London, 1980.

---. *Five Courtly Dances from 'Gloriana'*, arranged by David Stone, Boosey & Hawkes (19200), London, 1964.

---. *Folksong Arrangements* Volume 6: England. Boosey & Hawkes (18814), London, 1961.

---. *Lachrymae, reflections on a song of Dowland*, Op. 48. Boosey & Hawkes (17817), London, 1951.

---. *Night-Piece (Notturno)*, Boosey & Hawkes (19139), London, 1963.

---. *Nocturnal, after John Dowland*, Op.70. Faber Music, London, 1964. ISBN 0-571-50005-6.

--- .'The Second Lute Song of the Earl of Essex', Julian Bream, ed. Boosey & Hawkes, London, 2008, ISMN 979-0-060-11929-3.

---. *Sechs Hölderlin-Fragmente*, Op. 61. Boosey & Hawkes, London, 1958.

---. *Serenade for Tenor Horn and Strings*, Op. 31. Boosey & Hawkes (8934), London, 1944.

---. *Songs from the Chinese*, Op. 58. Boosey & Hawkes (18505), London, 1959.

---. *The Red Cackatoo & other songs* (1935-1969) Faber Music, London, 1994.

---. *Tit for Tat*. Faber Music (057150292X), London, 1973.

Falla, Manuel de. *Homenaje, pour le tombeau de Claude Debussy* (Tombeau de Claude Debussy). Paris: Durand, 1920.

Moeran, E. J., arr. *Six Folk Songs from Norfolk*. London: Augener Ltd., 1924.

Henze, Hans Werner. *Kammermusik 1958*. Koch Schwann, 310004.

Nadal, David. *John Dowland's Lute Songs; Third and Fourth Books*, New York: Dover Publications, 2002.

Stanford, Charles Villiers and Geoffrey Shaw. *The New National Song Book: A Complete Collection of the Folk-Songs, Carols, and Rounds Suggested and Arranged for the Use of Schools*. London: Boosey & Hawkes, 1905.

Walton, William. *Anon. In Love*. Cadenza Music, CAZWWANON01.

Whittaker, W. Gillies, ed. and arr. *The Hexhamshire Lass: Ballads and Folk Songs from the North Country*. London: Curwen & Son, 1978.

Films and DVDs

Balmer, Paul. *Julian Bream: My Life in Music*, DVD (Avie Productions, 2004).

Palmer, Tony. *Benjamin Britten: A Time There Was*, DVD Video (1979; Isolde Films: New Jersey, Kultur).

Dissertations

Milliman, Joan Ann. Benjamin Britten's Symbolic Treatment of Sleep, Dream and Death, and Death as Manifest in his Opera 'Death in Venice'. PhD diss., University of Southern California, June 1977.

Frame, Maire Brona. *The* Development of the Nocturnal Music of Benjamin Britten from Serenade to Nocturne. Masters diss., University of Manchester, 1990.

Moon, Kyung Soo. Balinese Influences in Songs from the Chinese. PhD diss., University of Texas, 1993).

Hse, Ti-Fei. Chinese influence in Four Twentieth Century Song Cycles by Roussel, Carpenter, Griffes and Britten. PhD diss., American Conservatory of Music, 1988).

Appendix I

Julian Bream's recordings on the lute as solo instrument, as an accompanist to Pears and in larger ensembles featuring the music of Dowland and his English contemporaries.

Julian Bream's Discography (207-215).
The Golden Age of English Lute Music (1961, RCA 16281 mono SB 2150 LDS 2560).
An Evening of Elizabethan Music (1962, RCA RB 6592 mono LD 2656).
Julian Bream in Concert (1963, RCA RB 6646 mono SB6646 LM 2819).
Music from the Royal Courts of Europe (1966, RCA SB 6698 LSC 2987).
The Dances of Dowland (1967, RCA SB 6751 LSC 2987).
Elizabethan Lute Songs (1970, RCA SB 6835 LSC 3131).
The Woods So Wild (1972, RCA SB 6865 LSC 3331).
Ayres for 4 Voices (1973, no catalogue information).
The Lute Music of John Dowland (1976, RCA RL 11491 ARLI 1491).
The Julian Bream Consort: Fantasies, Ayres and Dances (1988, RCA RD 87801).
Two Loves: A Sequence of Poetry and Music by William Shakespeare and John Dowland (1989, RCA RD87843).

Appendix II

While Bream and Britten must have spent many hours together discussing various technical issues, particularly relating to the guitar's rather idiosyncratic nature, it appears that, due to concert engagements and other commitments, they were often forced to communicate by post. Two such instances provide insights into early stages of the compositional process relating to *Nocturnal*. In one fascinating note, Britten enquires about a technical aspect regarding double octaves for a section that would become the central feature of Variation V.

Plate 7: Note from Britten to Bream regarding technical issues for *Nocturnal*, Variation V

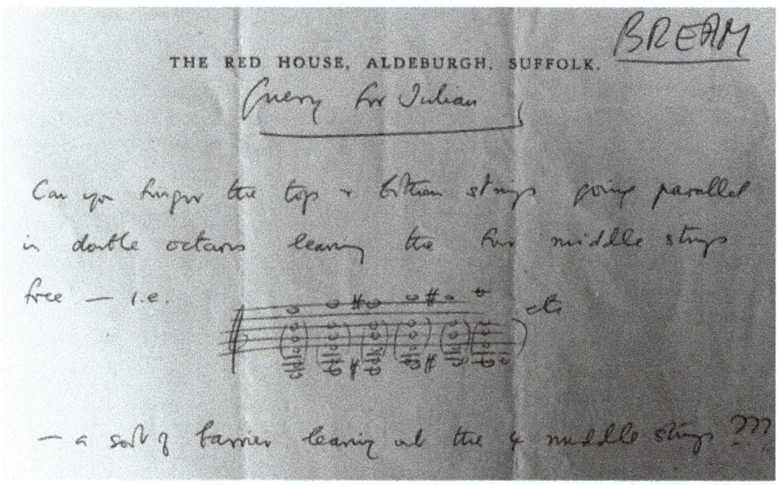

[BREAM Query for Julian: Can you finger the top & bottom strings going parallel in double octaves leaving the four middle strings free — i.e. — a sort of barrier leaving out the 4 middle strings???]

Here we get an intriguing preview of Britten's gift for understanding the specific characteristics of a given instrument. Though not a guitarist, in variation V of *Nocturnal*, Britten created one of the finest examples of idiosyncratic writing for the instrument. Another interesting note relating to *Nocturnal* was sent by Britten to Bream while the guitarist was on an American tour. Apparently, Bream was aware that Britten was composing an extended section with harmonics and obviously wished to check some technical aspects. This note refers to music that would form the basis for Variations VI and VII.

Plate 8: Note from Britten to Bream regarding technical issues for *Nocturnal*, Variations VI and VII

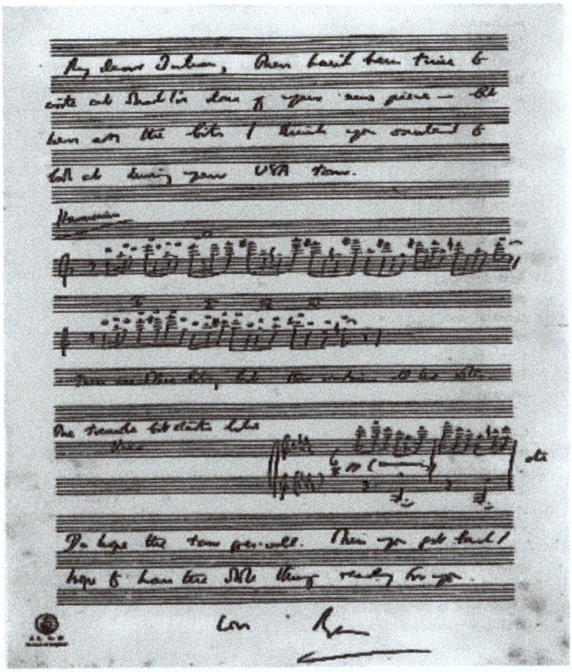

[My dear Julian, there hasn't been time to write out what I've done of your new piece—but here are the bits I think you wanted to look at during your USA tour. Harmonics [Variation VI]...There are other bits, but this contains all the notes...The tremolo bit [Variation VII] starts like this...Do hope the tour goes well. When you get back I hope to have the whole thing ready for you...Love Ben]

Appendix III

A short synopsis of *Gloriana*

At a royal contest, the highly motivated and politically ambitious Earl of Essex and Lord Mountjoy challenge each other. Mountjoy wins the tournament and the jealous Earl is wounded. Queen Elizabeth's solution to the ensuing skirmish is that, in future, both men must always attend court together. Being similar in motivation and character, they subsequently become friends. Sir Robert Cecil, Secretary of the Council, informs the queen about Essex's recalcitrant behaviour and political ambition, and also warns her of an impending Spanish Armada invasion. Essex enters, and suspecting (rightly) that the queen has feelings for him, compliments her. Although he has feelings for her, he also has an eye on securing the prestigious post of Deputy in Ireland, and the mission to quell the rebel Tyrone. Elizabeth hesitates in promoting the Earl, not only because his impulsive ambition is blatantly obvious, but also as she feels compromised by the political delicacy of such an elevation, and the possible dishonour such support might expose her to—a restraint based on her genuine feelings for him.

In Norwich the Queen is welcomed by the citizens and entertained by a festive masque. Meanwhile, in the Earl's house in London, the Earl of Essex, Lady Penelope Rich (his sister), and her lover, Mountjoy, hatch a plan to secure power through a *coup d'état*. At court, the Queen insists that all the ladies should change their clothes after a lengthy and energetic dance. Elizabeth reappears wearing the extravagant and identifiable dress owned by the Earl's wife—a blatant act designed to shame her. Though enraged, Essex is placated when Elizabeth declares the appointment he has so long desired and sends him to Ireland. The Earl's Irish campaign, however, is a failure, and on his sudden return he insists on access to the monarch while she is dressing in her private chamber. Unexpected, he comes upon her without her wig and wearing no make-up, and sees her suddenly as she is: an old and vulnerable woman. He defends his failures and beseeches her to view his political cause in good light, but she is unimpressed. Following this, Sir Robert Cecil warns her of the Earl's plot to dethrone her. In London, political factions close to the Earl fail in their attempt to win the people over to his insurgency. Consequently, his fate is inevitable; even the pleading requests of his wife, sister and friend cannot alter the decision. Elizabeth signs the warrant for his execution. In the final scene, the dying monarch recollects the trials she has endured during her reign.

Appendix IV

Biographical notes on Wu-ti, Po Chü-I and Lu Yu

Wu-ti (157-87 BCE)

Wu-ti was the sixth emperor of the Han dynasty (206 BCE-220), 'roughly analogous in extent, population, development and dates to the Roman empire'.[304] Some time after the death of his father, Emperor Jing, Wu-ti acceded to the throne in 131 BCE. Once in full control, he ruthlessly wielded authority more aggressively than any of his Han-dynasty predecessors. He had all but seven of his Prime Ministers executed, had many powerful families transported to distant regions in order to weaken them, and curtailed the power of kings and officials who had previously wielded significant political agency.[305] Where private capital was seen to challenge his monopoly of state power, it was curtailed.[306]

Wu-ti had a strong impact on Chinese society. He expanded China's frontiers, sent armies south to Vietnam, southwest to Tibet and Burma, west into Central Asia, north into Mongolia, and northeast into Korea.[307] Intriguingly, his aggressive expansionism and empire building was matched by an equally enlightened desire to revive past knowledge. He 'patronized the arts and literature...appointed erudite scholars who specialized in the Five Confucian Classics, and in 124 [BCE] he established the Imperial Academy for the training of future bureaucrats in Confucian philosophy'.[308] Given his aggressive geopolitical strategies and attachment to worldly power, it is striking that he was equally drawn to mystical phenomena such as witchcraft and black magic (or *ku*). This is evidenced not only by the influence that famous shamans such as Shao Weng and Luan Ta had on him, but also by extensive travels he undertook in search of 'immortal beings' and 'floating paradise islands' such as P'enf-lai.

---

304 Philip Watson, *Grand Canal, Great River* (London: Frances Lincoln Limited, 2007), 8.

305 Grant Hardy and Behnke Kinney, *The Establishment of the Han Empire and Imperial China* (Connecticut: Greenwood Press, 2005), 119.

306 Cho-yun Hsu, *Han Agriculture* (Seattle: University of Washington Press, 1980), 133-134.

307 I am using the modern names for these regions.

308 Grant Hardy and Behnke Kinney, The Establishment of the Han Empire and *Imperial China* (Connecticut: Greenwood Press, 2005), 119.

Po Chü-i (772-846)

Po Chü-i was one of the most renowned poets of the T'ang Dynasty (618-907), a highly significant epoch for Chinese poetry. Born in Shansi, he was the second son of a poor scholar. Possessing a natural intellect, he passed the daunting *chin-shih* examinations at the age of twenty-eight. His official career advanced quickly and in 807 he was appointed a scholar in the Han-lin Academy. Settling near the northwest borderland at Ch'ang-an, Po Chü-i held important government positions including the post of palace librarian and numerous provincial governorships. Despite his swift ascent through government ranks, he was very outspoken against official policy, and even though Confucian rule encouraged some criticism, Po Chü-i's remonstrations created many enemies in official circles. Not surprisingly, he was eventually demoted to the position of marshal of Chiang-chou, a remote rural region. Making the most of his exile, Po Chü-i spent much time studying Buddhism; and at the age of sixty he retired to a monastery outside Lo-yang (the eastern capital) where he built a temple. During this period, he was plagued by paralysis—a debility that darkened his writing considerably.

Po Chü-i's poetry expresses an unambiguous responsiveness to the suffering of ordinary people. It further displays a Confucian regard for deep egalitarianism using satire to attack government policies, the abuse of power by officials, and even religious doctrine, where he felt such criticism was warranted. In 815, Po Chü-i started cataloguing his own works into a collection that became known as *Po-shih Ch'ang-ch'ing chi* or *Mr. Po's Ch'ang-ch'ing Collection* (after the Ch'ang-ch'ing era in which it was collected, 821-24). Over the years, Po Chü-i continued to add to this anthology building it up to an impressive 75-chapter version by 845. The death of his son likely influenced his major themes, which include the futile waste of human life in pointless wars, exile, sickness, and the preciousness of time.

> ...Why is it that I,
> A white-haired man of three-score years,
> Am left behind,
> And you, a child of three,
> Must by Heaven's silent, stern decree,
> Precede me
> To that strange and far-off land
> Of death? ...
> (from 'A Lament for my Son Ts'ui', translated by Henry Hart)

Lu Yu (1125-1209)

Lu Yu was the most prolific poet of the Southern Sung Dynasty (1127-1279) having written close to 10,000 poems in most genres. He was born in Shan-yin during the politically tumultuous Northern Sung Dynasty (960-1126). When that dynasty was violently overthrown by the Jurchen Tartars (a non-Chinese people from Manchuria) who created the Chin Dynasty on the Sung's northern border, his family was forced to flee south. Numerous members of his family had previously held high positions in the old empire and were therefore disenfranchised as a result of the occupation. Consequently, his father became closely associated with a highly active militant group of officials who fiercely opposed the oppression of the new regime. He repeatedly sought to politically and violently undermine it, and retrieve the northern lands. Having inherited a good deal of his father's political fervour, much of Lu Yu's poetry expresses a strong desire for vengeance, highlights the conditions experienced by his fellow-countrymen still held in the North, and expresses the shame of exile.

Lu Yu passed the palace examinations in 1153, but his irredentist activities provoked the anger of Prime Minister Ch'in Kuei (1091-1155) who favoured appeasement in political affairs. As a result, he was denied further education. While he was temporarily back in favour when the Emperor Hsiao-tsung (1161-1189) ascended to the throne, a number of subsequent military campaigns against the Chin Dynasty, all of which failed, created a great deal of instability in his political life. With this instability came economic poverty, and Lu Yu was forced to accept a string of minor positions. One of these was as vice-prefect of what is now Feng-chieh, which required him in 1170 to leave his home in Shao-hsing, travel into the hinterland towards the western borderline by boat north on the Grand Canal to the Yangtze, and further upriver to K'uei-chou. During the five-month journey, he wrote a memoir known as the *Ju-Shu-chi*. The chronicle became a highly influential travel diary and a prominent model for future writers.

Lu Yu was a highly prolific poet. Even though he destroyed much of his early work, he eventually published about 2,400 poems. These writings embody numerous moods and styles, though two contrasting themes dominate: politics and the simplicity of rural life.

> [The first theme is Lu Yu's] longing to see the north, which he was too young even to remember, once more restored to native rule, a longing that often appears in his poetry in the form of fitful dreams in which he sees himself and his countrymen actually riding into battle against the hated barbarians. The [second] theme, wholly different in nature, is that of the quiet joys and experiences of everyday life. Lu Yu made no secret

> of his extreme fondness for wine, and in 1176, after being dismissed from a post on charges of 'drunkenness and irrespon-sibility', he adopted in a gesture of defiance the literary name Fang-weng, which means 'the old man who does as he pleases'.[309]

Despite his heavy drinking, Lu Yu was very interested in the notion of transcendence through Taoism and the *I ching* (the *Book of Changes*). Without ever losing his patriotic fervour or his willingness to criticize Sung bureaucracy, the poetry from his later life centred on themes stemming from Taoist philosophy, the customs of the peasants he knew (particularly the people of Shanyin), the celebration of wine and the tranquillity of rural life. He died without witnessing a satisfactory fulfilment of his political aspirations.

---

309 Burton Watso, trans., The Old Man Who Does As He Pleases: Selections *from the Poetry and Prose of Lu Yu*, translated by Burton Watson, New York: Columbia University Press, 1973), xiv.

Appendix V

Poems listed by Britten in annotations made into the index pages of his copy of Waley's *Chinese Poems*, but not included in the final selection for *Songs from the Chinese*.

The Five-String (by Po Chü-i)
The singers have hushed their notes of shrill song;
The red sleeves of the dancers are motionless.
Old Chao hugs his five-stringed lute;

Then his fingers dart, as he holds it close to his breast.

The loud notes swell and scatter abroad;
'Sa, sa,' like wind blowing the rain.
The soft notes dying almost to nothing;
'Ch'ieh, ch'ieh,' like the voice of ghosts talking.
Now as glad as the magpie's lucky song;
Again bitter as the gibbon's ominous cry.
His ten fingers have no fixed note;
Up and down - kung, chih, and yü.

And those who sit and listen to the tune he plays
Of soul and body lose the mastery.
And those who pass that way as he plays the tune,
Suddenly stop and cannot raise their feet.
Alas, alas that the ears of common men
Should love the modern and not love the old.
Thus it is that the lute in the green window
Day by day is covered deeper with dust.

The Spring River (by Po Chü-i)
Heat and cold, dusk and dawn have crowded one upon the other;
Suddenly I find it is two years since I came to Chung-chou.
Through my closed doors I hear nothing but the morning and evening drum;
From my upper windows all I see is the ships that come and go.
In vain the orioles tempt me with their song to stay beneath the flowering trees;
In vain the grasses lure me by their colour to sit beside the pond.
There is one thing and one alone I never tire of watching-
The spring river as it trickles over the stones and babbles past the rocks.

The Golden Palace (anon 1st century A.D?)
We go to the Golden Palace
We set out jade cups,
We summon the honoured guests
To enter at the Golden Gate
And go to the Golden Hall.
In the Eastern Kitchen the meat is sliced and ready,
Pounded beef and boiled pork and mutton.

Appendix VI

***I gave my love a cherry* [15th century]**
I have a yong suster [sister]
Fer biyonde the see; [far] [sea]
Many ben the drueries [gifts]
That she sente me.
She sente me the chery
Wythouten ony ston,
And so she dide the dowve [dove]
Wythouten ony bone.
She sente me the brere [briar]
Wythouten ony rynde, [bark]
She bad me love my lemman [lover]
Wythouten longynge. [longing]
How sholde ony chery
Ben wythouten ston?
And how sholde ony dowve
Ben wyhtouten bon?
How shold any brere
Ben wythouten rynde?
How sholde I love my lemman*
Wythouten longynge?
Whan the chery was a flour
Than hadde it non stone;
Whan the dowve was an ey, [egg]
Than hadde it non bon.
When the brere was unbred, [not yet sprouted, in seed]
Than hadde it non rynde;
When the mayden hath that she loveth,
She is wythouten longynge

The Railroader
I would not marry a farmer,
He's always in the dirt,
But I would marry an engineer
Who wears a striped shirt,
A railroader, mother, a railroader,
a railroader for me,
If ever I marry in all my life,
A railroader's bride I'll be.
I would not marry a blacksmith,
He's always in the black,
But I would marry an engineer
Who pulls the throttle back!
I've roamed this wide world over
Some pleasures for to see,
I fell in love with a railroad man
An' he fell in love with me.
I would not marry a sheriff,
For he is sure to die,
But I would marry a railroader

Who has them pretty blue eyes.
I would not marry a preacher,
He preaches too much hell,
But I would marry an engineer
Who rings the engine bell.
I would not marry a gambler,
He's always drinkin' wine,
But I would marry a railroader
Who runs the forty-nine.

The Soldier's Prayer
The first thing we'll pray for, we'll pray for some beer
That we may have plenty to keep us in cheer
And for each pint we now have, may we have ten
May we have a bloody brewery—said the sailor Amen.
The next thing we'll pray for, we'll pray for some baccy
That we may have plenty to keep us both happy
And for each pipe we now have, may we have ten
May we have a bloody shipload—said the sailor Amen.
The last thing we'll pray for, we'll pray for some wives
That we may have plenty to last out our lives
And for each wife we now have, may we have ten
May we have a bloody harem—said the sailor Amen.

Appendix VII

The Kontakion (Hymn for the Departed)
Give rest, O Christ, to thy servant with thy saints:
where sorrow and pain are no more;
neither sighing but life everlasting.
Thou only art immortal, the creator and maker of man:
and we are mortal formed from the dust of the earth,
and unto earth shall we return:
for so thou didst ordain, when thou created me saying:
'Dust thou art und unto dust shalt thou return.'
All we go down to the dust;
and weeping o'er the grave we make our song:
Alleluia, alleluia, alleluia.

Index

D

E

F

G

H

Y

Z

Benjamin Dwyer's *Britten and the Guitar: Critical Perspectives for Performers* is the first complete study of the guitar works of Benjamin Britten. This book offers more than an objective analytical study of these compositions. Dwyer draws upon his expertise as a classical guitarist, composer and musicologist to deliver a multi-lensed examination of this music providing broad contexts and unique insights.

Dwyer not only explores the intricate relationship between Britten, his life-long partner, the tenor Peter Pears, and the guitarist Julian Bream, for whom all the guitar works were written, but goes further in situating Renaissance composer and lutenist John Dowland as a central and inspirational figure who hovers over all of Britten's guitar works. In so doing, he offers new perspectives into Britten's compositional approach demonstrating how techniques of musical rhetoric, exemplified by Dowland, are central to his musical language.

Britten and the Guitar: Critical Perspectives for Performers is an essential guide for the professional guitarist and singer, the committed teacher, and those who simply wish to understand more about the guitar music of one Britain's foremost composers.

Benjamin Dwyer's Britten and the Guitar: Critical Perspectives for Performers goes on to my short list of great books about music and musicians. Dwyer steers deftly between the Scylla of pedantry and the Charybdis of gossipy klatsch to offer a treasure trove of interesting facts and vivid portraits of great musicians spanning a long arc of Western culture from the ancient Greeks through the Elizabethan era and on into the 21st century. Reading this book is an enriching educational experience, yet parts of it read like a thriller. As a guitarist myself, I am particularly gratified that Dwyer has ennobled our instrument by this captivating study.

Eliot Fisk

I was eager to learn how a fine composer like Benjamin Dwyer could enlighten us about the older Benjamin's compositional process. But this book is so much more. Dwyer makes a drone of cultural observation hover over Dowland, Purcell, folksong, philosophy and poetry. Britten's musical personality emerges magnified not by his unerring compositional decisions, but by the cultural affinities that led him to those paths. These works now appear to be even stronger. As a performer, reading this book has saved me many years of research, analysis and pondering. One shouldn't do without it.

Fabio Zanon

This is the first book to explore Britten's guitar works and it offers an extraordinary range of fascinating insights into the man and his music. Dwyer is a guitarist, composer and musicologist who has spent decades performing Britten's music and so comes to his subject not only as a researcher but also as an expert practitioner. This book is essential reading for all those who wish to perform or teach Britten's remarkable music for the guitar.

Xuefei Yang

Benjamin Dwyer is a guitarist, composer and musicologist. He has written extensively on Irish classical and contemporary music, and on the composers György Ligeti, Benjamin Britten and Alban Berg. Publications include Different Voices: Irish Music and Music in Ireland (Wolke-Verlag, 2014), Constellations: The Life and Music of John Buckley (Carysfort Press, 2011), and imagines (a limited edition publication with texts, scores and an audio recording by violist Garth Knox of Dwyer's imagines obesae et aspectui ingratae (New Dublin Press/Distinctive Repetition Design Studio, 2015).

Dwyer's music is forged from an intensive amalgamation of technical, improvisatory and interpretative elements. Renowned musicians and ensembles worldwide have performed his works. He has written extensively for the guitar including two guitar concertos, a guitar quintet and numerous solo works. His magisterial Twelve Études is described by Fabio Zanon as 'the summation of an entire guitar epoch.' As a classical guitarist and an exponent of contemporary music and free jazz, Dwyer performs internationally and has appeared as soloist with all the Irish orchestras, the Neubrandenburg Philharmonic, the Santos Symphony Orchestra, VOX21, the Callino Quartet, the Vogler String Quartet and Barry Guy's Blue Shroud Band.

Dwyer is an elected member of Aosdána, an Associate of the Royal Academy of Music, London (ARAM), and Professor of Music at Middlesex University.